Roland Kriewaldt's
CLEARING A PATH TO *Joy*

And finding contentment along the way

Aurora Sky Publishing
www.AuroraSkyPublishing.com

*I dedicate this book
to those who value the truth
even more than winning.*

First Printing:
"Author's Cut" Paperback Edition
Copyright © 2021 by Roland Kriewaldt

Published globally by
Aurora Sky Publishing

Ordering Info: www.AuroraSkyPublishing.com
Book website: www.ClearingAPathToJoy.com
Author's website: www.RolandK.ca

All rights reserved. No part of this book may be copied without the expressed written permission of the author. However, short excerpts may be quoted in print or electronic media for the sole purpose of review or promotion.

ISBN *978-0-9686823-1-9*

Cover / Interior Design / Typesetting: Roland Kriewaldt.
(This book uses a hybrid UK/US English spelling to annoy both sides.)

CONTENTS

Preface iv
Introduction v

No More Secrets
    Chapter 1   The Necessity of Joy 1
    Chapter 2   The Invisible Economy 13
    Chapter 3   A Matter Of Convenience 23
    Chapter 4   The Promise of Joy 37

The Material Path to Joy
    Chapter 5   Mind Over Matter 53
    Chapter 6   Losing Our Winning Attitude 67
    Chapter 7   The Comfort Trap 81
    Chapter 8   Selling Happiness 93

The Relational Path to Joy
    Chapter 9   A Balanced Joy Economy 111
    Chapter 10   Trading In Illusions 129
    Chapter 11   The Price of Love 143
    Chapter 12   Shopping While Hungry 159

The Spiritual Path to Joy
    Chapter 13   The Silent Partner 177
    Chapter 14   A Peaceful Mind 191
    Chapter 15   A Reverence for Life 205
    Chapter 16   Playing with God 219

The Global Path to Joy
    Chapter 17   Empires of the Mind 235
    Chapter 18   The Captive Society 249
    Chapter 19   The Greater Good 263
    Chapter 20   Life in the Balance 277

    Epilogue 298
    Glossary 299
    Index 304
    About the author 311

Preface

I was a thirty-one year old agnostic with no interest in spirituality or other such matters when a sudden and powerful Kundalini Awakening seized control of my life. Eleven days into that all-consuming event, it struck me that the relentless flow of insights streaming from my mind might also be useful to others in a book form. And so began my long and often confusing journey to sharing this information with you.

I did not obsess about what happened nor did I talk about it much, but I want to pay tribute to that peculiar and magical time in my life because this book would not exist without it, nor would I be the person I am today. In this way, it helped to clear my own path to joy.

Even now, I don't fully understand what happened to me. It felt like an internal switch had suddenly been turned on and I instantly became more self-aware, compassionate and insightful about matters that had previously never held my interest. It seemed that another aspect of me had awakened, or been reawakened. Was I remembering? Even in my dreams I was getting interesting new ideas to include in this book.

As a result, it was also a confusing time for my sanity as I underwent this dramatic shift of consciousness. Yet through it all I was enveloped by a profound feeling of love — much like what people describe during a near-death experience (NDE) that also dramatically alters their personal world view — chapter 15 addresses such experiences.

Unfortunately, I also soon realized that Kundalini Awakenings do not magically transform a person into a gifted writer. And so, after years of scribbling in notepads and working to tame my *class clown* within, I was finally able to give voice to what I'd learned.

I still marvel at how my unassuming life was seemingly hijacked to write this book and keep me determined to complete it. Many times I wondered: "Why me?" but found no answer. Regardless, that journey resulted in my creating a book that would have made my own early life far less wasteful and confusing had it existed back then.

And now that it does exist, I hope it serves you well.

        Roland Kriewaldt — Toronto, Canada.

Introduction

Clearing a Path to Joy was written to inspire a healing transformation of our ailing world by helping us all to live more joyful and contented lives. In serving this lofty ambition, it identifies many common aspects of daily life that can potentially impede our ability to attain this goal, both collectively, and as individuals.

Underlying this effort is a simple logic that the happier we feel, the less likely we are to hurt others, which will better ensure our long-term survival and that of the many other residents of this planet.

Furthermore, this book is the work of a lone individual and not an organized cell of subterranean lizard people. My apologies to anyone hoping for a more ominous plot behind the publishing of this book.

Aside from identifying various obstacles to joy, a further goal of this book is to expand our mental self-awareness to match our inherent joy potential. As part of this process, you will be exposed to uncommon insights, concepts, linguistic terms, analytic tools and theories as to how our lives might be improved. They include The IPSFA Sequence, The C–SIX States of Being, The Joy Coordinates and many others. Understandably, unfamiliar ideas can upset those who insist on reality being prescribed by some accredited institution or authority figure. However, it has long been typical for one person to introduce a new idea to their culture rather than councils of elders or angry mobs. This was true for anyone from Einstein and Buddha to Edward Van Halen. In short, being new is nothing new, and it's mostly not a team effort.

To maintain a more stable measure of objective truth, most claims made herein are supported by referencing animal behavior and natural laws. Human behavior will be analyzed using a "physics of psychology" approach based on our proven relationship to energy, the fundamental currency of all atomic structures in the cosmic marketplace.

To prepare for this journey, beginning is all you need to start. In moving forward, each chapter will propel you further toward resolving inner and outer conflicts that may be keeping you from experiencing life in a more boundless and enjoyable way. Ultimately, you will learn to enjoy a wealth of emotional riches without having to attain *a perfect life* because joy truly is just a state of mind.

Ironically, as a book about joy, humor herein is intentionally sparse to avoid distracting the mind of the reader — a daring act of restraint on my part, I must confess. This is because our quest for joy is actually a far more serious matter than what we might imagine. Subsequently, we will also be venturing into some disturbing aspects of our human behavior to better understand who or what may be blocking our access to a more joyful existence, both as individuals and collective societies.

Also, you will not find any references to modern-day nations, brands or technologies here as they are all but transient flickers in Earth's long history. A rare exception is *car culture,* which offers us a useful vehicle for exploring how marketers exploit our competitive impulses.

To promote honesty, this book also questions any value, belief or attitude that appears to be obstructing our collective quest for joy. This may cause some irritation among those whose emotional or financial comfort depends on preserving such a joy-adverse way of life. As such, we can each make our greatest contribution to a more joyful world by allowing others to think for themselves, as is every individual's right.

Finally, this book was not meant to be a disposable entertainment product but a lifelong travel companion to help you break down your mental boundaries in seeking a life of joyful adventure. So keep it near at hand, whether as a source of validation, or an unruly voice of dissent against your own habitual thinking. Use it to steer clear of conflicts or to avoid wasting your life on illegitimate pursuits of happiness.

As to what those pursuits might be, you'll find that answer and many more as we now begin clearing your own personal path to joy.

I would suggest putting on some comfortable shoes and to make use of the glossary found in the back to help you navigate some of the new ideas and terminology you will encounter along the way.

Ready? Here we go…

PART ONE
No More Secrets

CHAPTER 1
The Necessity of Joy

Survival and procreation are the shared ambition of all living things. As the guardian instincts of our earthly existence, they can also lull us into a trance-like state of selfish aggression from which some of us will never awaken. This unruly aspect of our body's *Bio-Psychology* is the single greatest threat to peace within ourselves, our families, and our global human communities.

Thankfully, there is more to life than existing to replicate ourselves — a fact to which any playful dog can noisily attest. And so, while the average fungus may be perfectly content to fulfill its biological duty without question or complaint, we human beings, on the other hand, also need joy to make sense of our journey through life.

Joy allows us to feel *complete* by giving our enduring struggle to exist a heartfelt sense of meaning and purpose. Yet even at our journey's end, we may hope to find an afterworld of eternal bliss awaiting us there. It is this constant, lifelong reaching for joy that imbues us with a higher calling to be more than the equivalent of an upright talking fungus, but a fully-realized and happy human being.

Beyond this ambition, our collective pursuit of happiness also has a practical use in that it offers us a powerful reason to live beyond mere instinct alone. In seeking to enjoy ourselves, we are not only inspired to thrive and excel, but also given a positive outlook on life and feeling of anticipation that protects us against apathy, depression and other mental threats to our existence. But more importantly, when we feel happy, we also feel no desire to engage in acts of violence, warfare or suicide. In short, joy keeps us alive by giving us the desire to live. As such, without it, our spirit will wither, as will our hope for the future.

In light of these facts, it is clear that the feeling of joy is a necessity of life, not only for our own long-term physical and mental well-being, but also for the survival of our planet and its many animal inhabitants whose lives can be adversely affected by our failing emotional health.

Given its wide-ranging importance, our lifelong need for joy also represents a significant aspect of our biological design. We know this is true because nature creates living systems that succeed without need of frivolous gimmicks. As with fear, we can assume that the emotion of joy is likewise necessary to our survival, otherwise it would not exist as part of our conscious inventory. Subsequently, if we ignore our need to experience this aspect of our being, we suffer the consequences.

We can even find evidence for this among the sullen captives of any ill-kept zoo. As sentient beings, animals can also experience emotions in ways that enrich their lives — or mentally torment them. And given how poorly some are treated, we can understand why we may not want to seek proof that animals are conscious of their suffering at our hands.

Among humans, we see the symptoms of joy's absence as a growing epidemic of anger, anxiety and depression caused by an obsessive focus on serving only the physical demands of our body while ignoring those of our spirit. In what is a familiar cultural trap, we intentionally dismiss our need for joy by abandoning our dreams for a practical career that may lead to our intellectual, creative and emotional stagnation.

In denying ourselves a rewarding sense of mission or a meaningful use for our creative talents, we can inadvertently condemn ourselves to a life of misery by failing to reach our inherent joy potential. And while our biological instinct to survive can keep us functionally alive for many decades to come, it is only in clearing a path to joy that we will experience the kind of life that can leave us feeling inwardly buoyant and wholly satisfied.

The Joy Compass

Contrary to media advertising, joy is not something that we are forced to buy at a local shopping mall. Given its importance to our physical and mental well-being, we should therefore first establish a clear and less costly interpretation of joy as a point of reference.

On the surface, joy is a pleasurable emotional reaction to positive stimulation, either mental or physical. We experience this as a sudden heightened state of well-being; a kind of mental orgasm that varies in intensity from soothing to sacred.

What we may not realize during these bouts of internal bliss is that they also temporarily free our minds from the prison of primal fears that binds us to our physical form. In what is a momentary lapse in self-consciousness, our minds are able to soar above the mundanity of our routine existence through a powerful surge in our appreciation for life. In short, joy allows us to experience a genuine state of spiritual transcendence — a loosening of our mortal coil.

In that fleeting moment, we are able to reconnect with the blissful, childlike essence of our being in its former *unconditional* state of trust. It is therefore no secret why our minds should want to return to this elated and carefree state of innocence as often as possible and by any means necessary given that it makes us feel so good.

As part of its function, joy also acts as a kind of internal compass that guides us away from conflict toward greater harmony with ourselves and others. Unlike anger, our growing sense of joy nourishes and heals us, while inspiring even total strangers to feel safer and more relaxed in our presence. In this way, our lifetime of investment in joy leaves us increasingly enriched by attracting a growing wealth of emotional goodwill into our lives. And if words should fail us, a friendly smile remains an international form of currency that is accepted worldwide and never loses its face value.

As the language of the naked, trusting heart, joy inspires the kind of unconditional harmony that cannot be imposed by way of political will or religious decree. It also creates enduring bonds between us that far outlast those fearful defensive clusters induced by war or other kinds of adversity. Moreover, once a crisis ends, we typically separate only to quarrel again, whereas when joy brings us together, we want to bask in the light of those who lift our spirits to soar above our daily struggles and make our lives seem even more worth living.

In short, joy achieves what mere survival alone cannot by giving us an inspired reason to look forward to each new day. And in allowing our lives to be guided by the true bearing of our innermost joy, we will always have a reason to smile in knowing that our every step is taking us in the right direction.

The Way Forward

We have now established a relatively robust argument for the necessity of joy to our lives, not only to endure its hardships, but also as a source of spiritual nourishment for our optimum functioning. Yet in a world so ripe with joy potential, there still remain too many of us without our fair share of its bountiful harvest.

And although there may be conspiracies afoot, it is certain that the most daunting obstacle to our emotional success is not some shadowy cabal of deranged aristocrats plotting against our happiness, but our own stubborn habit of thinking in various joy-defeating ways.

Ultimately, what we will discover is that joy truly is just a state of mind; a realigning of the unspoiled values, beliefs and attitudes that had resided within us at birth as the conscious foundation for building our future bridges to happiness. Intuitively guided and acting as if free, we then encountered the most daunting mental obstacle to our future joy, which is the socialization process of our culture.

Conditioned since childhood to uphold the standards of thought and behavior that animate our society, we were also taught to erect mental barriers to reality that may now be compromising our ability to seek out and experience greater joy — unless we overcome them.

Worldwide, we are all engaged in this struggle to remain true to the pure, joyful essence of our original being while various forces from the inside and out manipulate our fears to keep us obediently serving their selfish interests. For example, our fear of death can keep us from going into unfamiliar neighborhoods or speaking the truth. Meanwhile, we are also engaged in a lifelong battle to reign in our body's instinctual Bio-Psychology, whose hard-wired behavioral traits can cause us to be overly selfish and competitive, thereby undermining our attempts to create deeper, more meaningful human relationships.

In seeking a joyful life, our mission is to defend our mental freedom against all the many oppressive forces we can encounter along the four paths common to human existence. We will later explore each path in detail to identify its associated obstacles to joy. In the meantime, here is a brief overview to help us anticipate the way forward:

The Four Paths to Joy

The Material Path to Joy

Hunger and a need for protection sets us upon the material path at the moment of birth. Thrust into a lifelong dependency upon the physical realm, our first material acquisition is that of our mother's milk and her comforting embrace. Thereafter, it would seem only logical if we tried to ensure our immunity from all future suffering by buying our own milk factory and enlisting an army of female surrogates to shower us with a similar maternal devotion to our every need.

Today, whatever form our hungers take, we may hope to satisfy them with equally hopeful acts of overconsumption on the material path. Yet in defining joy as a state of acquisition, our insatiable urge to possess will always leave us feeling empty without some emotionally fulfilling use for all of our costly clutter.

The Relational Path to Joy

Relationships are the foundation of our human existence, bringing us food and comfort while defining our sense of place and identity. Their enduring necessity to our life also makes them a convenient conduit through which we may hope to find a lifetime's supply of happiness. Yet we cannot always choose our relationship trading partners, be they our parents or political leaders, while our daily need for other people's money and acceptance threatens our ability to negotiate for better treatment at their hands. This often tempts others to exploit us, which creates that familiar obstacle to joy wherein we must neglect ourselves and make the needs of others our priority while trapped in depressing circumstances that are often difficult to escape.

The Spiritual Path to Joy
Each day, millions of people engage with the invisible forces of fate in a ritual act of worship that we know as "playing the lottery." Here, even in gambling, we reveal our inborn tendency to sacrifice our lives and money in the name of faith, hope and superstition. Unfortunately, this also makes us easy prey for religious charlatans and other tricksters who exploit this age-old human tendency for personal gain.

Today, as countless forces compete for mental control over our lives, we must *know ourselves* impeccably to prevent others from leading our minds astray. Spirituality is how we maintain our inner joy by attaining greater self-wisdom against all outer threats. A decidedly lone journey inward, it unearths the fundamental truths of a universal creed of inner contentment that does not require us to buy our admission into heaven from some self-appointed ticket vendor for God.

The Global Path to Joy
The global path to joy blends the material, relational and spiritual paths into a cultural recipe for organizing society. Designed by the privileged few to serve the basic needs of the many, these mental scripts to ensure the social order require us to adopt a "one-size-fits-all" approach to life that can create obstacles to joy by imposing limits on our freedom to express ourselves intellectually, sexually, or otherwise. On this path, our challenge is to create more liberated cultures that do not thoughtlessly discriminate against anyone. In this way, we might all know the joy of remaining true to ourselves while being truthful in our relationships with others. Our willingness to share is also critical to creating a more contented world wherein we all can thrive in peace and prosperity.

Leaving Box World

In having made a rough assessment of our current human condition, we can see that our species faces many challenges. Primarily, it is to free our minds to experience greater joy while trapped in a body seemingly with a mind and agenda of its own — to be selfish, fearful and competitive. In addition, we are trapped inside the collective mind of our cultures whose pressures upon us to conform to some widely-accepted standard of thinking and behavior can be both intense and life threatening.

No matter the pace of our conscious evolution, whether as a species or as individuals, it must all begin with the act of "thinking outside the box" — which is just an easier way of saying that *innovative modes of thinking do not arise from restrictive mental programming.*

As individual seekers of joy, our goal is to break free from any kind of restrictive "box world" of habitual thinking as our journey demands. However, this is often quite challenging under the mental influence of the *four paths* as we navigate our way through life. In that regard, let us consider the following analogy which summarizes for many of us the kind of mental and physical obstacles we face as citizens of any nation or members of any oppressive social group or institution:

...

A rabbit in the wild can easily find food anywhere, from leafy plants to tree bark and pine needles. Free to roam, its choices are many. But when forced into a cage, perhaps as a child's pet, its freedom to choose or control its destiny becomes restricted as a captive to the selfish want of others. As a result, its life and joy potential is compromised in no longer being able to regulate its own diet or freedom of movement.

...

A similar fate awaits us as infants born into the cage-like world of adult society. Like the rabbit, our childhood journey also begins with a free-roaming body and state of mind wherein we can find joy almost anywhere. Limited in motion only by our infant clumsiness, our wild, untamed spirit and curiosity are free to explore the world until others try to force our mind into the mental equivalent of that rabbit cage.

Before captivity, we did not fear if our body met the standards of the chemical companies selling beauty products, or if an invisible God was eagerly waiting to punish us for thinking the wrong thoughts. Instead, our only concern was to keep our hungry minds fed through constant playing, which is how most sentient beings learn to think, feel, move and express their joy in being alive.

Like any other animal, we humans were not born to live in zoos. And so, as a result of this mental containment process, our childlike enthusiasm for life can also quickly erode as others increasingly restrict our freedom to think and do as we please in serving their own selfish agendas. This kind of a mental "box-world" existence has now become a global blight upon our once limitless human spirit.

The symptoms of this blight can be witnessed by viewing our human civilization from the skies above. Here, we will see an endless array of box-like land divisions that offer an ironic contrast to the fact that we live on a spherical planet where no other animal marks its territory with straight lines or right angles. This outward manifestation of our boxed-in state of mind betrays a relentless want for control by putting unnatural limits on everything, including how we choose to think and behave. Hence, we encounter the expression of *thinking outside the box* because most people are thinking from within it.

But the human mind does not exhibit the kinds of sharp angles and unnatural divisions that so often inform our rigid thinking on matters as race, gender, politics or the pursuit of happiness. And so, like any caged animal, it also begins to rebel against this kind of programmed mental captivity. Yearning for greater freedom yet unable to escape, we may then feel increasingly anxious or emotionally distraught, which has fueled a vast empire for selling alcohol, drugs and other addictive forms of mental distraction to keep us pretending that all is well in our increasingly boxed-in human existence.

In clearing a path to joy, we will stop pretending and begin instead the process of reclaiming our joy potential as the free-roaming spirits we have always been inside.

A Lesson In Laughter

In reclaiming our lives from the restrictive influences of our world, we must not only anticipate its many obstacles to joy, but also be familiar with the inner workings of our mind. In this way, we can increase our joy potential by understanding how the outer world might be adversely affecting our ability to experience greater joy.

As one of the many uncommon insights promised earlier, let us now consider the mental mechanics of laughter and how it frees our mind from the joy inhibiting *rabbit cage* of our social conditioning:

...

In a world of unavoidable suffering, it is one of life's most welcome pleasures to collapse into an uncontrollable fit of laughter. Yet looking deeper into this joyful aspect of our conscious life, we find that humor is no laughing matter, but serious business indeed.

At its core, comedy is an act of mental vandalism against our most sacred illusions and the fears that maintain them. Specifically, it targets our emotional need for certainty by subverting the authority of our beliefs — especially those concerning authority itself.

For example, The Duke of Bogstench sounds like a legitimate title until we recognize its satirical assault on the vanity of the aristocracy. Here we attribute the stench of a bog to those who pretend to exist above the coarseness of nature and the feral "lower" classes — both of which serve as an opposing repulsive force by which a status-conscious person maintains their illusion of being separate from and superior to others in our world. In this way, like a pie thrust into the face of the pompously proud, comedy finds a way to keep us humble, especially when we cannot afford to humble ourselves.

Underneath it all, laughter is how our nervous system has learned to react when it feels *safely* disoriented as we are losing control over what we believe is meant to happen. Ironically, this is both a pleasurable and therapeutic feeling because it releases inner tensions that can build up in maintaining those beliefs. This kind of full-bodied stress release is most explosive when comedy pushes against any mental boundary of certainty that is guarded by intense fear. This is why controversial jokes about sex, religion or government authority are apt to cause a more explosive emotional reaction in that they are contradicting our most sacred and well-established senses of moral and social order.

This also explains why laughter is "the best medicine" in purging the mental stresses caused by maintaining beliefs whose psychic torment could lead to mental or physical illness. A haunting fear of religious demons or romantic rejection, for instance, can fill our entire waking lives with a constant feeling of dread — which is why such fears must also be humbled through some courageous act of humor.

What many of us do not realize is that humor also accelerates our conscious evolution by forcibly expanding the limits of our mind. The word humor itself means "fluid," which aptly describes our emotional attitude upon breaching the restrictive dams in our conscious flow.

Ironically, we are unaware of making such mental progress, yet its proof exists in our inability to laugh at the same joke twice. Once our mind have grown to accommodate any new humorous idea or concept, no matter how trivial or crude, we can no longer be taken by surprise by that particular thought — and so we are no longer able to laugh as we did when we first breached that specific mental barrier.

In this way we are also engaged in a kind of unspoken conspiracy with comedians as they help us to blissfully break through our mental barriers and defeat our harmful beliefs with their aptly named "punch lines." In their role as impromptu spiritual mentors, they can inspire us to attain a more boundless state of mind and thereby make it easier for us to realize our joy potential. Even in using profanity, they are simply proving to us that words alone are nothing to fear.

...

Given the intense pleasure we can feel by challenging our cherished beliefs and sense of certainty through comedy, we therefore need not fear breaking down with equal enthusiasm any other mental barriers that may be inhibiting the natural flow of joy through our lives. Again, joy is a state of mind, which is why we must learn to make room for its enduring presence in our consciousness. And sometimes that means having to discard ways of thinking for which we have no further use.

Nature Always Wins

As will become evident with each passing chapter, our greatest obstacle to joy and social progress is our attachment to misguided beliefs that are often imposed upon our psyche by others. As a result, not only are we engaged in an outer struggle against the flawed thinking of others, but also internally against any self-defeating beliefs to which we may still be clinging from our unenlightened past. Here as well, an analogy can put into context this inner conflict between our need for joy and the mental blockades inherent to our socially-conditioned minds:

...

Untainted by cultural bias or wishful thinking, the natural laws that govern wild animal and plant behavior are a reliable gauge of objective truth. One such truth is that a weedless green lawn cannot exist except in our fertile human imagination. Yet to impose this synthetic vision of perfection upon our natural world, we must spray toxic chemicals on our lawn and its insect inhabitants, thereby poisoning native wildlife, family pets, our drinking water and everything that comes into contact with our man-made nature-killing products.

Moreover, each week countless homeowners mow their lawns with the equivalent of a *nature slashing machine* that has us indiscriminately chopping up not only the grass, but also each year's new generation of crickets, toads, rabbits and the many wildflowers that feed honeybees and other pollinators. We may then return indoors, never to use our freshly-cut yard again until the following week's mindless assault. And if we should fail to conform to this ritualized suppression of nature, we may even be fined by our government for being *irresponsible*.

This is just one example of how we thoughtlessly harm ourselves and others in a stubborn quest to control nature and all that is wild.

The dandelion is our sworn enemy in this ongoing botanical war against reality; a resilient plant that mocks our every futile attempt to control nature by pushing through the slightest crack in our defenses, including a freshly-paved driveway. In doing so, it also reminds us that nature always wins, having the power and patience to push a delicate flower through any barrier we erect to deny its right to exist.

As an allegory, our struggle against the dandelion teaches us to live a more joyful life by allowing reality to prevail; to free ourselves from the anger and destruction we create in trying to impose our will on all that resists our efforts to control it, be it the forces of nature, or some truth about ourselves trying to push its way through our denial.

…

In accepting the truth of our need for joy, let us agree that we were all forcibly assimilated into adult society as children to become its next crew of "honest, hard-working citizens." Whether such preparation for service has us obediently toiling to pay taxes or committing acts of war in foreign lands, it will always limit our options to whatever best serves the interests of our leaders and their systems of government.

Subsequently, as every rebellious child soon discovers, any behavior not serving those interests is quickly poisoned out of existence by way of ridicule, rejection and various painful forms of retribution. This is how human weeds are controlled to maintain the artificial facade of our cultures and their potentially toxic beliefs. It is also the tainted soil from which we each must rise as seekers of joy.

In clearing that path, we must show equal determination to that of the dandelion in breaking through any barrier of resistance to the truth of our nature and need for joy. Let its tenacity and resolve become a symbol for the boundless child-like spirit that we must reclaim, along with our innate gifts of curiosity and the unbridled courage to explore life as though it was all new to us again.

Above all, we must not allow ourselves to fall victim to the frustration that consumes those fighting a lost battle for absolute control. Instead, let us surrender all such futile ambitions and their associated anger lest they also poison our flowering hope from within.

Ultimately, no matter how foreboding the future may appear, joy is always within reach. So trust yourself and step forward, for not only is the darkest soil often the most fertile, but like the dandelion and even the most crooked tree in the forest, so are we also constantly growing toward the light, for that is our nature.

CHAPTER 2
The Invisible Economy

Life may be an unfolding mystery, but we cannot leave that unfolding to chance if we expect to live a joyful life. Even just to survive we must feel confident in what we can predict about our own uncertain future.

Luckily, our early life teachers worked hard at filling our minds with certitudes. And trusting in their authority, we may have never thought to question those teachings, even now. Yet eventually there will come that day for each of us when we encounter someone who may strongly disagree with what we believe. And yes, we could dismiss them as living in a fantasy world, but they could accuse us of the same, leaving neither side the wiser from this unsettling clash between opposing realities.

What we learn from such interactions is that human certainty is a very uncertain thing — the truths in which we believe need not even be true for us to passionately defend them. And while our own slippery hold on truth poses little threat to family life at the dinner table, it can be lethal if two highly-trained physicians disagree about how to treat our child's sudden illness. That threat is further increased by warring factions of political and religious zealots fighting to impose their own preferred truths upon the governing of our nations — also regardless of whether their claims are true or merely a self-serving ruse.

In response, we could always talk about the weather to avoid arguing over what is true or "the right thing" to do. But we still need reliable facts to navigate this increasingly complex human world in our quest for joy. In short, life can be more than just something that "happens" to us if we take the time to learn *what is happening*.

Our first challenge is to think outside the box of our culture with its soothing cocoon of simplistic answers to calm our fears and keep us all hopeful in often hopeless circumstances. Furthermore, our leaders may lie to control us, which makes them unreliable as a source of authentic truth or wisdom. In fact, their antics are why we live in a world full of conflicting truths and reality distortions wherein the things we believe may have most of us living in some version of that "fantasy world."

In clearing a path to joy, we must first gain a strong, reliable foothold in reality by understanding our mind and how others can tamper with it. But like any electronic gadget, we use it each day without actually knowing how it works. Yet in peering beneath its slick grey surface, we find a bustling marketplace where our intimate thoughts transact with complex biological impulses to form the expression of our unique identity. What happens here affects all things, from our daily survival routines to how we define joy. It is here in the invisible economy of our mind that our quest for truth must begin, for in identifying its various currencies and methods of trade, we can gain the kind of certainty we need to realize our greater joy potential.

The Value Of Meaning

Living on a planet made of stone, we may find little reason to celebrate holding a small piece of it in our hands. Yet as an avid rock collector who has spent decades searching for this one specimen, this could well be our happiest day ever. And so we encounter one of life's open secrets in that joy is our reward for living with a heartfelt sense of purpose.

Whenever we imbue our actions with a personal sense of meaning, we will truly value them and respond to our success in ways that allow us to feel emotionally enriched. Best of all, even if we never reach our intended goal, we will still feel that the journey itself was worthwhile in having allowed us to do what we felt we were meant to do.

As this rock collecting analogy reveals, our feeling of joy can easily be engaged, even by making the pursuit of a unique stone a valuable currency within the invisible economy of our mind. In doing so, we are offered the emotional reward of feeling inspired by a sense of mission while the feeling of anticipation for our future success will increase our appreciation for just being alive. In short, our greatest asset in life is knowing what we want from life itself.

This notion is proven by the stark contrast in our attitude when we exist without a meaningful sense of purpose to guide our steps. We may then feel more like an emotional drifter on an aimless road of random events whereupon our actions have no greater purpose other than to ensure our daily survival. And if we should come to feel that our life is utterly worthless and disposable, then we may begin to treat all things in much the same manner, including our need for joy.

Moreover, without a heartfelt sense of meaning, life itself can begin to feel like a form of punishment. In trying to escape our suffering, we may then imbue any trivial pursuit with a false sense of importance to use as a form of emotional distraction.

There is evidence for this among those chronic shoppers who hope to find their happiness on the shelves of a discount store, and people who enter into loveless relationships just to escape feeling empty. Even among the wealthy, we find a competitive squandering of time and money on costly items whose only value is that somebody else might want them even more. And while such pursuits can keep us distracted for decades, they are not genuine paths to joy but only a way of coping with our spiritual disorientation as to who we are and what we want from our journey through life.

Frequently, such wasteful behavior arises when our Bio-Psychology has seized control of our mind because our spirit is not making better use of it. We may then revert to a more primitive use of our bodies and minds to serve equally primitive ambitions based on themes of basic survival and procreation or aimless hunting and gathering to feed our hunger for emotional nourishment. Thankfully, we can reverse this condition of spiritual inertia by simply allowing our minds to explore the world beyond the familiar bounds of our daily life routines where new sources of inspiration await to be discovered.

A Change In Attitude

Our quest for a meaningful mission in life may require broadening our emotional reach. This often means exploring unfamiliar worlds of joy potential that we may never have considered before.

For instance, a selfish person may find greater joy in serving others rather than withholding their time and energy out of fear. The same is true for a habitually submissive person who might also experience an increase in their joy potential by reclaiming a leadership role over their life. As such, we may find our lifelong path to joy by simply moving in an opposite direction to where our fear-based character inclinations have always been leading us. In this way, we also find new meaning in that familiar saying, "opposites attract."

Also worth considering is that our joy potential increases by inviting change into our lives; a theory supported by the fact that we also cannot keep laughing at the same joke throughout our lives. Instead, we must find new ways to shake the foundation of our established thinking to stir up our emotions.

However, any effort to change will be met by the powerful adversary of our biological resistance to change itself. Given our lifelong need for predictable access to food, family and other resources, we tend to anchor our lives to a single location or mental state to maintain control over life's uncertainties. As a result, our body and spirit tend to be at constant war with each other over the future direction of our life.

As an analogy, *we live as sea captains who value more the weight of our anchor than the lightness of our sail.* As such, we may also go down with our ship in fearing to let go of some anchor of security to which we are clinging. Yet the solution is not to go overboard by abandoning all that we know and love, but to simply trust ourselves to leave our familiar harbor of safe routines to explore new horizons. As many of us will discover, our values, beliefs and attitudes can often weigh us down and cause us to sink into despair in trying to protect ourselves from the threat of uncertainty. Yet ironically, it is often within that uncertainty wherein awaits our greatest potential for future joy.

Entering The Funnel

Let us invoke one last shipping metaphor as we consider that nautical tradition wherein "the captain goes down with the ship." Here, his fate rests not only with his own skill, but also with those drawing up the charts. As captains of our human vessel, we may also be navigating life by the charts of others, perhaps by trying to fulfill the dreams of our parents or embody our society's idealized notions of womanhood or patriotism. If we then add to that potential life disaster a co-navigator who refuses to change course without considering what is best for us, we can then understand why our joy may run aground in following the misguided directions of others into murky, uncharted waters.

We all face this threat of being misled, beginning in early childhood. In the wild, there is a natural life progression wherein animal mothers will teach their young to survive in this world. As human children, we are not only taught how to survive, but also how to think and become the kind of person who others prefer. We may even be assigned our father's name, which suggests we are but an extension of another's life and identity. Whether this proves flattering or a hindrance, it reveals that our inner sense of direction and freedom to choose can be easily compromised by the people who make such early life decisions on our behalf. In short, we may be treated as though our life belongs to others, and that may even include our foreskin, if born a male child.

In addition, our early life mentors may overload our minds with an ill-informed cargo of values, beliefs, attitudes that can further sabotage our future success in many aspects of adult life. Tragically, such mental tampering begins so early that we cannot defend against it. For that reason, our joy potential may also have been "funneled" into the narrow confines of someone else's limited knowledge of life or censorship of reality to become a mere trickle of its formerly majestic flow. Given our limitless creative potential, this would be like trying to force the ocean into a garden hose to control its output.

Not surprisingly, governments and religions also recruit us early in life for mental conditioning, for once their ideas are firmly anchored into our young minds, they are often difficult to eradicate or replace with better ones. We are all victims of this phenomenon whenever we refuse to hear other sides of an argument to defend our beliefs.

Whether done for reasons of virtue or villainy, the funneling process has lasting consequences for our joy potential by limiting our freedom to think, act and dream as we might have done without such mental interference. And just as our body limits our choice of physical activity, so may our mind now be limiting our choices of how to seek joy. As a result, we come to define reality by our limitations and limit reality by our definitions. In short, we become what we believe we can and often little more. In response, we must learn to dream bigger dreams and not only the kind that fit comfortably into another's garden hose.

Cropping And Wedging

As earlier stated, our fear of change derives from a need to control our access to resources for our survival in an uncertain world. This is also why our parents, teachers, governments and most others want to force their way of thinking upon us. Their simply logic is that by controlling our life, they can better control their own. Later as adults, we may fight to the death to defend our list of borrowed values, beliefs and attitudes upon which our survival and emotional comfort now also depend.

Our strategies for defending this mental territory may include lying, denying, name-calling, refusing to listen, shouting, making threats or even killing those who disagree with us. As for our motive, it is simply to ensure that our preferred version of the truth prevails.

This kind of defensive behavior is part of a "cropping" and "wedging" strategy that our mind utilizes to ensure that the external reality of our world conforms with the contrived inner reality we have created to feel safe, certain and in control of our life circumstances.

Cropping is a term derived from photography where we cut away the unwanted parts of an image to narrow the viewer's focus on our chosen subject. Our minds engage in a similar act of censorship by removing contradictory elements from reality to maintain our focus on what we want to believe. For example, we may ignore a spouse's affair to avoid disrupting our dreams for a financially stable future, or that our church minister is buying personal luxury items from our donations to avoid disrupting our faith in his moral virtues.

Wedging is a similarly self-serving act of mental propaganda wherein we forcibly attribute positive events to our beliefs to validate them. For instance, we may credit God with saving our life in a car accident, or shower praise on our preferred political party in good times and then conveniently blame the opposing party when things go wrong. In this way, our mind engages in a reflexive filtering strategy to keep the good reputation of our beliefs intact by not associating them with failure. This also ensures that we are never wrong or uncertain about anything, which explains why *cropping* and *wedging* are so widely popular.

Unfortunately, our world is divided by fear into feuding groups and nations seeking to protect whichever version of the truth best ensures their own continued access to power and privilege. Subsequently, this creates ironic paradoxes, such as when atheists and religious believers both find comfort in speculative myths about our human origin.

In clearing a path to joy, we must accept that the truths in which we believe may also have been compromised by our over-protecting them against scrutiny. For that reason, we must not ignore evidence that could bring the wisdom of our thinking into question. After all, we will feel a far greater level of certainty and mental order if guided by beliefs that we need not lie about to make them seem believable. It is best that we accept all evidence without prejudice as we find it, for no matter how much we feel the urge to defend our pride or emotional comfort, our ultimate goal is not to always be right, but to always seek the truth. And the motive for the one is mutually incompatible with that of the other. Moreover, the search for truth does not end for our personal comfort or convenience — nor that of our proud leaders.

In The Beginning

Now that we have thoughtfully explored our mind's development and its arsenal of mental defenses, we are better prepared to understand why some of us might want to reject the following information:

…

In light of the many conflicting versions of *the truth* being promoted to guide our future, our world is clearly in need of a more reliable basis for peacefully organizing and improving human life on a global scale. And while there has always been an abundance of defensive shouting and killing, verifiable *proof* of such claims remains in short supply.

Ultimately, in promoting greater self-awareness worldwide, we are best served by a truth that does not rely on our faith in what others are telling us but what we can prove for ourselves. In short, we need a truth that does not rise and fall with its proponents. A legitimate truth must be able to survive without need of myth or law enforcement and affect all things equally instead of favoring only one human group or species over another, as many of our currently held truths tend to do.

Our only suitable remaining candidate also boasts a proven record of having attended the origin of life itself — namely, that ancient and omnipresent force known to us as "energy."

Here is an undisputed and all-mighty animator of life whose eternal presence we can actually see and feel throughout our lives each day. Yet acknowledging energy's influential presence does not discount other invisible forces from also acting upon our lives, whether love or even forces from other dimensions. Everything is possible, but believing is not enough to make it true. We must instead be wiser in our approach to interpreting reality so that our truths will stand, even without us.

What energy offers is an objectively provable foundation by which we can better understand ourselves and one another. In this way, we can begin to move away from our historical paths of tribal violence and moral hypocrisy toward a future time of enlightened contentment that would ideally see all of us thriving in peace. This will require not only standing on common mental ground but also seeing in others what is equally true within ourselves. In short, a worldwide consensual truth based on provable, non-subjective evidence.

In providing us with that common mental ground, energy presents us with a universal form of currency that determines the fate of every least fragment of any celestial body, including ours. It is what each of us requires to live as we continually feed the flowing river of electric impulses being conducted by the moisture in our bodies. As an aside, this is why we die faster from thirst than starvation as water contains the electrolytes needed to conduct our body's electrical charge. And as that energy surges through our being, it also influences who we are and who we desire to be by conducting those thoughts and behaviors that result from our various states of *physical* and *spiritual* hunger.

In this way, energy is an invisible guiding force that can manifest in countless ways, from a myriad of biological life forms to inspired acts of artistic creativity and the laws and forces of nature. In short, nothing escapes energy's all-pervading influence. And each day we must also consume energy to maintain that electrical spark of consciousness that is anchored within this hopeful biological vessel we think of as "me."

The Physics of Psychology

In having reviewed energy's glowing resumé, we can finally put it to work to help us explain ourselves to ourselves. In future chapters, we will delve more deeply into the physics of our human psychology, but first we should get better acquainted with our new invisible friend.

Energy can take many forms. For instance, we hunger not for food but for the energy contained in food. Plants and animals are all merely energy in disguise, for as we consume them, our body converts their physical forms into nutrients to sustain us. Yet each nutrient is made of atoms whose core essence is energy. In this way, energy connects each of us by an invisible cosmic thread to all that exists; we are all but one form of energy consuming it in another to feed our shared hunger for existence, eternally — a real-life version of the mythical vampire.

Yet once we have eaten our fill, we continue to hunger for various other forms of energy in disguise. Here, our mind acts like it own kind of digestive system by converting one form of energy into another. This often involves turning solid objects or human gestures into emotions within our invisible economy in conjunction with our physical senses.

For example, we may convert eating a delicious meal into the feeling of pleasure, or watching a sports match into a feeling of triumph. Such *symbolic energy conversions* explain our endless list of social hunting and gathering behaviors through which we attempt to feed various kinds of spiritual hunger. In this way, we can convert anything into a form of emotional nurture, from a bouquet of roses into feelings of romantic love to the wearing of a uniform into feelings of pride and power.

Yet all such emotional responses exist only as invisible transactions inside our minds. This makes them *subjectively true and real to us,* but not to others. In short, one mind's rock is another mind's pleasure. This kind of symbolic energy conversion also makes possible the creating of consensual illusions, such as the imaginary power of money to control our lives by whatever amount is permitted to reach our hands.

In closing, we now have a basis for understanding why we might cling to illogical beliefs due to our constant need for energy in various forms. We also understand why we behave much like the alchemists of old in seeking to transmute anything from a street brawl or catching a trophy fish into the emotional riches for which we yearn. However, as we will also discover, our quest for joy has little to do with amassing symbolic energy in our bank accounts, wielding power over others, or exercising unlimited selfishness branded as "freedom." Yet such lessons are not taught in schools, nor can any authority figure tell us what path to joy is best for us. Instead, that mystery is ours to solve by fearlessly facing ourselves each day to ask "Why?" of all we do and dream about. It is our curiosity that will lead us forward, not our fear of what we may find. Ultimately, in gaining a greater awareness of our spiritual needs within the invisible economy of our mind, we can set ourselves upon a path of limitless encounters with joy. And thereafter, all we need do is take our first step forward in courage and trust.

CHAPTER 3
A Matter Of Convenience

Knowledge is power and no joy school education is complete without also knowing how to make ourselves perfectly miserable. Thankfully, such training is provided free of charge by the many masters in that art.

Among them are those angry drivers speeding frantically past us on the fast lanes of life while waving their fists and yelling insults at us for slowing their progress. Ironically, their impatience is the unintended side effect of a modern technology-based lifestyle that had promised to leave us with more time to relax and enjoy ourselves. Instead, it is not only our hurried lives but also our opportunities to experience joy that can become just another passing blur in our haste to get ahead.

Not surprisingly, a quick scan of media advertising reveals that *fast*, *free* and *easy* are also the most common words of mass seduction in use today by promising those conditions most attractive to every human energy-combusting organism in search of greater convenience.

But as *faster* foods and a heavily-polluted planet reveal, convenience does not always improve our quality of life and may even increase our overall suffering. Yet we continue to deploy this strategy to decrease our efforts while conveniently ignoring that our desire for convenience is always relative to the speed we have already attained. In other words, even as our life is racing along faster than ever today, by tomorrow our incessant drive to further decrease our expenditure of time and energy may have us feeling that our current pace is already too slow. And as each new generation dismisses the last for having fallen behind, this impulse to constantly accelerate has all but eliminated our ability to connect with life in a more tactile and emotionally-fulfilling way.

Today, where once a skilled craftsman had patiently carved wood into furniture by hand, he now pushes buttons on a furniture-making machine. No longer permitted a sensual and creative interaction with the natural world, his only means to experience joy is represented by the symbolic harvesting of a weekly wage to spend on machine-made products by other button pushers working in equally unfulfilling roles.

As for joy, it must also come to us *fast, free* and *easy* as a matter of convenience in a life too distracted and short of time to ponder its own purpose or direction. Today, this hasty path to misery is fast becoming acceptable in a world that defines the human race as a race itself. Let us therefore slow down for a moment to consider how a corruption of our fundamental relationship to energy itself has come to undermine countless aspects of our collective quest for joy.

The Path Of Least Resistance

We can better understand the cause of our haste-filled lifestyles and their growing negative impact by identifying similar behaviors in other forms of energy. For instance, as water under the influence of gravity, it exhibits a similar behavior seen in the physics of our own psychology by taking the path of least resistance down the side of a mountain. In this way, water proves to be as opportunistic and lazy as we can be in choosing not to overwork ourselves.

Similarly, under the biological gravity of our instinct to survive, we also favor taking the path of least resistance to avoid losing time and energy. A classic example is when we clear a trail through a forest to hasten our future travels there. Wild animals will then also use our trail to save energy in not having to push through the dense undergrowth. Meanwhile, a fallen tree across a winter stream becomes an improvised bridge to avoid the loss of energy to a longer detour or the loss of body heat in having to wade through the frigid water. Each such decision to avoid making a greater effort represents an act of *convenience*, which is a survival strategy that all creatures utilize *to save energy by expending the least time and effort to accomplish any task.* And naturally, we feel compelled to use the same approach for attaining many other goals in life, including the fulfilling of our need for joy.

As an aspect of natural law, convenience-oriented thinking is also part of our Bio-Psychology, which is why this natural tendency toward convenience exerts such a powerful influence on all aspects of how we live and govern our societies. For example, it is easier for us to buy fast food than to cook for ourselves, or to conform to the demands of our boss than risk losing our job. Likewise, it is easier for leaders to control us by removing our freedoms of choice and inciting our fear, which has created countless obstacles to joy for many in our world.

Peering into the darkest aspects of convenience-oriented behavior, we also find the causes of slavery, theft and rape, which are all a means of stealing other people's energy to avoid the inconvenience of having to invest more of our own time and effort to achieve our goals.

Whether seeking greater convenience for logical reasons or out of a primal fear of losing to others, such examples teach us that we may also be losing countless opportunities for emotional fulfillment in wanting everything to come to us in an increasingly *faster* and *easier* manner.

As a musician, for example, we will deny ourselves a lifetime's worth of pleasure if, rather than investing the time and effort to learn how to play an instrument or compose music, we buy instead a machine that can create music for us. And what lofty summits of achievement might we have already conquered in science, medicine or in the protecting of our planet's ecology had we not always withheld our best efforts to save time and money in reaching for a lesser excellence?

Unfortunately, our collective progress toward healing this condition is hindered by those political leaders who, as a matter of convenience, only want to treat the symptoms of our ailing societies to avoid making a greater long-term effort to achieve a genuine cure. As such, it is the burden of ordinary citizens to excise this growing social malignancy of convenience-oriented thinking from our lives so that our need for joy does not also become yet another inconvenience on this rapid decline toward doing more and more of nothing at all.

The Avoidance Of Suffering

Convenience-oriented thinking is designed to protect us against the loss of energy. Yet hidden beneath this ambition is the far more serious motive of avoiding the suffering associated with energy loss, which our biology interprets as a direct threat to our survival. This is confirmed by observing similar behavior in other conservative-minded animals.

For instance, the northern black bear is best known for her winter hibernations wherein she sleeps to conserve energy during the coldest months. She does this because searching for food in deep snow would cause her to lose too much energy, thus resulting in her death. Instead, her survival depends upon a strategic hoarding of potential energy as body fat, which she accomplishes by eating in excess of her needs in warmer times of plenty. In this way, she awakens from her slumber a thinner bear, but very much alive to raise her newly-born cubs.

Humans are equally conservative-minded in sharing this impulse to hoard against future adversity. We do this by filling our cupboards with excess food or saving money "for a rainy day." But unlike the bear, how we define *suffering* can be a subjective matter. As such, while some of us may barely whimper in having broken our leg, others are reduced to fits of primal screaming in having run out of coffee.

Such a frail emotional state may often result from a lifestyle of being overly-protected against adversity, which can cause us to feel helpless without an army of servants to suffer on our behalf. Ironically, we find a parallel for such spoiled behavior in the wild. Here, the *slave-making* ant becomes so dependent on its parasitic relationship to enslaved ant servants that it can starve to death in the presence of food in having forgotten how to feed itself. As such, it has become a victim of its own fast, free and easy lifestyle in the wild.

Similarly, it has long been a matter of convenience within human societies for those at the top of the dominance hierarchy to enslave the *lower classes* to avoid suffering the loss of their own energy. Ironically, in having to become a human sacrifice to their gods of greater comfort, we are also drained of income tax and enlisted to fight in wars whose cost is conveniently financed by diverting funds from essential social services into bullets and body bags. And while this has kept countless generations of men gainfully employed in dying for their country, it ultimately robs our nations of their spiritual health by creating joyless divisions among its privileged and those being sacrificed for the sake of protecting those privileges.

Thankfully, we do not all hunger for unlimited power over others. Yet we may also be tempted to lie, cheat, steal or withhold our kindness in an attempt to avoid suffering the loss of our energy under that popular conservative strategy wherein we take as much as we can while giving back as little as possible. Yet thankfully, we do not all behave this way, which proves that there can be differences in our human behavior not accounted for purely on the basis of biology.

Crimes Of Convenience

As a quick review, convenience-oriented thinking is a natural survival strategy among animals in the wild. Yet once it is translated into the foreign language of human culture, it promotes a selfish way of life that threatens both our joy in the present and our existence in the future.

Here, where the love of money stands falsely accused as "the root of all evil," we find instead that a want for convenience is evident at the scene of every crime. Even our legal justice systems fall victim when a prosecutor or police officer seeks a path of least resistance to a fast, free and easy conviction or political career advancement by hiding evidence and knowingly sending an innocent person to languish in prison.

We can define crime itself as *an unbalanced, often violent exchange of energy forced upon us by others* — the threat of which incites a fear of loss and suffering that compromises the joy of every society.

Here as well, we can connect our convenience-oriented thinking to the motive of any criminal act. Even senseless acts of violence often betray an attacker's symbolic attempt to convert the conquest of others into *self-esteem energy,* the way athletes do in defeating a rival team.

Meanwhile, to avoid facing his own inner failings, a serial killer may conveniently project them onto his victims, who now symbolize those faults he must ritually slay to perfect himself. Ironically, a similar kind of behavior can afflict political or religious groups who conveniently blame "outsiders" for their inner discontent. Their actions demonstrate that familiar energy-saving ruse of conveniently blaming others for the problems we create. Aside from justifying our prejudices, it also saves us the time and effort of having to improve ourselves.

Child sexual abuse is also a crime of convenience because nothing is easier than to exploit the trust of a helpless dependent. And just as any child must trust its adult protectors, so must we also trust one another as citizens to protect us against the threat of all such selfish crimes.

Unfortunately, the convenience-minded quest for economic power ensures that criminality runs rampant in our societies. This also causes many to exhibit the cunning of a wild predator in gauging the field of social opportunity for whichever human prey can offer them the path of least resistance to ensuring their own selfish gains.

Convenience-oriented predation explains why the young of society are targeted by the sellers of addictive and meaningless mass consumer products. Meanwhile, the poorest are subject to a constant plundering of their land, labor and freedoms by those seeking a faster, easier route to increased wealth or the building of a self-glorifying empire. And to make their conquests even more convenient, they enlist the services of armed mercenaries to convince their protesting victims that it would be far more convenient for them to surrender or just stay home.

Despite what apologists for unchecked greed or economic growth may claim, such behaviors are not incidental flaws in the fabric of our societies but purposeful acts of human predation that encourage in politics and business the kind of ethics and stalking tactics mirrored by serial rapists and pedophiles. In short, for the most part, our societies are *a crime in progress.*

Killing Risk Management

Ironically, we may have less to fear in facing a well-fed wild lion than a predatory business empire driven by an insatiable appetite for profit and power — as both the nicotine addiction and war industries have shown in their disregard for human life. Yet even the most shameless of human predators must abide by laws from which they cannot buy their immunity. Instead, they may enlist the laws of nature to gain an unfair advantage in hunting humans for economic sport. And just as magicians do not divulge their trade secrets for creating illusions, so are we best preyed on as consumers if unaware of how these licensed hunters of our incomes exploit our biological relationship to energy for their own selfish gain.

In defending ourselves against such attacks, let us consider first the hunting behavior of a wild lioness. Sleeping much of the day and only targeting the weak and vulnerable, the lioness also saves vital energy by assessing her risk of energy loss while hunting. This often leads to her giving up a chase to avoid fatigue, which could make her vulnerable to attack by other apex predators. In human economics, we refer to this as "risk management," which is *the strategic avoidance of unnecessary loss by assessing the risks inherent to our social hunting and gathering behavior.*

Insurance companies represent a perfect example of this strategy by expending the least revenue on outgoing claims to ensure the highest incoming profits — a motive which their advertising conveniently fails to declare. As with all businesses, they exist to make money, not to give it away — and this is clearly demonstrated by their hunting style.

Credit cards demonstrate a form of economic predation wherein our impulse to manage risk is being used against us. Here, the illusion of our having easy access to *free* money without immediate consequences allows us to conveniently override our own impulse to conserve energy by delaying the feeling of loss. This creates the illusion of our having greater financial vitality so that we will keep hunting for our happiness at the local shopping mall as the targeted prey of money lenders in a growing *debt industry*. Credit lending is also profit-driven and thereby not beholden to any moral or ethical concern for our future suffering.

In the meantime, having access to credit delays the discomfort we would otherwise feel by having to save and spend our own money for each purchase. This can also tempt us to take greater financial risks, as seen by the behavior of many governments who amass insurmountable debts that future generations will still be paying interest on — perhaps for abandoned sports stadiums built to accommodate a singular event. This makes it even more ironic when we borrow money to finance such trivial, fleeting vanities yet allow our societies to languish from neglect.

But the greater subplot of this story is loss itself, for credit debt also allows for the economic ownership of entire nations by a wealthy few. In this weaponless war for global conquest, the more money we owe as a nation, the more we are owned by our lenders.

Thankfully, the power of money is just another illusion summoned for the convenience of the magicians of the economic class. Nor could they hide their trade secrets from view in a world that has transitioned toward a state of direct democracy where informed consent is the law.

Ironically, on either side of this symbolic energy equation there is a quest for greater convenience: as the borrower, it is the convenience of not having to spend our own savings to hunt and gather; for the lender, it is the convenience of being able to control people or entire nations without having to raise a fist or fire a single bullet.

The Lazy Mind

Credit is not the only convenient tool for killing our risk management impulse. Guns achieve a similar result by emboldening police officers, criminals and sport hunters alike to bravely challenge some defenseless citizen or wild animal to a mismatched contest for dominance. Yet the most advanced social predators have no need for guns because they can solicit our surrender by simply wearing down our mental resistance.

The effectiveness of their strategy is assured because proper thinking is not a fast, free and easy activity. In fact, it requires a great investment of time and effort that not only depletes our energy reserves but also stresses our mind the way hard labor stresses our body. In short, if done properly, thinking is hard work.

The ensuing mental fatigue from deep thinking can also cause us to feel agitated or be careless. As a result, a student may even fail an exam for having studied too much. To guard against such energy loss, our mind's own path of least resistance is to avoid thinking in favor of acting on impulse to gain our desired rewards — perhaps by cheating on an exam instead. As such, "laziness" is our mind's default setting.

Impatience is the symptom of our mind struggling to conserve its energy. This is evident whenever we start randomly pushing buttons on a new device to avoid the effort of reading the manual. This impulse to avoid thinking while acting in haste is also what makes us easy prey for economic predators who intentionally exploit our mental laziness for their personal gain.

Among their familiar traps is the small print used in advertising. Here, distracted by our haste to enjoy some promised reward, our mind conveniently ignores the unpleasant information that might otherwise trigger our objection to buying the product. A further example is the exhaustive length and language used in legal contracts. This hastens our signing as we try to save time and energy by not questioning what unfair advantages the seller is trying to gain by making their motives such a struggle to understand.

In seeking a similar competitive advantage over our minds, leaders in government and business may hire skilled lawyers and marketers to distract us from knowing the entire truth. Their job is to increase our mental struggle to understand what we might be losing through our social contract as citizens or consumers. Not unlike a pack of hungry wolves wearing down a deer in the deep snow, their tactics paralyze our minds with such fatigue that we may willingly forfeit our every right to defend our interests so that our liberties or incomes can more easily be preyed upon. Yet in promoting unfair-play, they also promote an air of suspicion in our dealings with them — and even lifelong feelings of regret. For that reason, there is often a distinct lack of conscience and ethics among those who take advantage of us in this way.

Shallow media distractions can further prevent our thinking about social and political issues that adversely affect our lives if our intellect, like our body, becomes sluggish for lack of exercise. Yet beyond mental fatigue and distraction, there is an even greater threat to our individual freedom of choice if we intentionally refuse to think as a matter of convenience. In doing so, we then risk not only becoming our own worst enemy, but also a grave threat to any peaceful society.

Easing Into Prejudice

We have seen many examples of how convenience-oriented thinking can create obstacles to a joyful life. Yet no obstacle is more tragic than those needless social divisions we promote by unfairly discriminating against others in a fast, free and easy way to save time and effort.

By focussing only on the race, gender or income of others and then conveniently ignoring the finer details of their character or personal contributions to society, we also make it easier to justify mistreating them out of a fear of losing our own social advantages to any potential new rival. Thankfully, we need not succumb to this thoughtless mental tendency toward prejudice if we give some critical thought to its three primary causes. These we can identify as follows:

The Need To Stereotype:
In the wild, a sudden rustling sound in the grass may signal that we are about to be attacked by a predator. Our body's instinctive reflex is to turn toward that sound to identify its source because we cannot risk ignoring it. While it may only be the wind stirring, it could also be death approaching us in stealth mode.

This survival reflex is also why loud and unexpected noises startle us; a reaction commonly exploited in horror films to induce fear. In always turning to face that sound, we also demonstrate a biological *prejudice* against all unfamiliar sounds by impulsively and thoughtlessly treating them as a potential threat to our lives. This demonstrates the forming of a stereotype wherein we see the fault of one in all others of its kind, be it a sound or an unfamiliar type of human being.

Like the printing industry from which the term "stereotype" derives, our mind also tends to use a single template to make multiple copies of the same prejudicial judgment against others. That is why we may hear ourselves saying: "Those people are all the same!" even if such a statement is entirely untrue in judging "our own kind." After all, we do not all act the same as others of our own race, gender or income.

Animals also share this same defensive stereotyping impulse because we could all potentially be another's next meal if caught off guard. As humans, we are already ill-equipped to defend ourselves and must be even more cautious to avoid being attacked by a superior predator. In anticipating that threat, our earliest defense is to *visually identify* who is a friend or foe from a safe distance. This gives us time to prepare to fight or flee from that danger and explains why we make convenient use of people's appearance to visually judge their threat or social value relative to ours. This lessens our risk of losing by avoiding close contact with people who may have the strength or motive to defeat us and steal our energy resources — or even take our lives.

In constantly surveilling our world for threats, what we fear most is the unknown, as also represented by people from a foreign culture or who wear unfamiliar clothing — which signals that they may engage in other unpredictable behaviors. This is why young rebels often dress to intimidate as a way to defy any attempt by their parents or society to shape their personal identity or future life narrative.

Fortunately, all such social discrimination can easily be managed by making direct contact with those we fear and learning to understand them. Yet this also requires making ourselves vulnerable and investing time and effort that our lazy, fearful mind may claim we cannot afford on behalf of world peace. As a result, we may continue in the habit of not talking to strangers while treating them all as being equally guilty of some unknown crime until they have proved themselves innocent.

The Need For Certainty:
A fear of strangers may sometimes be warranted when a loved one has failed to return home as expected. During such anxious moments, our mind can fill with an overwhelming fear of the unknown as we wonder to ourselves: *Where are they? What has happened to them?*

In struggling for answers, our survival instinct can prejudice us to fill that mental void with unsettling thoughts of what dangers our loved one may have encountered. The resulting feelings of emotional agony from worry and helplessness causes our entire being to feel weak and drained of energy. And if our worst suspicions are confirmed, then the process of grieving will only increase our feeling of loss and confusion.

Given the emotional and physical gravity of such a fear response, it is obvious that beyond unfamiliar sounds, we also face a further threat of energy loss and suffering from our *feelings of uncertainty*.

In the domain of natural law, uncertainty makes us feel unsure of ourselves, whereas being decisive makes us potent. This is as true in the wild as in any competitive human society wherein *the slow to choose are quick to lose*. And in observing our global proliferation of spy agencies and surveillance equipment, we can see that the uncertainty caused by our fear of the unknown drives our quest for knowledge even more so than natural curiosity itself — even magazines use fear-inducing cover questions to trigger our want to pay for their glossy answers.

Yet even as we fill our textbooks and intelligence databases with ever more worldly knowledge, the vastness of our planet alone ensures that we can never be certain of knowing everything. And naturally, we have a convenient way of coping with the threat of our being overwhelmed by the many uncertainties of life as well.

First, we invent *reassuring myths* that offer a simple explanation for all that we feel uncertain about — whether by offering up an almighty God or an all-in-one evolution solution to calm our fears. This brings us a comforting sense of knowing in facing the greater unknown.

Secondly, we employ superstition, a ritualized physical interaction with the nonphysical world to create the illusion that we can control the unknown and thereby our fate. Such behaviors range from wearing good luck charms and praying for personal favors to eating tiger parts to gain courage. This explains why people throughout the world have adopted *a regimented lifestyle based on faith or objectivity* to gain control of their interpretation of reality. And best of all, it matters not if what we believe is true as long as it allows us to feel certain. And this is why nearly everyone we meet seems remarkably sure of what they know in that it helps them to cope with their fear of not knowing.

The Need For Control:
In adopting various cultural myths and superstitions, we demonstrate an instinctual want for control over our circumstances to ensure our survival. School and other forms of institutionalized learning further increase that feeling as we adopt various values, beliefs and attitudes that allow us to negotiate for greater power within society.

During our learning process we may also be exposed to what we can refer to as "fear fencing." This is the convenient practice of mentally dividing our world into a two-tiered hierarchy of "right versus wrong" or "us versus them." Fear fencing makes it easier to train our minds by causing us to fear any "wrong" way of thinking that could undermine our faith in those belief systems that offer us greater certainty. It also gives others greater control over our lives in declaring what is the *right* or the *wrong* way of thinking in our society.

Fear fencing is an aspect of stereotyping and a troublesome element in forming *Acquired Social Identities* (ASIs) that we will investigate in the coming chapter. It allows us to conveniently discriminate against anything not residing on the "right" side of our newly-erected mental border against uncertainty or reality itself by dismissing it as being "wrong" — the way an atheist might dismiss religion.

Fear fencing can have a practical use, such as when teaching our child that playing with fire or knives is *wrong*. But serious mental obstacles to joy can arise if we tell our child not to speak to other children living on the "wrong" side of a fear fence we have build to avoid our own inner feelings of uncertainty. Moreover, driven by our urge to compete for dominance, we also defend those mental territories that elevate our status or ensure us of always being *right*. This explains a worldwide human trait wherein people adopt simplistic systems of thinking that allow them to achieve a feeling of certainty in life while also declaring them to be superior to anyone outside of those systems.

Although a complex topic, its expression is easily recognized in a world divided into warring factions of "us" versus "them" where facts and fine details do not slow our quick judgment of those on the wrong side of our belief system. This explains why even the most dull-minded of individuals can be seen strutting like a peacock in having adopted some conveniently thoughtless interpretation of life that claims to favor them above all others. Why would we give up such a rewarding delusion, especially if its only requirement is to be born into the *right* race, gender or social caste? Better yet, why not flaunt our favored status to draw attention to ourselves? And as we can see, many do.

As for our own feelings of certainty, we now better understand how the fear-fencing process is used to create social prejudices based on our competitive need to feel superior to others. This also creates mental barriers to attaining a global state of joy as governments, religions and academic institutions fight to maintain their own proprietary systems of social control by dismissing all rival systems of governing or modes of thinking as "the enemy" to be defeated.

In completing this lesson on how to achieve a perfect state of misery, let us also consider the "Gender Wall" that every culture erects to offer us greater certainty and control in our social role as men or women. Separated at birth according to our sex organs, we are then offered two stereotypical gender lifestyles whose inflexibility promotes a fearful and competitively-driven disdain for anyone seemingly confused as to which side of that gender wall is the *right* one for them.

This explains our often reflexive prejudice against homosexuals, who embody a hybrid human identity that defies any narrow interpretation of gender or reality itself. And so, like any angry driver who wants to recklessly speed ahead, we may also wave our fists and shout hostilities at such people for creating yet another obstacle to a *fast, free* and *easy* life of thoughtless convenience in our black and white world.

CHAPTER 4
The Promise of Joy

Temptation is a nagging presence in our daily lives as we are mercilessly bombarded from every direction by emotionally-charged enticements to buy, choose or believe in what others have to offer.

Today, the promise of joy is the primary sales tool used to promote anything from cars, houses and can openers to the religious identities in which we place our unwavering faith. And with seemingly every product, service or ideological lifestyle promising to lead us to joy or its symbolic equivalent, we might even begin to hope that a cure for unhappiness is within our collective reach. But sadly, we are instead more likely to lose a significant amount of money and trust in greater humanity to the deceptive practices of various skillful liars.

After all, a promise is a worthless commodity in trade, running just behind money and gold in its value to our biological existence. Costing nothing to make and affordably within reach of anyone's lips, it acts as an invisible form of collateral with which others try to secure a line of credit on our trust. Thereafter they can boldly demand from us almost anything in advance of their having to pay for it, whether it be money, sex or our lifelong servitude in return for empty assurances that we will "soon" be rewarded for our efforts. And given that no one likes to lose in our human race for more — be it their pride or the ill-gotten money in their bank account — we are as unlikely to hear a confession of guilt from these abusers of the public trust as we are to see a thief return our valuable possessions.

Human history is also mostly just a recounting of our victimhood at the hands of various deluded despots and articulate psychopaths. In defending ourselves against these high level abuses of the public trust and those of the average street level grifter, we can employ one of three potential defense strategies:

The *first* is impractical because it requires us to reject all promises outright and always demand immediate results. The *second* is the least popular option because it requires us to reassess the joy potential of all those values, beliefs and attitudes by which others can seduce us, be it our want for fame and fortune, or to enter a storybook romance. Our *third* option is the most convenient in that we simply continue to live in denial as unwitting accomplices in the sabotaging of our future joy. In short, business as usual for both victim and perpetrator.

However, given that any credible path to joy will require choosing the more challenging second option, let us investigate how to create the feeling of joy and inner contentment for ourselves so that we no longer have to trust in those who promise them to us.

A Cry For Attention

In recalling our childhood and later transition into adulthood, we may remember them only as a slow aging process punctuated by a number of emotionally-charged events. Yet also interwoven with them was the subtle process of our learning to gain acceptance through conformity.

It all began upon entering our world with a somewhat fitting cry of distress and a sudden, overwhelming need for attention. And as is the good fortune of most helpless newborns, nature ensured that we were immediately attended to by our mother's warm embrace and given the necessary comforts and nourishment we needed. However, not long thereafter, a noticeable shift began to occur in what may have seemed like an unconditional relationship between mother and child.

As a natural response and out of necessity, our mother then began to teach us — within the limits of her own life experience — how we are to interact with our environment to ensure our own future survival.

Our father may also have participated in this teaching process if he was present and actively engaged in family life; yet just as in the wild, our mother was perfectly capable of doing this work alone.

At this early stage in our development, we were asked to behave in certain ways to earn our mother's positive attention. In doing as we were told, we might have heard her say "yes" or "good girl," which was accompanied by an enthusiastic smile or even a delicious treat. In stark contrast, we may have been offered an angry scowl or physical pain as punishment if we failed to do as requested, accompanied by words of scorn and rejection, such as "no" or "bad boy!"

Whether or not we recall such teaching moments, they nonetheless signaled the beginning of a lifelong process of external manipulation wherein we are tempted to conform to the demands of others to earn their positive attention and acceptance or simply to avoid the various kinds of pain associated with their rejection of us for being "bad."

Although a human mother will often remain a valuable ally to her children for life, she must also eventually stop responding to our every distressed whimper for help in allowing us to grow more confident and self-reliant as she herself had to do. And so there will come a day when we must also set out upon that inevitable human journey of trying to ensure that our needs will be met by gaining the positive attention of others within our society — to "make a living," as is often said.

But much to our dismay, what we find is an overwhelming demand for such attention, making it a valuable commodity for which we must now selfishly compete. And this we do by engaging in various kinds of attention-seeking strategies.

The Fisherman's Hook

Gaining social attention is very important because it promises to give us access to the time and energy of many people, which can lead us to the energy rewards we seek, be it employment, career advancement, friendship, marriage, or just frivolous sexual pleasure. And logically, the more positive attention we attract to ourselves, the more opportunities we create to negotiate for our desired rewards.

Like every peacock or positively-charged atom, we accomplish this task by making ourselves appear more "attractive" than our rivals for attention. The unspoken secret of this enticement game is to appear *rewarding* so that others see some selfish advantage in approaching us, be it for our money, sexual favor, or to increase their perceived social standing by being seen in our esteemed company.

This also explains our often obsessive grooming and self-adornment rituals in preparing to display our reward potential in public. Like the fisherman, we must then also present our bait and wait patiently in the hope that the fish are biting. This is how we all must lure our intended catch into energy transactions for our benefit, be it for marriage, to sell them a used car, or to win their applause as an aspiring entertainer.

In more recent historical times, our gaining of positive attention and acceptance has become essential to negotiating for our basic survival. As such, we are forced to compete ever harder to ensure that our rivals do not monopolize the many potential energy rewards of an admiring society. However, our oft-heated battles for attention can also have a number of destructive social repercussions.

Among them is that we now promote the winning of attention itself as a path to joy. This has caused many to thoughtlessly pursue fame and fortune for their own sake rather than as a byproduct of choosing an emotionally fulfilling career. It is also why many successful entertainers will feel disenchanted in having nowhere higher to ascend emotionally as the inevitable landslide of celebrity status pulls them down again.

Self-confidence is also important to gaining positive attention and acceptance. This is why we flaunt our physical assets while concealing any flaws that could invite rejection. But like any young animal finding itself inexperienced, alone and struggling to survive, a desperate desire for acceptance can also attract opportunistic social predators who prey upon both our want for attention and fear of rejection — perhaps by offering us the chance to be sexually humiliated in the porn industry.

And naturally, all of this frantic energy-trading activity does not go unnoticed by the more sophisticated apex predators of our society.

Today, there exists a thriving "fear economy" for selling products and services that exploit our fear of losing the attention of others or being rejected for our lack of reward potential. Here, the images of our social rivals are even broadcast directly into our homes as hyper-sexualized fashion models who our daughters must emulate to also be considered worthy of a man's celebrated few thrusts of sexual attention.

And as we slouch before our flickering screens with our bodies and ambitions on pause, our televised minds are overrun by a stampeding herd of happy-faced actors all pretending to have found eternal bliss in using a particular brand of toothpaste, hair shampoo or nail polish that may well be the key to our own emotional salvation.

Ultimately, it is our unspoken fear of loss, suffering and death that has always made beauty products and military arms perennial favorites as we try to evade the threat of being caught with our defenses down.

The Perfect Stranger

As noted earlier, our mothers teach us to conform to their demands by rewarding us for our "good" behavior while punishing us for what she deems as "bad." Such early childhood training establishes a lifelong pattern wherein we must *pay* for other people's positive attention and acceptance — or just to avoid being rejected — by conforming to their demands. And this policy remains constant within all relationships, be it with our parents, teachers, lovers, employers or political leaders.

Included with our many outgoing energy payments may also be the purchasing of the latest fashions or home furnishings to avoid falling behind our more visually-appealing neighbors. This kind of symbolic status warfare is evident even in attending to our basic necessities, such as when we dine on overpriced "high fashion" foods in a prohibitively expensive restaurant to draw attention to our income or social rank. However, such boastful public displays of vanity can have destructive social repercussions if naive young onlookers see our behavior as the evidence of living *a joyful life* when it may only be our desperate cry for social validation or a wasteful symptom of our excess wealth in an otherwise boring life of obsessive material hoarding.

Unfortunately, our absorbing of these kinds of social values, beliefs and attitudes is nearly unavoidable because mimicry is an important survival mechanism among young animals and children alike. It is by imitating the proven life strategies of our mother or older adults in the wild that we will better ensure our future success. This also applies to human society and explains our common desire for fortune, fame and physical beauty, which are also proven strategies for attracting social and sexual success — as any rich and famous celebrity can attest.

As expected, this can also have us mimicking the lifestyles and life strategies of people who are secretly miserable while pretending to be happy for the sake of appearances. And so we may choose to mimic the stereotypical indicators of their counterfeit happiness, be it the sipping of only the most expensive champagne or snorting powdered charisma while moored in some exclusive harbor for the rudderless rich.

Sadly, it is in our desperate attempts to win acceptance by proving our superior reward potential that we may also begin to reject ourselves as a joyless impostor — that so-called "perfect stranger" who seems able to win everyone else's admiration but our own.

Nonetheless, here at the opposite end of the fear economy, obscene profits are also being made by a glory-seeking industry that promises to sell us ever-bigger, better and more financially-prohibitive ways to win the attention of our envious onlookers. Often set apart in exclusive boutique districts or tropical resorts for the wealthy, we can purchase here a vast array of obscenely priced vanity products, from exclusive club memberships and jewel-encrusted watches to privileged private school instruction on how to become a dominant attention seeker in the world of politics, industry or finance. And if empty promises of ultimate joy cannot entice us to keep buying, then the fear of losing our lofty position in this costly uphill race for attention surely will.

Yet in tirelessly working to financially sustain our attention-seeking enterprise, we may pay little attention to the ironic fact that as we are learning how to succeed in this shallow pageant of materialist illusions, no one is actually teaching us how to feel happy. Instead, like most, we may naively assume that joy is a natural byproduct of following in the celebrated footsteps of our social idols toward what may actually be a lifetime of unconfessed loneliness and spiritual poverty.

Plotting Our Joy Coordinates

Typically, we are born with an unlimited potential for creating joy in our lives. But as demonstrated by leaving an empty toilet roll for others to replace, some of us may choose a *path of least resistance* approach to making ourselves happy. This we may do by pursuing one of the many convenient "Joy Stereotypes" being advertised for mass consumption.

Joy Stereotypes are generic one-size-fits-all recipes for happiness that cater to our desire for convenience rather than our need for spiritual fulfillment. Best sold in haste from the impulse aisles of life, they have us believing that money can buy happiness; that marriage will lead to romantic love, or that joining a religion will make us spiritual.

However, like any stereotype, the finer details are often conveniently missing or hidden from view. Instead, it is like receiving an empty box with attractive packaging that leaves us wondering how to fill it. As such, we can achieve great success and still feel empty in waiting to be filled with more than just symbolic representations of the joy we had been expecting for our many years of hard work and dedication.

In seeking to fill our lives with a legitimate and substantive feeling of joy and inner contentment, *how we feel* must lead the way because a rewarding life truly feels rewarding to those living it.

Toward that end, let us consider the following list of what we can refer to as "Joy Coordinates," which are the full-bodied sensations that we must feel to achieve a genuine state of emotional success. They are defined as *full-bodied* in that we will simultaneously feel them in body, mind and spirit, like the intense, spine-tingling exhilaration felt during moments of creative inspiration or the all-surrounding comfort we may experience from a heartfelt sense of belonging.

The Joy Coordinates identify and define the emotional energy rewards that feed our spiritual hunger. This also makes them useful in verifying any joy map we are following because they identify the conscious states of emotion that we must experience along the way. These act as the "true north" of our inner joy compass and are defined as follows:

The Joys Of Inspiration:

- ☑ Feeling enthusiastically committed to a personally meaningful goal.
- ☑ Feeling a healing sense of mission that awakens us to our own humanity.
- ☑ Feeling our inner essence expressed through any creative outlet.
- ☑ Feeling a child-like awe, wonder and curious fascination for life itself.
- ☑ Feeling a constantly fulfilling desire to learn and grow in self-awareness.

Between our fleeting episodes of joy, we also require a feeling of inner contentment. This is even more valuable in the long-term as it will sustain us between those short-lived dramatic bursts of exhilaration so characteristic of the joy experience. As such, let us also identify the Joy Coordinates of our contentment as follows:

The Joys Of Contentment

- ☑ Feeling a sense of belonging, connection or being "home" where we are.
- ☑ Feeling valuable to the lives of others, including our animal companions.
- ☑ Feeling love for ourselves; being our own best friend at all times.
- ☑ Feeling a trust in our own inner guidance and what we are doing.
- ☑ Feeling no fear of competitive judgment or criticism for being ourselves.
- ☑ Feeling a sense of eternal being that allows us to accept death.
- ☑ Feeling sufficient empathy for others to tame our instinctual selfishness.
- ☑ Feeling that the success of others is not a personal judgment against us.
- ☑ Feeling that our suffering has also brought us wisdom, and not just pain.

The Joy Coordinates clearly reveal their significance to our emotional enrichment when we compare them to the modest conditions required to sustain the survival and procreation needs of human life:

The Survival and Procreation Coordinates

- ☑ The environment must not be perpetually hostile to our existence.
- ☑ The land must offer adequate food, water and shelter to survive.
- ☑ The female must be healthy and capable of raising offspring to maturity.

The Joys of Inspiration, as listed, are the currency of our enthusiasm for life. They offer us a sense of adventure and a feeling of emotional wealth while displacing feelings of apathy and spiritual poverty. They can also act as emotional signposts by guiding us away from a joyless marriage of utility toward an authentic spiritual union, or bypassing a heart-numbing career for a more heartfelt sense of mission in life.

In addition, we are more likely to identify a person who is happy in their chosen life's work because they seem to have a tireless energy for accomplishing their goals. Conversely, those at the opposite end of this heartfelt spectrum will try to do the least at the lowest quality and feel no sense of accomplishment in what they are doing. Subsequently, their lives suffer for lack of a quality joy associated with the pursuit of personal excellence. In short, we cannot excel at something that we do not enjoy — and will thereby lose the opportunity to feel fulfilled.

To best assure our own future feelings of joy and contentment, we must embark on some personally-meaningful path that nourishes our spirit with these Joy Coordinates. Thankfully, there is often sufficient reward potential in each one to fill our entire lifetime with everlasting hope and inspiration. And as we carry that burning ember of hope into the emotional battlefield of human society, we must enlist the Joys of Contentment to guard against any envious empty vessel who wants to extinguish our hope, or divert us from our chosen path with a costly detour to the local shopping mall or legalized drug dispensary.

The Joy Bureaucracy

As we learned in chapter one, our inner joy compass intuitively guides us toward activities and lifestyle choices that we will enjoy. It is during childhood that we often "feel" most clearly the unique path to joy that awaits us. We must then protect this inner sense of knowing from the socialization process, which typically disregards our emotional needs altogether. Instead, we may be assailed by a torrent of demands from our parents, teachers, employers, government, media advertisers and greater society to become an advocate for their preferred values, beliefs and attitudes — often by negating our own.

Ultimately, what most people want is for us to become like them so that we will support their personal ideas, products, lifestyle choices or projections of social identity. And if we get caught up in their selfish stampede to serve those ambitions, our own needs may wind up being trampled into the dust and left behind.

Subsequently, by the time we reach adulthood, we may have already long-abandoned our rightful path to joy. Instead, what we often bring with us is a confusing array of *Acquired Social Identities* to help us mimic the "perfect stranger" that others want us to portray to win their love or acceptance within society.

We can refer to this as our "Joy Bureaucracy" — a mental layer of administrative bloat and corruption that keeps us from living a more authentically joyful and contented life. We experience this by way of *Acquired Identity Conflicts* that can erupt as we try to meet the often contradictory demands of the many social roles we are asked to play.

For instance, in trying to be a "good" employee, we may be forced to be a "bad" mother by not giving our children the attention they need and deserve. Meanwhile, in being a "good" patriot, we may be enlisted to behave like those very evil-doers that our religion had warned us about. As a result, knowing ourselves is no easy task, especially if we are trying too hard to be someone else for the sake of others.

Fortunately, the socialization process uses a common framework for recruiting us to a lifetime of conformity by having us to adopt various social identities that we can deconstruct using "The IPSFA Sequence."

The IPSFA Sequence

As a brief introduction, the IPSFA Sequence was identified specifically for this book to help us understand the means by which we are being mentally programmed to believe and behave as others want, for better or worse. It can now be shared globally to promote mental freedom.

The IPSFA Sequence mimics the structure of an atom in achieving its own unique purpose of creating Acquired Social Identities (ASIs). It offers a reliable visual means to identify the scripted thoughts and behaviors we must adopt to create those characters we portray on the social stage to earn our energy rewards.

As a diagnostic tool, it can be used to resolve inner identity conflicts that arise when the values, beliefs and attitudes of two or more social identities contradict or *repel* one another.

The IPSFA Sequence also allows us to chart the framework of any social identity or relationship to assess its inherent joy potential — or lack thereof. In this way, we can more effectively chart a path back to the authentic individual we were born to be.

To better understand how the IPSFA Sequence works, let us refer to the now-familiar DNA sequence, which acts like a genetic recipe for creating the *fixed* biological identity of all terrestrial life forms. In following the human recipe, untold numbers of converging atoms are instructed to create the unchanging physical traits inherent to our own fixed human identity, including our species, race and gender.

In the wild, our own fixed identity allows us to survive by extracting energy through our relationship to the various fixed identities of other plant and animal life forms. Yet upon entering the artificial, monetized landscapes of our modern human cultures, we are also forced to adopt a number of Acquired Social Identities to facilitate exchanging various kinds of energy with others to ensure our survival.

For example, in adopting the identity of a doctor, we trade both our physical and mental energy for money, a symbolic form of energy that we then exchange for food and shelter — which are their own forms of energy. Subsequently, our survival no longer depends on our skills as hunters and gatherers but on how well we can meet the expectations of others as an acknowledged partner in the human energy trade.

Like the fixed biological identity created by our genetic code, we can also create an Acquired Social Identity by following its recipe of social behavior instructions in the form of an IPSFA Sequence; an acronym derived from the first letters of its five unique elements.

Acting like "thought genes," each element instructs us to conform to a scripted way of thinking or behaving to earn our energy rewards. But unlike our fixed biological identity, we return to a state of *non-identity* if we are not constantly proving ourselves to be who we claim.

The IPSFA Sequence is defined as follows:

Identity	The energy-attractive social character that we choose to portray.
Promise	The energy rewards we are promised for portraying this identity.
Script	The scripted values, behaviors and attitudes we must express to prove this identity.
Fear	The repulsive outer "fear fence" of threats that keeps us loyal to this identity.
Apathy	The resulting mental conflicts that we must ignore to maintain this identity.

Using this new IPSFA Sequence framework, we can now construct a simple Acquired Social Identity based on our previous insights about early childhood mental conditioning wherein we are taught to pay for the acceptance of others through our "good" behavior.

I	**A Good Boy / A Good Girl** (A virtuous, positive energy-attracting social identity given to a child).
P	To win the acceptance of our parents and avoid being punished.
S	Do as we are told — no matter what our parents tell us to do, or else…
F	Rejection, pain, suffering and ultimately, death from abandonment.
A	What a parent defines as *good* behavior may not always be good for us.

In this "Good Boy/Good Girl" example, we see how the motives are front-loaded as *the promise of joy* to lure us into adopting this script. This is followed by actual instructions on how we must think or behave to attain our promised reward. Below this is a *fear fence* designed to keep us following that script to avoid various negative consequences.

The IPSFA Sequence is highly flexible in allowing us to create any kind of social identity, including those of heroic or fictitious characters. Here is the basis for creating one such heroic social identity familiar to anyone ruled by a centralized form of government:

I	**Police Officer** (The enforcer of government control over citizens and society's consensual reality).
P	To feel like or be seen as a heroic public figure; to exercise uncommon power over others (etc.).
S	To serve and protect gov't leaders against angry protesting citizens; to disrupt chaotic predatory or combative behavior that threatens to undermine the orderly controlling of society.
F	Being killed or dominated by a challenger; losing our position of social power and authority.
A	Seriously injuring or killing a fellow citizen in our determination to dominate them.

In the above example, "etc." denotes that more information can be added to this or any category within the sequence to complete the full identity. We can assume this for all IPSFA Sequence examples in this book — some could span several pages to list all of its traits.

Acquired Social Identities benefit the organization of human society by creating less confusion and greater certainty in how we are to trade energy with others for our survival. Unfortunately, we also find them used as a method of mind control for the purpose of social domination.

Here we are forced to surrender our money, power or freedom to an empty promise of future joy or out of a fear of social or otherworldly persecution. As such, the IPSFA Sequence can also be used to create hateful divisions in our society by having us adopt a scripted identity that promises to make us *superior* to others for belonging to particular kinds of exclusive social groups or associations. In the example that follows, we will recognize this familiar form of mental trickery:

I	**The Happy Clappers** (A fictitious religious order).
P	To gain greater certainty or social privileges for belonging to a self-proclaimed "superior" group.
S	Engage in clapping for God; denounce non-Happy Clappers to prove our group allegiance.
F	To be shunned as a non-Clapper; to lose our social and Heavenly rewards as an outcast.
A	Living in denial that non-Clappers also deserve to be happy, accepted and loved for who they are.

Like atoms and DNA, the IPSFA Sequence also has a "God-like" ability to take any form in the mind of its creator, including objects or even actions. For example:

I	**Littering** (The act of disposing our waste in a thoughtlessly destructive manner).
P	To keep our personal environment free of unsightly waste in the most convenient way.
S	Roll down car window; discard beer cans and fast food wrappers; keep driving.
F	Police officers finding empty beer cans in our car; losing time to disposing waste responsibly.
A	Finding toxic waste in our water, air and body when others share the same reckless attitude.

The usefulness of the IPSFA Sequence will become more apparent in the upcoming chapters. For now, in having come to the end of this first section of the book, there now remain no more secrets to keep us from taking our next meaningful step toward clearing a material path to joy.

PART TWO
The Material Path to Joy

CHAPTER 5
Mind Over Matter

Joy is our proof that *it's good to be alive* and the material path to joy is where we collect the mounting physical evidence of our happiness.

Here it fills our closets, attics, basements and garages with countless possessions, each holding the ghost of some long-departed emotion that we felt in buying it. Yet in seeking to give eternal life to the thrill of new ownership, we also risk turning our homes into a graveyard of neglected consumer artifacts while burying our future beneath a pile of growing debt. And if our entire culture encourages us to direct our ambitions toward the quest for material gain, then it is little wonder why we may find ourselves engaged in a lifelong futile struggle to buy the evidence of our joy in some costly material form.

Unfortunately, this can also lead to the destruction of our personal health, family life, communities, planetary ecosystems, and all hope for the future survival of our species as governments, industries and those of incredible wealth vow to fight to the death to maintain their own undying faith in this all-consuming way of life.

Trapped by our economic dependency in societies designed for our constant spending, we can no longer escape the monetary matrix and its myriad merchants of material bliss. Enticing us with joy decoys and symbolic substitutes for a meaningful life, we are tricked into believing that our happiness is being held hostage inside whatever item happens to be on sale that day. Duped by a shameless act of mind over matter, we may then be willing to pay almost any price to ensure its safe release and return into our possession.

In clearing a path to material joy, we must learn how to navigate this mesmerizing maze of material seduction so as not to become lost in its costly illusions. Yet once free of its trappings, the material path can offer us a wealth of joy potential even without a price tag, whether in witnessing the majestic wonders of our natural world or in sharing the erotic pleasures of our naked form. It can also provide us with practical tools for improving our quality of life or artfully stroke our minds with a soulful harvest of other people's creative self-expression.

Ultimately, there is much we can gain from our various relationships to the material world — even spiritually — if we can just avoid being owned by what we own, or consumed by what we consume. In seeing material assets as the tools for creating joy rather than its essence, we can avoid arriving at that ill-fated crossroads wherein we feel ourselves emotionally impoverished amidst a growing pile of needless junk.

As seekers of joy, our goal is to maintain a balanced relationship to material gain by refusing to waste our life, income and joy potential on vain displays of personal power, or on futile attempts to fill a nagging spiritual void with *random acts of spending*.

To assist us in that pursuit, we can enlist the metaphor of religious devotion to give us a fresh perspective on the behaviors we may engage in to pursue our vision of paradise in material form. Now let us embark on an enlightening journey to understand this energy-depleting urge to spend our way to happiness.

A Faith In More

To live as a joyfully self-aware person, we must renounce all illusions. Yet in taking that stance, we stand in direct opposition to the agenda of a growing global economy that seems intent on having us embrace them more and more. One such illusion is the life-enhancing value of diamonds and gold, which resides as a belief within our imagination.

In reality, neither adds much value to our existence except in making cutting tools or electronics. Yet through another masterful act of mind over matter in our invisible economy, the merchants of material bliss have imbued them with mystical powers over love and future financial security. And now we worship them as powerful talisman in the service of "Materialism," a kind of superstitious religion that demands our unquestioning faith in consumption as the road to our salvation.

As true believers, our temple of worship is the shopping mall where we hope to buy our entry to a paradise of material bliss. Guided by the missionaries of media advertising, we are promised everything from perfect love to eternal youth in devoting our life to the invisible god of *Credit* — that all-powerful animator of cash registers summoned by a secretive monetary priesthood to facilitate the ever-growing cost of our faith and devotion as consumers.

The creed of consumerism promises that we will *feel more by having more* — the more we buy, the better we will feel. And this leads us to overspend not only in hoarding basic necessities to avoid suffering, but also in trying to buy our sense of meaning and purpose in life. In short, for many of us, shopping has become our life's mission in hoping to maintain a state of joy through our constant spending.

And so, as we slowly come down off that mountaintop, we realize that we have been socially-conditioned to deal with both negative and positive emotions materially instead of spiritually; as though spending is the answer to all of our problems and questions in life.

Yet in contemplating this dogmatic belief of "excess leads to joy," we need only observe any wealthy person who, after a lifetime's worth of excessive spending, is no closer to joy than if born into poverty.

Fortunately, reality and facts still matter. But like many religions, materialism has its share of fanatical crusaders who insist that selfish personal gain is humankind's only hope for the future. It is an ideology that also justifies the joyless parcelling of our world into privately owned territories whose captive workforces are leased to the lowest bidder for that greatest good of society known as shareholder "profit."

As devout followers in this cult of materialism, we are encouraged to keep spending our way to the promised land, guided by a faith in that our ultimate joy is always just ahead and only one purchase away.

Yet betrayal awaits us there, for a purchased joy is a fleeting joy. Here again, we mark into evidence those wealthy persons compelled to buy a tenth luxury car after the first nine cars failed to keep them satisfied. Often referred to as the "hedonic treadmill," we may also find ourselves caught in this perpetual cycle of aimless spending to relive that thrill of buying our first car, home, appliance or rare minted coin. However, neither advertisers nor credit-lenders seem interested in warning us of the dangers of overspending borrowed money at high interest. Instead, they keep us aimlessly speeding along on our costly treadmill by loudly and cheerfully advising us to — "Just keep shopping!"

And while some will shout *blasphemy* at such claims, the truth of consumerism is that, even as we are waiting in line to pay for our latest infusion of joy in material form, our insatiable urge to possess will soon have us searching once again for our next symbolic conquest. In reality, we never truly satisfy our hunger to possess but only transfer it to each new object of our desire. And here again, our joy will be held hostage until we can afford to pay the ransom for its release.

Today, no matter our reason for recklessly overspending or drowning in debt, it is met with the blessing of retailers and tax collectors who want nothing more than for us to keep repeating this same predictable pattern of trying to buy our escape from pain or passage to pleasure in perpetuity so that they themselves will never be caused to suffer.

Yet as seekers of a more enduring and legitimate joy, our salvation on the material path depends on reaching an enlightened state of inner contentment that will not see us spending our way into damnation in trying to buy a piece of paradise. And as always, this will require us to have a deeper understanding of the underlying processes responsible for our impulsive spending behavior and a state of self-awareness that will allow us to make the best use of that information. Fortunately, this chapter can offer us a helping hand in both regards.

A Joyful Matter

As earlier stated, joining a religion does not make us a spiritual person. At best, it facilitates our passage to a life of greater introspection. The same is true on the material path where it is best to see material gain as facilitating our joy rather than representing joy itself.

In that regard, what we feel from material gain and ownership may not be joy at all but only a temporary sense of relief. For instance, we may buy something to make ourselves appear "normal" or agreeable to others — perhaps a new coat, shoes or popular electronic device.

We may also misidentify the feeling of arrogant pride as that of joy when we parade our newly-purchased items in public to gain a fleeting sense of being "better than" others. However, these emotional reactions are no more a genuine expression of joy than the cruel and derisive cackling of cynics and sociopaths. As such, let us free our minds from this cult of consumerism by understanding how our deep emotional attachment to matter has been socially programmed.

Toward that end, our primary human relationship to matter is one of necessity due to our lifelong biological dependence upon food and shelter. Yet unlike other life forms, we have extended this relationship to become a complex mental reward system for extracting emotional nourishment from solid objects.

Yet object-oriented joy is largely symbolic. Like a coveted trophy in sport, it may only represent a single day's victory at best and little more. Subsequently, we may feel a sudden burst of excitement in buying a new "trophy" sports car only to watch our joy quickly speed away while we remain stuck in the same old emotional traffic jam.

Ultimately, whether upgrading products to keep competitive fears at bay or paying retailers a hefty ransom for the temporary release of our enthusiasm for life, we are often just buying another weapon in our ongoing mental war for inner peace and contentment.

In that regard, our recruitment to feeling emotionally-attached to material objects already begins in infancy as we innocently stare up at the ceiling and wait for the world to come to us. And so it does.

First to arrive is our mother who offers us many material pleasures, not only in the form of food, comfort and loving attention, but also as toys that stimulate our awakening mind and physical senses.

Making her wide-eyed *happy mommy face* and blissful sounds, she also inadvertently teaches us *how to react emotionally to material objects* as they come within reach of our selfish little grasp. This reinforces our mental perception that *joy comes from outside of us* as objects and people begin to enter our lives. In later years, this can prejudice our quest for joy as we reflexively shun the inner path of spirituality for the outer path of material gain. And if our parents were true believers in that joy can be found in the aisles of a store, then we may also dedicate our lives to shopping at the temple mall for our own future happiness.

The Objects Of Our Desire

As infants eagerly grasping for any new toy within reach, we remain unaware that every car, doll, plastic gun or board game is a miniature aspect of the adult society into which we will soon be assimilated.

Upon closer inspection, we can see that toys act as symbolic tools to ease our mental transition toward consumerism by ensuring that we all share the same material values and expectations in society. On a more sinister note, this also creates opportunities for economic predators to program the minds of children for future consumption of questionable products. In two such historic examples, candy cigarettes and toy guns were sold to small children to subliminally link them to the attaining of adulthood. Subsequently, once those children grew older, they were more likely to buy those products to prove their own maturity. For that reason, many grew up smoking cigarettes or owning guns, even if they had no practical use for either one in any lawful, healthy society.

Toys also train our minds to invest inanimate objects with life giving importance. Here as well, it has inspired our ironic behavior of treating money as the protector of all life while destroying the natural world upon which our life actually depends in a misguided effort to earn ever more of something that has no "real world" value at all.

This kind of early childhood "Object Value Training" also introduces us to scheduled buying events, such as birthdays and other gift-giving holidays. In becoming adults, we are then prompted to give *presents* to others based on the dates on our calendar rather than a genuine desire to be generous. Conversely, this also trains us to expect that our family and friends must celebrate our presence in their lives by buying us gifts as material evidence of their love and gratitude. This can also lead us to feel rejected in not receiving gifts, or even insulted if the cost of someone's gift signals our having a lower position of honor in their life. And that may well be true if we are actually so vain.

Today, we even objectify love through the giving of flowers, jewelry and toys, whether as proof of our genuine affection or just a substitute for having to offer the more generous gift of our time and attention.

Media advertising further reinforces our emotional bond to material objects by encouraging us to interpret the value of ordinary consumer goods for their promise of joy. As a result, we buy cars, houses, clothing and furniture not only for practical reasons, but also to feel joy in our possessing them. And if we no longer feel happy with what we possess, then we must interpret this as a sign to go out and buy something even bigger, better or more expensive to revitalize our spirit.

Yet in working to extract emotional nurture from inanimate objects, we also divert precious time and energy away from activities that could actually be bringing us the spiritual nourishment for which we hunger. Equally significant is that those who do reach the symbolic summits of material wealth often make a full circle return to their infantile seats of power by employing a host of substitute mothers and manservants to soothe their every childish whimper. Ironically, in such well-served families, the children may not even be taught to tie their own shoes.

As such, based on the evidence, it appears that the ultimate goal for some on this material path is to return to a state of spoiled, child-like dependence — a somewhat ironic destination for anyone in pursuit of greater personal power to only surrender it later as a sign of success.

Given such observations, there is much to criticize about our human relationship to material gain. But this is also not a celebration of its joy potential but an attempt to identify its obstacles to genuine emotional fulfillment. However, we can assume that anyone truly committed to a life of material-based joy-seeking may find some way to conveniently *crop* away its negative aspects to remain faithful to their chosen path. Among them are the many social predators who profit by undermining our quality of life and joy as citizens trapped by our circumstances.

The Monetary Ecosystem

Worldwide, our collective material quests for joy and obsessions with wealth are due to the changing nature of our relationship to matter itself. In contrast to the hunting and gathering lifestyles of our early ancestors, many of us now live in the resource barren urban landscapes of industrialized and post-industrialized nations.

Built as protective fortresses against the hazards of the wild, what we gain in convenience as city dwellers we have lost in direct access to land and natural resources — the only true currency of value in the economy of life. Trapped inside these "monetary ecosystems" — a kind of *economic rabbit cage* for humans — we are forced to use the symbolic energy of money to trade for the real food energy we need to survive.

Consuming factory-processed foods and chemical-laden tap water, this newly-adopted artificial lifestyle also allows us to live as remote, self-absorbed individuals no longer in need of communities or contact with neighbors. This further promotes a feeling of remote detachment that makes us easily-isolated prey for our governments and others to exploit us for selfish gain — perhaps to acquire those costly material items that promise them a more *exclusive* and *prestigious* kind of joy.

As toys and school teachers prepare us for the rigors of living in this artificial world, we cannot escape knowing that, like the caged rabbit described in chapter one, our survival now depends entirely on those controlling this closed-in, locked-down system of supply and demand, especially the flow of money that determines our right to exist.

As such, life in any self-proclaimed "free world" is anything but free for those forced to pay taxes or other fees in trying to survive, but also legally obligated to lay down and die from hunger within arm's reach of food if they cannot afford to pay for it. Morally this may never occur due to volunteer food charities, but legally it is entirely permissible.

Ironically, this path of communal isolation and profit-driven *combat economics* is the same one that many political leaders claim will lead us toward a shared future state of peace, prosperity and happiness. It is an ironic delusion, yet one being promoted by the ceaseless expansion of human civilization as we continue to overrun fertile farmland and decimate rare wildlife habitats in paving the way for the future profits of those bankers, developers and politicians in charge of humankind's destiny. And all they need do is convince us to keep spending.

In a monetary ecosystem, the surrounding natural world becomes a host to the parasitic needs of inner cities that must constantly feed on its natural resources to survive. This kind of exploitive relationship is unavoidable as cities do not grow their own food and must rely on outside producers. Such trade also requires the practicing of mind over matter wherein money is "borrowed" at interest to fuel a constant state of growth, whereupon it is distributed among city dwellers who work to convert outside natural resources into commercial goods that allow them to survival in these unnatural, unsustainable settings. And while few know money's deepest secrets, our repaying of these growth-debts requires a constant selling of goods to keep our nation's money-based energy trading system from collapsing from its own state of poverty. This has resulted in a consumer culture that now demands our constant spending while also causing us to live grossly out of balance with the natural world and the fundamental needs of our biology for a healthy and secure living environment.

Today, we are placing unsustainable pressures on both our natural ecology and our human sanity in trying to keep these dead zones alive. This is also why we are encouraged from early childhood to buy our joy, acceptance, success, self-esteem and even our feelings of love in some sellable product form. And while this keeps our economies well-fed, it can also leave us feeling alone, adrift and spiritually malnourished.

The Body Nation

Admittedly, such insights do not paint a very flattering picture of our current human condition. However, our deeper understanding of the many challenges we face as inhabitants of these monetary ecosystems can prepare us to better negotiate our future joy as we begin to evolve beyond these increasingly alienating systems of human organization.

In that regard, many aspects of human life now exist as a condition of mind over matter. In the future, for instance, we may realize how the imaginary medium of money was used as a weapon of global warfare to enslave nations with debt, thus making their leaders beholden to a privileged few lenders. By appealing to their greed or vanity, leaders are easily enticed to borrow money for wasteful projects that they cannot hope to repay, including as earlier discussed, sports stadiums that only serve the public for two weeks while generating for its lenders revenue from interest for perhaps generations to come.

We may then wonder: how can our societies ever evolve if all we are doing is repaying loans for wasteful vanity projects or gambling houses while genuine progress towards life sustainability and true democracy are being derailed for lack of public funding? Until we resolve such issues, our species will continue to live in a compromised state in these unsustainable communities while locked into an economic grid that is governed by greed and political treachery. And so we must make due with our fishbowl-like existence while media advertisers set us upon a lifelong misguided quest for a material-born happiness to ensure that we all can live in a state of constant debt.

We can work to counteract some of these negative external pressures by becoming more aware of our innate human impulses. This includes learning how our natural Bio-Psychological urges toward selfishness and sexual competition can undermine our quest for joy when they are being *intentionally triggered* and *redirected* toward material gain.

Ideally, we will each attain a state of physical and spiritual balance that prevents us from wildly swinging toward the extremes of material gluttony or those of ideology-based self-deprivation that keep various cultures from evolving beyond a fearful hand-to-mouth existence. The middle ground is a far better option than inertia or extinction.

To more easily guide our life vessels toward such a balanced state, let us also think of our bodies as nations in their own right, wherein our mind acts as its uncontested and all-powerful leader.

To fully embrace this metaphor, like any nation, our bodies also have their own form of government by way of our beliefs; an economy by way of what we value most, and a military force by way of the fears that defend our physical boundaries and mental culture.

Furthermore, we are inwardly divided into regions whose individual demands exert a powerful and conflicting influence upon the whole of our being. These regions we can refer to as *The Six States of Being*, our knowledge of which will better ensure our ability to thrive in a shared future state of peaceful prosperity and joy within our own body nation and that of the greater political body we share with others. Therefore, it is critical that we understand how these six states can influence our decision-making along each of the four life paths, especially here on the *Material Path to Joy*.

The Six States of Being

As a general summary of the previous chapters, we now understand the importance of the Joy Coordinates to our quest for joy and how our mind symbolically converts matter into meaningful emotional energy. We also learned how the promise of joy recruits us to adopt *Acquired Social Identities* that can limit our joy potential by seeking counterfeit forms of happiness through shallow Joy Stereotypes, or by mimicking the success strategies of people who may be secretly unhappy.

To better organize these and future insights, we can categorize all human behavior as being directed by the Six States of Being (C-SIX) of our body and mind in relation to our journey through life. These are comprised of two opposing sets of three *physical* and *spiritual* values which guide our lifelong existence and decision-making by way of the various influences they exert. They are categorized as follows:

The Physical States of Being:

(C1) **Comfort:** The purpose of comfort is to defeat discomfort, whose warning signs include hunger, thirst and pain. Our body's discomfort detection system can protect us against most physical suffering, yet we may also seek mental comfort through emotional contentment, whose subjective values defy objective measuring. As a result, our body can live in luxury while our mind lives in poverty — perhaps for lack of a genuine heartfelt goal or the courage to live as though our life matters.

(C2) **Convenience:** The purpose of convenience is to conserve energy by saving us time and effort; a value demonstrated by doing the least to achieve any goal. On the material path, this attitude can result in a lowering of quality in our life, perhaps by eating inferior food or by wasting time and money to correct errors that result from our haste or neglect. Conversely, an enduring sense of joy requires from us a higher level of personal engagement; a standard of mind that we cannot attain by withholding our best efforts to save energy by every means.

(C3) **Control:** The purpose of control is to ensure greater certainty in tending to our survival and procreative needs. Such control is defined by gaining power over our personal freedom of choice. In theory, the more we control, the greater our power to choose. Yet this relentless pursuit of power often finds us being controlled instead by what we control as our every effort is focussed on amassing ever more control or protecting what we already have. As a result, we risk living a joyless life in our constant fear of losing control over all that now controls us, including our freedom to choose a more contented way of life.

The Spiritual States Of Being

(C4) **Curiosity:** The spiritual purpose of human curiosity is to inspire our conscious evolution. It is through our urge to explore that we also gain greater wisdom and self-awareness. However, our curious nature is directly opposed by our need for mental comfort from a predictable life routine. Meanwhile, mental laziness, competitive vanity or a fear of the unknown can also potentially sabotage our mental exploration of the world. We may then pretend instead to know all the answers by *cropping* away the truth or reality itself if they oppose us. However, this can also make us susceptible to mental conflicts caused by our willful ignorance or contradictions to what we force ourselves to believe.

(C5) **Creativity:** The spiritual purpose of creativity is to express mind through matter by way of our imagination. This represents another tool of conscious evolution that fuses the knowledge we gain through our curious exploration with our active intelligence to manifest what has never existed before. Creativity transcends our mental boundaries as we synthesize seemingly unrelated realities into cohesive structures. In doing so, we use our world as a canvas by transforming thoughts and emotions into solid evidence of our being. Our creativity is opposed by our physical want for convenience, which may seek to inhibit our free spending of energy if it does not serve our biological needs.

(C6) **Communion:** The spiritual purpose of communion is to have us engage in various intimate forms of contact with other sentient beings. Such connections can occur between people, animals, or in the form of a "cosmic alliance" with all of existence. In the latter, we embrace all things as we transcend fear itself to become part of a unified whole. Fulfilling this desire for communion can create immense joy, but our instinctual fear of physical vulnerability may incite us to take a more defensive counter-stance to regain control over our circumstances. This can result in an overly-guarded attitude, thereby blocking our access to deeper channels of intimate communication. In short, fear may not afford us the trust we need to share ourselves with others.

The C–SIX are defined as *states* because each of these aspects of our being desires to exist in a particular state, as defined by its name. Also, the three states sought by our physical being serve the interests of our survival and procreation and can often play an adversarial role to the spiritual states which serve our emotional quest for joy. We can find the evidence for this rivalry both internally within our own bodies and also externally in our social and political relationships with others.

One obvious place to look for such conflicts is in our sexuality. Here we express our desire for physical and/or spiritual communion with others, which may then be opposed by our want for control, either over our partner or ourselves, be it their threat or our safety. This can result in conflicted thoughts and behaviors if we simultaneously feel lustful and competitively fearful of losing our status or showing any sign of weakness or vulnerability.

The values of our invisible economy also play a significant role in our negotiating for sexual pleasure by determining to whom we may feel attracted and why, as well as other facets of this intimate experience. Even our urge for sexual release can be seen as *seeking comfort* from an agitated state of mental and physical arousal. In this way, achieving orgasm allows us to regain our prior sense of balance or *resting state.*

Socially, we find proof of this internal C–SIX rivalry in the various philosophical divides between voters of a *conservative* and *progressive* mindset, wherein one side appears to live predominantly inside their bodies while the other lives more inside their minds. This would also explain the escalation in selfishness, aggression and hostility expressed by those who feel their existence threatened by the prospect of social *change* or ideas that trigger their feelings of mental *discomfort.*

Perhaps more significantly, we find evidence of this conflict between the physical and spiritual in the rebellion of artists and others creative freethinkers in rallying against any mentally rigid, creativity-stifling form of government that is designed to ensure the material comforts, conveniences and controlling interests of its rulers.

Fortunately, our political nations are but a macrocosmic expression of the divided nature of our own body nation. This offers each of us a lifelong opportunity to promote greater social harmony by working to balance within us our dissenting spiritual urges with the tyranny of our selfish biological impulses.

In this way, both sides will ultimately share in our victory, as will the rest of the world once we have each gained the wisdom to attain such balance within ourselves.

CHAPTER 6
Losing Our Winning Attitude

Pride and panic are two highly profitable states of mind at any casino gaming table where they can trigger our frantic refusal to lose against the house that always wins. And given the odds, the longer we attempt to prove ourselves a winner, the further we will fall behind.

Legalized gambling is just one of many economic traps waiting to exploit our instinctual urge to win to keep us losing to the true winners of that game. But losing our money or pride is the least of our worries when the future survival of all earthly life is being recklessly gambled away by this same insatiable compulsion to win at any cost — even if it means losing *everything*.

While competition is a natural behavior in the wild, it becomes an aberration in the artificial confines of our monetary ecosystems where overcrowding forces us to compete for money not only to survive, but also to win more attention for what we possess. Already living under the shadow of a selfish biological reflex to guard our territory against all intruders, this instinct now rages dangerously out of control among those who have an irrational emotional attachment to material wealth as proof of their winning status over others.

Whether a sprawling mansion estate, an imported luxury car, or the mounted head of an endangered Rhino, material goods of extravagant price and exclusivity have always been used as symbols to denote our social victory over others. Yet our symbolic wars for social dominance also promote an unnatural level of competition that now threatens all life on our planet for a victory whose ultimate winner may not survive their own deluge of destruction to savor its spoils.

As seekers of joy on the material path, our healthy relationship to money and material gain depends on a refusal to be coerced by credit lenders or business interests to fight these pointless territorial disputes with excessive spending. By losing our winning attitude, we can regain emotional control of our energy outflow and free our minds of costly materialistic conflicts that are meaningless to all but those who profit from them. Best of all, we can walk away feeling like the true winner in being able to attend more peacefully to our legitimate needs with an empowered sense of focus in seeking our ultimate purpose in life.

The Fear Of Losing

To heal our dysfunctional human relationship to money and material gain, we will be better served by studying the dynamics of competition rather than trying to reach a consensus as to what size of house is best to avoid triggering the competitive envy of our neighbors. It is only through understanding our instinctual urge to win that we can avoid being defeated by it.

Toward that end, our primal instincts serve to keep us alive and safe from serious injury. But while triggered involuntarily, they often give us some choice as to how or when we wish to react to them. For instance, we can reject our body's hunger for food and even voluntarily starve ourselves to death. While this may be a negative outcome, it proves that our mind is capable of overpowering some of our body's natural instincts.

Fear is another such natural instinct whose role is to protect us from danger, yet it also offers us the choice of whether to fight or flee from a threat if escape is an option. We can even mentally suppress fear, such as our fear of rejection when asking some attractive stranger to dance with us. Likewise, we can also mentally suppress our competitive urge to win by regaining control of our fear of losing to others — especially if the ultimate prize for victory exists only within our imagination.

Fear-based flight has a practical use in allowing us to flee needless violence rather than risk dying or being injured to prove that we are the better fighter. This is why most wild animals also favor such evasive behavior because a serious combat injury can make it impossible for a wounded animal to hunt or eat its food. As such, running is our wisest choice given that life itself matters more than any fleeting victory.

Subsequently, if natural law dictates that flight is our wisest choice when faced with a threat, then it is equally wise to flee the battlefield for material dominance rather than lose precious time and money by being drawn into meaningless symbolic combat. It is in succumbing to our competitive urge to win that we will limit our options in facing any challenger, whether by swinging our fists or buying a more expensive sports car to prove ourselves a supreme commander of attention.

In all such rivalries we lose our energy, whether as blood and fatigue or from buying extravagant material goods that have no practical value beyond their use in competitive social display. Unfortunately, those who make such vanity products are actively engaged in promoting our surrender to the fear of losing so that we will keep trying to spend our way to victory in any symbolic contest they tempt us to enter. And as we each spend a relative fortune in vain, it becomes obvious that the only winners in all of this arrogant material posturing for glory are the sellers of these useless vanity products and those lending us the money to pay for all this symbolic social weaponry. In short, the more we fight to win on their economic battlefield, the more we stand to lose because *the house always wins*. It is the seller of weapons who wins the war.

World Champions

Winning serves a simple function in the wild by rewarding the victor with access to preferred territory and mates. As part of nature, we share this same urge to win and have made competition a defining aspect of every human society for those same reasons.

However, to avoid getting blood on our carpets and fine linens, we *sublimate* our territorial aggression through symbolic displays of power.

In this way we can protect our society and its rulers from the threat of our unrelenting and often violent urge to win at any cost. And this is also a way of ensuring that only those with the most money can win.

This purposeful redirecting of violent aggression helps to explain money's use as a modern weapon of social warfare, most notably in the purchasing of costly material items to convey our winning status. As one would expect, the top economic dominators of our society also monopolize a wealth of prized real estate territory and material assets, while the defeated, in having lost access to land and power, must fight for what scraps fall from the master's table — hence, we get "chitlins."

Our sublimated social combat can take many forms. For instance, just as in nature, a responsible human mother cannot risk engaging in violent clashes for power as this would endanger her offspring. Instead, she may compete for social glory in a passive way, such as displaying her physical beauty, family wealth, or the achievements of her children, which draws attention to her superior skills as a mother.

In stark contrast, *adolescent males* are the most physically aggressive statistical group in this social competition for status. At this age, their undeveloped minds are no match for their awakening sexual chemistry and its insistence that they compete for mating status and territory. As a result, many also succumb to a constant urge to prove themselves the equal or better of others at any cost. Aside from winning the race for highest mortality rate from thoughtless accidents, their impulsive use of aggression also features prominently in daily news stories of street gang violence, robberies, rape and murder or attention-seeking acts of religious terrorism — for which they may be promised personal glory in heaven and a lineup of eager virgins. And being more war-like than wise, they will not understand the error of their ways until it is too late.

In response to this constant threat of adolescent male violence, our social leaders have learned to disarm these restless juvenile gladiators by sending them off to fight in wars or directing their lust for conquest into organized sports where they engage in a futile cycle of competing for trophies that symbolize their dominance over one another.

Later as adults, *economic* might will defeat mere muscle in the sport of conspicuous consumption wherein we buy luxury items that are too expensive for our rivals in social combat to afford. And if all goes well, we will be incredibly rich while everyone else remains poor. And once we have conquered our communities and nations, then it is time to move on to conquer the rest of the world. And then, other planets.

And so, while entertainment media focuses our collective attention on foreign wars, sports and random street-level violence, the truly epic battles for social dominance are being fought in the arenas of politics, industry and finance. Here, the boys who once clashed over academic rank and backseat body counts must now wear prohibitively expensive suits while continuing to play the same self-serving measuring games for glory as in the days of their youth. The only difference is that now their losses and victories have the potential to destroy entire nations and biological ecosystems throughout our world, from jungles to the frozen arctic poles. Oil spills, chemical poisoning, resource looting and costly, unending warfare are but a few casualties of their manly sport.

Largely immune from public scrutiny due to backroom dealings and the censorship of a privately-owned or government-controlled media, these are the true world champions of global domination and to whom winning is all that matters. Here, where neither age nor muscle play a role in social victory, young and old men alike set forth each day to compete for the most coveted of all trophies — to control worldwide everyone else's ability to win against them. And with nation crushing debt as their secret weapon and young adolescent male soldiers armed and eager to fight for dominance, victory for these small but influential groups of apex social predators is all but assured.

The Urge To Win

As consumers of broadcast media raised on a diet of social violence and war as entertainment, we are constantly exposed to human contests for dominance wherein both sides will stop at nothing to win, be it in war, sport or beauty pageants for six year old girls. But what we cannot see are the underlying motives of those battling to the last breath to ensure that they prevail over their rivals. In many instances, that combatant is equally driven to win by their fear of losing.

The intensity of such fear can cause us to engage in equally vile and destructive behavior — not for the sake of victory, but simply to avoid suffering from loss. For instance, we may lie to our family or employers to avoid losing our good reputation or economic status. And as each lie increases our distance from the truth and our integrity, we face even greater threats of loss from corrupt politicians and greedy businessmen seeking to defend their privileged status from loss by lying to us about various social, economic or environmental threats that can destroy our collective health and ability to survive their reckless reigns of glory.

As joy seekers surrounded by a world full of selfish social predators, we can better protect ourselves and our future joy by understanding the two primary impulses at the root of our competitive behavior. In this way, we can work together as global citizens to lessen the deadly impact of both military and economic warfare upon our lives.

...

Toward that end, our urge to win originates from those very same biological impulses of selfishness and lust that also incite competitive behavior among wild animals. But whereas our selfishness is triggered by the *fear of losing*, our lust is triggered by an *urge to win;* notably, the desire to win preferred access to sensual pleasure via sexual intercourse or other forms of physical intimacy and interaction.

While selfishness and lust often work in tandem, it is important to realize that each is its own distinct biological urge. It is also helpful to reassert that these are both natural and necessary biological impulses whose intended purpose we now distort in competing for survival and mating privileges in the artificial confines of crowded cities that offer us no escape from our alpha dominators or their monetary ecosystems.

In the wild, the biological urge toward selfishness is demonstrated by wolves fighting over a carcass, whereas lust is what incites the noisy, boastful displays of male peacocks to attract a female or intimidate a rival. Both of these impulses are active in humans to varying levels of intensity and may find expression in our competitive hoarding and displaying of material assets, or boasting of our membership in some exclusive social club or academic institution.

Let us now explore each of these instinctual impulses separately as the coming chapters will require us to have an understanding of both.

Selfishness And Lust

Despite their popular usage, the meaning of *selfishness* and *lust* remain vague and metaphoric at best. Subsequently, for the sake of clarity, let us consider the following CPJ book-specific explanations, along with some practical examples of how they each can manifest in our lives:

What is Selfishness?

Selfishness is the unbiased protector of life; a self-preservation instinct that defends our existence by having us avoid or overcome any threat in our surroundings. Its unconscious nature is seen in the behavior of newborn kittens as they engage in aggressive shoving matches against rival siblings to win access to their mother's milk. Deaf, blind and only aware of their hunger, selfishness is what keeps them fighting to exist. As such, selfishness is not a character trait, but a reflexive extension of our inborn biological fear of death and suffering.

This helps us to identify human selfishness as a kind of impulse to *push others away* to prevent our suffering from loss. In human societies, selfishness continues to serve our survival needs by causing us to push away our rivals for a better paying job, a newer home or any other kind of advantage that might help us to avoid suffering in the future.

Selfishness is also not triggered in isolation but by a fear of losing to a challenger. And given that it serves our physical survival, such losses typically relate to our bodily comfort, convenience or control. Our fear in being challenged initiates a fight or flight urgency that propels us into action, whereupon we may lose all objectivity — and sometimes our good reputation. As such, our displays of selfishness may be quite common, but they are not very popular.

Anticipating our fearful reaction to the threat of loss, politicians may then exploit voters by provoking their existential fears. A common ruse is to demonize any opposing party as a threat to our way of life. In this way, we can be tricked to vote against our own best interests. Ironically, this mental strategy of divide and conquer also distracts us from the real threat we face, which is the selfish gluttony of wealthy donors who pay corrupt politicians to divert our anger away from their own greedy exploits toward trivial foreign threats or volatile moral issues. As such, *the fat cat feasts best when the mice are fighting over crumbs.*

In our family homes, selfishness can take many forms. For instance, a husband may dominate his wife or an older child his younger sibling, each to protect their access to greater comforts or sensual pleasures. As such, an unhappy family life can often be less the result of poverty than of the distrust created by our selfish unwillingness to share.

Outside the home, our panic-stricken contests to avoid losing our place in line or a seat at the front of the bus can often lead to tragic consequences. And given that our social dominators are using every legal, financial and military means to protect their dominance over our nations, we can understand why our political systems and Democracy itself cannot evolve wherever selfishness is allowed to thrive.

Ironically, we can deny our selfishness, but it is in plain view as those advantages we often gain at the expense of others losing theirs. And if we have not forgotten our history, we will recall that neither women nor slaves had the right to vote because the *free men* of that era fought with political might and brutality to avoid having to share their power.

I	**Selfishness** (a biological survival instinct often characterized by extremes of self-interest).
P	To protect our life against any loss of comfort, convenience or control.
S	Push others away, at any cost, from the energy resources we need to avoid suffering.
F	Suffering and death; feelings of vulnerability for lacking sufficient resources to survive.
A	Hoarding; refusing to share; causing others to suffer by preventing their access to resources.

What is Lust?

Lust is an always-inadequate term for describing a powerful feeling of attraction for something that exists outside of us. For the male gender of most species, that object of desire is an estrous female holding the promise of a spastic, frenzied orgasm for whichever suitor is successful in the fight to fertilize her eggs. And clearly, this reward incentive is both highly effective and infinitely popular among males.

Logically, the inclusion of an orgasm proves that "nature," no matter its true architect, is not only a brilliant designer of biological systems but also a cunning social strategist in manipulating our selfish lust for pleasure to keep us replicating ourselves. After all, without this brief, opportunistic episode of sensual self-indulgence, a good many of us alive today would not have been born at all. In this way, lust serves the greater good of many species by ensuring that we continue to procreate for the sheer selfish pleasure of it.

Equally clever is that nature has created a competition for mating privileges among the males of many species. This is done to ensure that only the strongest, most resilient male combatants will pass their genes to the next generation. Contests for genetic dominance can be physical altercations or symbolic acts of display, whereupon the top performer is then allowed to claim his fertile female prize. In this way, nature *automates* the entire process of ensuring the future biological health of a species by allowing only its proven winners to forward their genetic code to offspring.

It is the male's fear of losing his position of sexual privilege to other male challengers that introduces *selfishness* into the lust equation. This explains the increasing magnitude of display among young men as each contestant tries to outperform the other to win dominant status within their peer group. This also explains why many young men meet with an early death due to violence, car racing or alcohol poisoning during a binge-drinking contest to determine the dominant drinker.

Ironically, a female need not even be present for such male rivalry to escalate, as evident in the heated battles for alpha status among male prison inmates. Here as well, our selfishness is triggered by the mere presence of a rival for control of our territory. Naturally, this is all about power and privilege, even if no female is present to reap the benefits.

Once translated into the symbolic language of material dominance in our monetary ecosystems, these contests for sexual dominance can take many forms. They include heated social leadership battles wherein our top gladiators can even be those frail old men who control the flow of money by way of their alpha status in finance, industry or politics. Moreover, where there is only one seat of power available, it becomes an attractive option to lie, cheat or murder our way to that top position. As a result, although portrayed as being the "best" of humanity, many leaders actually exhibit its worst traits — apathy, greed and hypocrisy.

Women are also raised on symbolic equivalents of male dominance, which is why they may enter sexual union with sickly old men who appear "alpha" for their wealth, not their bodily condition. As such, our battles for symbolic dominance are defeating nature's true objective.

Meanwhile, far from any genuine seat of social power, the winning lust of society's true dominant males is being sublimated into symbolic athletic warfare for the benefit of a ticket-buying audience. Herein, the *scoring* of the "goal" typically requires overwhelming our opponent to penetrate their territory and insert a rounded object into their guarded central opening. In this way, spectators are unwittingly paying to be aroused by a simulated act of sexual conquest and penetration in the less than romantic setting of a sports stadium.

However, the desires of our heroic gladiators of sport to generously spread their seed remains aligned with nature's own ambitions.

I	**Lust** (An instinctual attraction to external sources of sensual pleasure).
P	Joy; ecstasy; deep feelings of satisfaction; a sense of purposeful direction in life.
S	Act on impulse to secure the object of our desire; engage our selfishness to win such access.
F	Failing to indulge in the sensual pleasures of the five senses; a lack of meaning or purpose.
A	Having to make room in our life for anything from heartbreak and herpes, to a jealous lover.

The Glory Seekers

A deeper understanding of selfishness and lust can help us to lead a more joyful life by increasing our awareness of how each physical urge can undermine our spiritual needs. This is especially important on the material path where their incessant mental and physical prodding can lead us to indulge in excesses of material consumption.

Overeating, for instance, can be linked to feeling a constant loss of "comfort" energy, whether physical or emotional. This feeling can also be induced by watching distressing television programs, which allows media advertisers to increase our consumption of energy by provoking our fear of loss; a remotely-induced form of selfish hoarding behavior. This may explain our constant reaching for snacks or impulsive buying of dubious diet plans and exercise machines, seduced by the three most comforting words in advertising — *fast, free* and *easy*. And this barely scratches the surface of psychological manipulation in media.

Under the influence of countless internal and external forces, it can be difficult to know if our actions are being directed by a sincere desire for joy or whether they are merely an outward expression of our primal urges translated into various symbolic acts of fearful hoarding, social competition or outward dominance display.

To assist us in that regard, we can further classify our more cowering impulse toward selfishness as promoting *comfort-seeking* behavior, and our more attention-seeking lust as promoting *glory-seeking* behavior.

In making this distinction, we will notice that some people's selfish urge to seek comfort is stronger than their lust for glory. This we can confirm by watching media advertising which intentionally targets the fears of comfort seekers to sell them "reliable" cars with safety features, while appealing to the boastful nature of glory seekers with offerings of fast, expensive cars that promise them more social attention. We will later explore comfort-seeking behavior in detail and how marketers exploit our various innate instincts to stimulate our spending. For now, let us focus on the destructive influence of the glory-seeking impulse in making us feel joylessly-obsessed with winning at any cost.

...

Glory seekers must always be in the lead, which is the primary cause of road fatalities as drivers recklessly speed ahead to avoid losing "the big race" underway in their competitive minds. The popularity of sex and violence as media entertainment is also no coincidence because it mirrors our relentless biological grasping for dominant mating status with sex being the prize for men getting bloody. That same competitive urge attracts us to shows featuring themes of conquest wherein human strength, beauty, skill or talent are judged in media measuring contests. And then we have sporting events, game shows and political debates.

In the monetary ecosystem, our instinctual desire to be recognized for our genetic dominance is symbolically translated into ambitions of becoming *a leader* in business, politics, sport, fashion or entertainment media. Yet that nagging compulsion to always prove ourselves a winner can leave us feeling perpetually dissatisfied, even upon achieving great success because that contest is never over, and someone better is always eagerly waiting to take our place — which can also make us paranoid.

In personal relationships, our lust to win is a joyless hindrance that can cause us to feel angry in losing a friendly game of cards because we may treat everything as a contest to prove ourselves *better than...*

This obsession with staying "on top" also creates vast fortunes for drug companies offering to resurrect the withering pride of aging male combatants so that they might continue pushing bravely forward into uncharted female territory — if their arthritic knees can hold out.

In this way, we are all being unwittingly *gamed* by an instinctual urge to win our genetic immortality; one that keeps us at constant war both within ourselves and a world full of people dying to play this game.

Counting Our Losses

Ironically, while its victors claim that social competition brings out the best in us, it also brings out our worst when desperate to avoid losing within the selfish confines of our monetary ecosystems.

In competing to save money, for instance, governments, industries and home owners may hire the lowest bidder to oversee a construction project. Yet in being paid the least, that contractor can also least afford to make the best effort without risking their own economic survival. As such, public buildings, bridges or even our bedroom ceiling may be in danger of collapsing upon us whenever material or labor costs are being competed over to accommodate our selfish hoarding of energy.

And as we each compete to avoid losing money to one another, we create a fast-food kind of mentality in our societies wherein quality in manufacturing plummets as we make the lowest selling price the most significant aspect of every product or service. In short, we compete by doing our worst in seeking to gain the most for ourselves; a bizarre and disturbing ideological trend that explains our use of automated phone systems so that angry customers can no longer reach the guilty party.

Overcrowding has also proved to be a recipe for social disaster as it places unnatural pressures on natural resources while overstimulating our innate competitive instincts. This further makes a mockery of that motivational maxim of social profiteers in witnessing how our selfish competitions, instead of improving our societies, may only tempt us to become better at lying, cheating or stealing when the odds of winning are hopelessly stacked against us. It also ensures our reckless grasping for wealth as our only hope of salvation when our societies abandon us in times of economic recession or when our debt-ridden governments must enact austerity measures because they cannot afford to both serve a captive herd of taxpayers and still offer tax cuts to the wealthy.

What makes all these desperate efforts to win so ironic is that while the underemployed, elderly, infirm and culturally disenfranchised must suffer for lack of basic life necessities, we find that those living in the upper stratosphere of wealth have no actual use for more money except to keep score in their various money sports for personal glory. In the meantime, our world needlessly suffers for their competitive vanity.

As such, all facets of our lives, both physical and spiritual, are at risk because of systematic corruption and unchecked greed, including the institution of democracy itself. Here, tempted by the promise of glory and social dominance, political profiteers are selling unfair access and economic advantages to their most generous of private donors.

Equally tragic is when we see vain religious leaders strutting amidst opulent excesses while sending the poor into battle for control of God and the lucrative toll gates to immortality. Their urge to conquer and control the masses is the same as that of any other lust-filled beast.

And then there is the unspoken threat of nuclear war and poisoning of our land and oceans from chemical weapons as pro-war profiteers arm even the most mentally unstable of world leaders with the means to kill all of us with the simple push of a button.

Today, in competing for absolute control over the lives and incomes of all citizens, nations are building ever more glorious weapons of mass destruction whose killing power has turned selfishness and lust, once natural allies in assuring our collective future survival, into our greatest enemies. And that is why at any moment, even as you are reading this sentence, any self-deluded dictator in one of many weaponized nations can, in a moment of competitive pride or sheer panic, launch at their convenience a planet-killing missile assault that would cause us to lose everything because *winning* was the only thing that mattered to him.

And thereafter, we will have no time for regrets or second thoughts. It will all be gone just because a lone, fearful individual unknown to us except perhaps by name from newscasts, could not live with the fear of having to lose control over the rest of us.

As global citizens, we might then ask ourselves how we feel in being forced to live in such a competitively hostile and vulnerable condition for the sake of a privileged few dominators, many of whom suffer from mental delusions that make them unsuitable as our leaders. And as the next chapter will reveal, sometimes we deal with such fears by making our own flight from danger, or even reality itself, into a way of life.

CHAPTER 7
The Comfort Trap

Nature is never intentionally cruel but only practical in making use of energy in any form to perpetuate its ongoing miracle of life. Taking no sides and showing no favor, nature has created a world in which every plant and animal is under the constant threat of being consumed to ensure the survival of another life form.

Here, not even our top predators can escape the selfish ambitions of parasitic flies to earn a living wage of flesh and blood at their expense. Surrounded by all these potential hazards, we also cannot reasonably tend to our needs or raise our offspring in feeling a constant urge to fight, flee or cower in fear. In response, it is the highest priority of every earthly sentient being to attain a level of physical security that ensures its continued survival. And so, just as roses grow thorns and skunks spray offensive odors, so do we humans express this urge to defend ourselves in our desire for *comfort.*

Comfort is the absence of discomfort; it is when our hunger has been satiated, our thirst quenched, and our body is warm, dry and free of pain. Comfort is when our shoes fit so well that we no longer notice them on our feet. Unfortunately, our need for joy may also go equally unnoticed if that quest for comfort does not end at our toes. After all, it was not for joy's sake that we humans first stepped on the moon, but rather to aim future military weapons at our rivals below.

Today, as "intelligence" gathering satellites track us from above like radio-collared ruminants in wanting to control our every thought and movement, we now live in nations designed by our fearful response to threats both real and imagined. However, in living this way, we have also created a world that is effectively a "comfort trap."

As a frequent obstacle on the material path, comfort traps are those ironic circumstances wherein we cause ourselves to suffer even more to avoid suffering itself. For instance, in treating every stranger as a threat, we also lose the opportunity to make new friends. And so, in choosing to surrender our freedom of choice for greater security, we may also prevent ourselves from exploring life beyond our familiar boundaries of comfort where new paths to joy await. In the extreme, they keep us chained to such a rigid routine of self-preservation that nothing can progress in our life except for the dates on our calendar.

Yet the human spirit does not tolerate enslavement by any means, including our body's own needful clinging to material comfort. And so it will exact its revenge by causing us to feel restless and bored with our existence. And while we may find temporary relief in shifting furniture around or shopping for shoes, we can altogether avoid this nagging symptom of our spiritual stagnation by abandoning all hope that joy will magically appear one day in a safe, predictable manner.

Instead, we must escape the selfish tyranny of this instinctual fear of death that seeks to revoke our every right to enjoy life.

The Comfort Seekers

As we have already learned, comfort-seeking is a necessary aspect of our biological existence. But just as we can become lustfully-obsessed with winning glory, so can we become fearfully-obsessed with trying to prevent the loss of our comfort.

This has created yet another unique human relationship to matter wherein we use material gain not as a weapon of self-promotion, but as a weapon of self-defense. And whereas our glory-seeking impulse can manifest as reckless acts of greed and vanity, our comfort-seeking impulse is typically expressed in selfish acts of conservatism out of our fear of dying or suffering from loss. In some of us, this can lead to an excessive and aggressive guarding of our material resources against depletion, thereby creating an impenetrable barrier to experiencing a more rewarding emotional life outside our materialistic comfort zone.

For example, a selfish aversion to sharing can cause divisive conflicts in any family or have us living a guarded life in a gated community for fear of losing our hoarded energy to others. As a result, our life will be defined not by friendly smiles and handshakes but fences and guns.

As a comfort seeker, our main ambition in life on the material path is to build a protective fortress of physical comforts. As such, our every purchase is meant to counteract a potential threat of death or suffering. As with all extremes of behavior, this creates an imbalance in our life as our attention becomes focussed on the biological utility of tending to our survival at the cost of our spiritual quests for joy.

While a seeker of joy will allot time and energy for spiritual pursuits inspired by their *curiosity, creativity* and desire for *communion*, we as comfort seekers may intentionally avoid those Spiritual States of Being (C4–C6) to not endanger those predictable *conveniences* and *controls* that ensure our continuing *comfort* into the future. As a result, the sum of our life's expression may simply be building and mending of fences against countless forms of adversity, real or imagined. In short, while the open-minded seek more responsible immigration laws, we may be shouting for higher walls and more armed guards at our borders.

Our goal in overcoming this joyless imbalance in our priorities is to identify how we translate our fear of death into various life-numbing forms of private terror. We can then learn to identify how we attempt to buy our protection against them through the "fear economy" of the monetary ecosystem. Once aware of the various fears that undermine our joy potential, we can begin to free ourselves — and those affected by our fear — from our mental bondage to various forms of comfort.

Ultimately, we can never entirely avoid suffering, but we can ensure that our happiness is not sacrificed to an overwhelming urge to cower from all that makes life worth living. Toward that end, our thinking and behavior are influenced both consciously and unconsciously by three distinct categories of comfort-seeking. These are expressed as our *physical, mental* and *social quests for comfort*. Each triggers various fear reactions of which we must become aware to reclaim ownership of our body, mind and spirit from comfort's selfish grasp. Let us now examine each of these comfort categories separately:

The Physical Comfort Seeker

Our quest for physical comfort has us attempting to avoid all forms of danger that may lead to our biological death from cold, hunger, injury or other serious threats. Although a logical and legitimate concern, we can also lose countless opportunities to celebrate life to our obsessive focus on preventing our premature death.

The typical human response to a fear of physical death is to surround ourselves with an impenetrable fortress of defenses against adversity. This may find us living in seclusion with vicious guard dogs roaming inside an insurmountable fence that discourages unscheduled human intrusions into our protective sanctuary.

Inside our fortress, we may be heavily fortified with guns and other such weapons, padlocks, burglar alarms, extensive insurance policies, as well as ointments, antiseptics and magic potions to calm our every fear of encountering some threat beyond our ability to control. In this way, our life is a microcosmic reflection of our equally fearful and fortified nations, which reflect the private terrors of our leaders in not wanting to lose their own hold on comfort to an attacker, foreign or domestic.

This aversion to physical pain and suffering is most dramatically expressed through our adversarial relationship to nature and its host of wild and unpredictable forces. Today, our mass exodus into synthetic dwellings and urban landscapes has caused us to feel disoriented in our former ancestral home and hypersensitive to its once familiar threats of darkness, mysterious sounds and biting insects. Armed with an arsenal of toxic weed and insect killers, gas-powered habitat-slashers, human scent-masking soaps, disinfectants, wildlife assault rifles and various other kinds of anti-nature weaponry, we now also seek comfort in a cosmetic defense industry that promises to defeat the very last and most lethal natural enemy remaining in our midst — the withering affects of our own biological aging process.

Here too, we can enlist the help of the IPSFA Sequence to chart our common and understandable fears in regard to getting older:

I	**Youth** (A biological indicator of our fertility and vigor).
P	Gaining sexual attention and access to social opportunities for personal growth and pleasure.
S	Conceal signs of aging through cosmetics, clothing and surgery.
F	To be treated as worthless by our society and abandoned to die alone.
A	Chronic fear and self-loathing in being unable to escape the reality of our aging body.

Our growing physical and mental detachment from the wilderness and natural world has also encouraged an opportunistic kind of elitist attitude toward the more "uncivilized" roaming among us on our dirty little foul-smelling planet. And so we will hear others condemned as *pigs* for displaying any kind of unsavory behavior normally reserved for the secretive hypocrisy of our private life, such as expelling gas from our intestines or picking mucus out of our nasal passages.

Socialized to deny our true nature, our membership in polite society demands that we conceal our naked, animal-like crudeness by eating our food with utensils, engaging in various hair removal rituals, and loudly condemning our natural body fluids and odors as "disgusting." Subsequently, when company arrives, we must also put on a mask of refined civility, lest we die prematurely from embarrassment in being labelled a "savage."

The Mental Comfort Seeker

Our quest for mental comfort has us avoiding circumstances that may cause us to feel anger, confusion, grief and other forms of emotional suffering. But unlike the predictable causes of physical discomfort, our feelings of emotional discomfort can be influenced by a combination of many factors, from our unique upbringing, individual temperament and cultural influences to the particular mood we are in. As such, this leaves each of us with our own unique collection of private terrors to manage. And that is also what makes our quest for mental comfort so subjective in that others may not share those same fears.

On the material path, mental discomfort compromises our joy by causing us to buy products or services to solve problems that may only exist in our imagination. In anticipating those threats and our often dramatic emotional reaction to them, we may then engage in various *suffering avoidance behaviors* that become our personal comfort traps. This typically involves engaging in repetitive routines or rituals that are meant to defend us against death or suffering from such threats.

In this category, we might buy an excess of hand soap or antiseptics to neutralize the threat of germs or other invisible hazards to which we may never be exposed except through news media fear-mongering.

Our mental discomfort from aging can also inspire various suffering avoidance behaviors, such us buying herbal remedies to "protect our health." Exploiting this fear among the elderly, crooked supplement companies offer dubious health products as miracle cures for any kind of age-related health issue. This can lead to a costly form of emotional dependency wherein we obsessively buy supplements for fear that if we stop using them our body will deteriorate faster. As such, we often use them more to manage our fear of dying than to gain proven results.

Another suffering avoidance behavior is adopting a cynical attitude to avoid exposure to any kind of risk and threat. Here we preemptively reject all that could theoretically endanger our life or cause us mental discomfort. Far exceeding typical risk assessment behavior, cynicism is an obsessive comfort trap that undermines our joy by causing us to even avoid engaging in emotionally-enriching activities.

Even without the mental urging of various obsessions, we all engage in some form of suffering avoidance behavior each day. For example, we may constantly look in the mirror to check for flaws that may cause us to be rejected — what must we buy to fix ourselves? We may also engage in various kinds of superstitious behavior arising from our fear of death and suffering in facing the unknown. This has us engaging in various superstitious rituals to counteract those fears. In some cultures, we actually pretend that the 13th floor of a high rise building is the 14th floor, as though this better ensures our safety. And certainly, there are material costs involved when catering to such mental terrors.

Other threats to our mental comfort include attacks on our beliefs and traditional ways of survival. This may have us choosing to live only in neighborhoods where others will not challenge our existing values, beliefs and attitudes. Aside from leaving little time for joyful thoughts as we vigilantly defend our mental territory, we also create imposing mental barriers to our conscious evolution in our attempting to avoid any encounter with uncertainty or confusion. This also creates material consequences, such as limiting our choice of lifestyle options.

A feeling of inferiority can also be a threat to our mental comfort by undermining our self-esteem or self-confidence. Reacting to that fear, we may even make a preemptive strike to eliminate that threat, as is seen in our indiscriminate killing of wild animals that pose no actual or immediate danger to our existence, especially if we must travel to a foreign country to *neutralize* that dangerous offender.

I	**The Bear Hunt** (A yearly ritual slaying of a dominant predator).
P	Using a gun to disprove our inferior status among dominant animal predators.
S	Buy a gun; enter the bear's home; kill the bear; boast of our courage and skill to friends.
F	To be hunted as prey in the same manner without our courageous gun in hand.
A	Cross-species recreational murder; the taking of another's life as a trophy.

Ironically, in wanting to control all that makes us feel threatened, we often become an even greater threat to those innocent people, animals and various forces of nature that have caused us to feel so afraid. It is therefore important to realize that we can choose how we feel and that the dangers we perceive may not be genuine threats at all, but just our own emotionally-charged mental projections of a frightful world that only exists in our imagination. That is not to say that a lion will never attack us, but if we must board a flight to Africa to provoke the attack, then our violence against wildlife is more a *glory-seeking* venture.

The Social Comfort Seeker

Ironically, the most recognizable form of comfort-seeking also makes us unrecognizable in a crowd because we are so adept at blending into it. As masters of social camouflage, we use mimicry as a self-defense strategy to avoid ridicule, rejection and other such threats of suffering for failing to meet the expectations of others. But even more ironic is that this is the same strategy employed by psychopaths, sociopaths, charlatans and garden variety grifters in hoping to make us their next victim. In short, the means to our end could be the means to our end.

But how did we get here? We can anticipate the answer in recalling that the socialization process trains us to avoid punishment by doing as others desire — this is how we pay for their acceptance. And so we begin to mimic those behaviors that best allow us to avoid their harsh criticisms or negative reactions, perhaps by becoming a chronic people pleaser or closet hypocrite. Social acceptance is also critical to our daily survival. As such, we must find ways to ensure our broad acceptance by co-workers and especially our employers.

From thereon, we begin to push the limits of how far we can venture from authenticity before losing ourselves completely to the pleasant character we have chosen to portray. As social comfort seekers, this is the nature of our comfort trap as we live to avoid rejection by avoiding detection, often at great cost to ourselves, especially in our ability to experience a more genuine, freely-expressive and joyful life.

On the material path, social comfort-seeking traps us into spending time, money and effort to maintain a flawless facade for others. For example, we must ensure that our hair is cut to an *appropriate* length or style, and our clothing and footwear be to the satisfaction of others to ensure we look *presentable* and *respectable*. Here again, that is exactly what career criminals do in wanting to win our trust, as demonstrated in the apathy category of the following IPSFA sequence example:

I	**The Suit** (A type of men's clothing worn to display our civility in public).
P	To be seen as a respectable, hard-working citizen by society; to show we are a "good" person.
S	Buy a suit; wear it wherever and whenever we may be judged for our outward appearance.
F	To be rejected for appearing uncivilized, uneducated, poor or otherwise unrewarding to others.
A	Witnessing all manner of criminals wearing suits to court to appear respectable before the jury.

As a social comfort seeker living in any community, we try to put the minds of our neighbors at ease by reassuring them of our commitment to their values, beliefs and attitudes. We may then display our nation's flag or religious symbols in our yard to prove we are not "one of them" who they may collectively hate or fear. In this life of trivial pursuits, our comfort trap also represents a profitable merchandising opportunity if this competition to prove ourselves the better patriot or true believer escalates into a frantic display such as often seen among teenaged boys competing for group acceptance or glory. We may then spend a small fortune on loyalist flags, bumper stickers, t-shirts and baseball caps to avoid triggering the suspicions of our always vigilant neighbors.

As a social comfort seeker, our life is pre-scripted and prescribed in that our only role is to "fit in" wherever we go, no matter the cost to ourselves in terms of price or personal integrity. And as we go to work each day looking like everyone else and spend our weekends to ensure that both our lawn and family are up to the neighborhood code, we do not realize that we are also engaging in the creation of a homogenous culture of mediocrity wherein we aspire to meet a shared low standard for which everyone is reaching as we slowly become indistinct from one another in our fear of being seen as different.

The Selfish Sleeper State

We are all comfort seekers out of biological necessity, with variations based on how often we answer the call of fear. Yet our fear can also turn necessity into obsession if we begin taking unnecessary precautions in all aspects of our life. In ironic contrast to this approach is the attitude of those daring thrill seekers who purposely challenge their instinctual fear of death to feel more alive. But while skydiving and mountain climbing are not a requirement to make our life feel worth living, there are equal hazards at the opposite extreme of such risk-taking when we succumb to the "selfish sleeper" mental state. Then, instead of a sudden end to our life, we may suffer a long and lingering spiritual death.

Here our endless daily repetition of the same thoughts, behaviors and survival routines lulls us into a trance-like stupor. And that is how we remain unless we invite some meaningful new forms of conscious stimulation into our life to break up the monotony. Much like the bear hibernating to escape the threat of winter's cold, so does this condition of lowering our mental activity protect our comforts from the threat of change. Yet in doing so, we also become trapped in a life of spiritual poverty as we barricade our minds against any form of learning that threatens to contradict or force change upon our predictable lifestyle.

As a selfish sleeper, our frozen mental state is not only a threat to our own joy in life, but also to those who attempt to awaken us from our walking trance. If that should occur, we may exhibit the symptoms of a drowning man as we grasp for anything within reach to avoid going under. And naturally, we may pull our potential rescuer down with us.

Similarly, in denying our need to change, we may lash out angrily at others to avoid leaving our protective sanctuary of mental or material comforts. Some classic examples of this are when elderly parents refuse to abandon a home they can no longer maintain; when parents insist that a child adopt their archaic cultural traditions; when followers of a religion refuse to question their borrowed truths, or when academics struggle to wedge a problematic piece of metaphysical evidence into their limited materialistic worldview. In the latter case, we can use the IPSFA Sequence to investigate why this might happen:

I	**Materialism** (An objectivity-based philosophy to govern our life).
P	To gain control over our life through absolute mental certainty.
S	Using our five physical senses to define the limits of reality.
F	Losing control; being vulnerable to the exploitation of charlatans and our vivid imagination.
A	Limiting our joy by restricting the reach of our curiosity to the familiar or predictable.

The selfish sleeper state is yet another hazard to joy that is caused by convenience-oriented thinking. Here, we behave not unlike birds who return each day to the same feeder because it offers fast, easy access to free food. In developing a habitual way of thinking, we may also keep returning to that same old convenient mental feeding station each day. Yet there are times when that feeder is nearing empty and yet we keep pecking away at it out of habit or sheer desperation. Instead, we must dare to move on to look for new sources of conscious nourishment.

Creatures Of Habit

We have now absorbed a lot of information in assessing how the quest for comfort can inhibit our quest for joy. As "creatures of habit," we tend to create many such obstacles, including to our collective social and spiritual progress. Understandably, we tend to repeat our daily life routines because this is just a faster, easier strategy than having to learn a new approach each day to meeting our needs. It is also safer, because we are assured a predictable outcome. That is also why we may exhibit irrational or even violent behavior when others attempt to force any kind of change on our minds or its well-worn routines. This also helps to explain why governments may violently oppose much-needed social reforms or why polluting industries refuse to adopt ecologically safer technologies in that each feels an existential threat in having to disrupt their own *tried and true* patterns of social behavior that allow them to maintain a comforting sense of control over their enterprise.

Unfortunately, this kind of fearful resistance to change can also keep us from evolving as a society. For instance, the medical industry might not be tempted to find a legitimate cure for any disease when selling a costly treatment for its symptoms is more profitable in the long term. This kind of self-defensive reasoning also creates a tragic social paradox wherein our attaining an optimum state of public health, peace or social equality actually poses a threat to any industry or institution that depends on our continued suffering for their own survival.

In short, finding genuine cures or social solutions can be bad for business, thereby making our future joy or health an acceptable loss.

However, we need not shun any legitimate need for comfort but simply rebalance our approach to life so that our fear of suffering does not needlessly limit our joy potential, nor that of others. As any seeker of joy has come to realize, discomfort is the unavoidable price we must pay for the pleasure of facing new challenges to nurture our personal growth. We can either face those challenges as courageous explorers of our joy potential, or reject them as cowering prisoners of our lingering fear. Always, the decision is ours to make, until it is too late.

And so in closing, let us entertain a final ironic thought in that, after a lifetime of running from every imaginable threat to our existence, we simply die from old age. In reflecting upon such an uneventful demise, we might then reconsider investing so much valuable time, money and effort into continuing to live in fear. However, should we come away from this still believing that we might eventually buy our joy as part of some discounted gift basket of consumer comforts, then the coming chapter should sell us on the idea of abandoning all such hope.

CHAPTER 8
Selling Happiness

The Angler Fish is a master of disguise. Appearing as just another rock in its underwater terrain, he effortlessly hunts in plain view of his prey because no one can detect him. Growing from his forehead is a long, worm-like tentacle that he wiggles vigorously to attract the attention of passing fish. And there he waits for some unwitting victim to give chase to that counterfeit bait only to find itself being consumed by its deceptive owner.

Using the hunger of others to satisfy its own selfish appetite, the Angler Fish offers a useful metaphor for the equally cunning marketer of commercial goods and services. Here lurks another kind of hidden angler who also makes an easy meal of others by eliciting their hungry emotional response to his advertising message and its own tempting worm of enticement — *the promise of joy*. As to why he dedicates his life to selling such promises in material form, the simple answer is that so many of us are hoping to buy it.

Like the Angler Fish, the satisfying of our hunger is not a marketer's intended goal. Instead, he is seeking to win his own economic angling tournament by delivering us like a flopping-wet trophy fish into the eager jaws of his client; the seller of any product, service or idea. And thereupon they will raise a glass of liquid cheer to celebrate their covert victory over their unsuspecting victim — the consumed consumer.

Admittedly, we are all selling something — be it ourselves, our skills or even our own products. However, our concern here is not with the selling of goods but with the purposeful mental invasion of our psyche by marketers preying upon our ignorance or emotional vulnerabilities as buyers. This is especially true for young adults with low self-esteem or those desperate for love, comfort or acceptance. In believing their advertising promises, any of us can fall victim to spending our way into hopeless debt and misery as we try to buy our happiness in some costly counterfeit form.

Understandably, the manipulative tactics of marketers are not being advertised in media, lest they lose their strategic mental advantage over their unsuspecting prey. In addition, the use of such tactics to promote political and religious conformity further discourages public disclosure of those selling secrets — no one wants to give away the game.

As seekers of joy on the material path, we must therefore educate ourselves about the mental sport of marketing as it seeks to control our minds and spending behavior. And while not all marketers are villains, we must be prepared to protect ourselves and our communities against those sociopaths whose broken moral compass would allow them to sell cigarettes and other kinds of dangerously addictive substances to healthy teenagers not only to earn a living, but also as a form of mental sport. It is their reckless disregard for the public's trust that demands our quick and enlightened response to neutralize the threat of these remorseless social predators who see us not as a fellow human beings, but only as herds of targeted "game" to be hunted and consumed.

The Need To Sell

Our human relationship to material goods and their acquisition is fraught with many hazards, as already revealed. Aside from our falling into financial or moral ruin, those hazards include our ingesting of dangerous chemicals in processed food and losing valuable time and money to the joyless pursuit of hiding our perceived flaws with costly beauty products and surgical procedures.

Meanwhile, the reckless exploitation of our natural resources for profit pollutes our water and air while generating excesses of wealth far beyond anyone's actual needs. Subsequently, our excursions to the mall and grocery store are not just a superficial act of buying necessary goods or entertaining distractions but a means by which we can decide the future fate of our world in choosing how and what we buy.

In that regard, let us consider the toxic legacy of gas-powered cars, which once seemed a rewarding choice, yet now overwhelm our world with their deadly consequences, including the countless wild animals being smashed to death on roads or dying in oil spills. Are we really so much further ahead once we include these additional high costs, or is it time for us to move on to some wiser mode of transport?

Working against us in making such wiser purchasing decisions is society's constant need to sell. Quite literally, unless we are constantly buying and selling in our monetary ecosystems, we will quickly die for lack of money to pay for food and shelter. This necessitates a perpetual cycle of constant aggressive marketing and selling to ensure the daily survival of the product manufacturers who are also employing us.

Unfortunately, our need for money also spawns products of dubious value, such as elite underwater sport watches for landlocked men. And whereas the merits of food need not be advertised to the hungry, the act of compelling us to buy items of no practical value always requires some degree of mental intimidation on the part of advertisers. It is this kind of psychological sorcery of which we must be aware to defend against its subversive attacks on our unsuspecting minds and incomes.

Today, as stores offer products that fulfill more the economic needs of their sellers, marketing companies are enlisted to create some reason for us to buy those products. Here again, cigarettes demonstrate how a useless product can become widely popular yet offer no actual benefit — while killing us with its toxic ingredients. And although we benefit from being made aware of our buying choices through media, we must always be alert to the more sinister practice of convincing us to buy the promise of joy within products for which we may have no actual use.

Toward that end, let us expose yet another metaphorical angler fish hiding in plain view inside our homes where it also tries to bait us into spending our money with its loud, urgent appeals to the impulsive and less rational parts of our brain.

The Clandestine Selling Machine

Historically, the craft of advertising began through direct contact as street vendors and swindlers alike announced their wares to passers-by. This helped to establish the language and theatrics of selling, just as print media advanced its visual presentation, and radio its aural assault.

Today, all of these selling strategies are combined to create the aptly named "commercial" of television infamy. And although television was not invented for selling, that is now its primary function in our homes, often for hours each day, from early childhood onward.

The programs that it offers are also not free but rather a costly form of entertainment bait used for catching a "target" audience of desirable viewers. In short, it is a device for remotely generating retail sales leads based on viewer preferences. The attention of viewers is then leased to marketers who promote specific products to targeted viewing groups on behalf of their clients, who may want to sell furniture or makeup to women, utility trucks or beer to men, or toys and sugary treats to the young. The goal of television advertisers is to offer each type of viewing audience a favorite show to watch so they will turn on their clandestine selling machines at the allotted time to watch those targeted ads.

A most revealing aspect of television commercials is that everyone acting in them must always look happy, with very few exceptions. This demonstrates the theatrical aspect of selling wherein the promise of joy is conveyed through the fake smiles and laughter of paid actors. The reason for their counterfeit happiness is that we are far less likely to be enticed by a product that leaves others looking sullen or indifferent. And so, instead it becomes: "Yay, tampons!" and "Yay, laundry soap!"

Knowing this, we can identify a wide range of exaggerated facial expressions of joy — from the orgasmic delight of the woman closing her eyes while eating creamy yogurt, to the wide-eyed "happy mommy face" of actors pretending to have won the lottery or a casino jackpot.

Nor is it a coincidence that they are using the same face of delight our mothers used in pressing teddy bears and other joy paraphernalia into our happy little infant faces so that we might also feel safe and satisfied in our blossoming emotional relationship to material gain.

As spectators of this strategic selling spectacle, our obligation is to believe that everyone in commercials is a happy customer and not just a paid actor faking that emotion for the camera. Our second obligation is to believe that the promise of joy being conveyed could also be ours by simply buying that product. Yet suspiciously absent is any warning that our joy in owning that product *may not be exactly as shown.*

Selling medicine or other comfort-oriented products, however, will require a more serious tone and message. Cold remedies, for instance, promise women the reward of being "good" mothers for not allowing their children to suffer from coughs, fevers or stuffy noses. Ironically, by artificially suppressing a sick child's autoimmune responses, those medications may actually be undermining the body's natural efforts to heal itself. We may also question the wisdom of using an injured limb just because a powerful pain-killer has completely numbed our brain's ability to detect further threats of injury through warnings of pain.

However, such medical paradoxes go seemingly unnoticed by that mystery panel of experts known as "9 out of 10 doctors recommend…"

And as that selling machine sucks away our time and money like an insatiable electronic vampire, it can also keep us disengaged from the real world outside. Today, television is for many our only community experience wherein we may care more about the lives of fictitious play actors and media celebrities than our families and neighbors. And all the while, the selling machine must keep on selling, lest there be no more free television for us to watch tomorrow.

The Unseen Truth In Advertising

Beyond its overtly manipulative nature, media creates further obstacles to joy by censoring truth and reality to protect its lucrative relationship with advertisers. That relationship also gives media the unique feature of being *a product for selling products,* as we quickly realize when buying a magazine for its articles only to find it full of advertising. This would also suggest that media's true loyalty is to the act of selling itself, which is why we cannot expect it to defend us against the ill affects of product marketing when its very survival depends upon facilitating it. This may explain media's seeming indifference in helping to ensure our mental surrender to the often misleading appeals of its most valued customers.

That threat is further escalated when media is owned or directed by groups of anonymous investors or nomadic corporate mercenaries who feel no personal sense of social responsibility in failing to protect us from such purposeful manipulations of our mind. As a result of this conflict of interest, truth in media and advertising is not something in which we should invest our trust.

Further justifying that position is the food featured in commercials, which is artificially colored, glazed and sculpted into a misleading state of perfection so as to appear more appealing to our eyes. The same kind of artificial enhancements are made to those alluring fashion models being used to draw our attention to products by way of our sexual lust. Their tempting presence creates a further hazard by leading young girls and boys to mimic social values, beliefs or attitudes that are unrealistic or outright deceptive. As we have learned over the years, this can also result in ill mental states causing willful starvation, self-loathing and a life of "have-not" misery that may already begin in early childhood.

Aside from trolling its attractive models as sexual bait for our hungry eyes, media also makes use of proven "experts" to overcome our buying objections, especially if that product is a political candidate or the toxic views of industrial profiteers. In that regard, the now-popularized term of "gaslighting" refers to the act of causing others to distrust their own eyes, ears and intelligence; an activity for which media advertising has long been known in convincing us to buy whatever it is selling.

In advancing the public careers of fashion models, entertainers and politicians, media also proves to be a promotional vehicle for selling people as products. This "public relations" aspect of marketing finds anyone from famous actors and future monarchs to industrial polluters hiring marketers to create a flattering public image for them through constant favorable media exposure. As a result, the perceived humanity of a political candidate photographed holding a baby or serving soup to the poor is often as illusory as are their campaign promises.

Media also promotes its own authority by creating boisterous award ceremonies that celebrate and advertise its top-selling people products. Meanwhile, our conflicted emotional impulses to both praise and envy those we admire spawns a lucrative celebrity gossip empire that invites us to simultaneously worship and mock our beloved idols.

In witnessing its confusing array of paradoxes and overt pretensions, we can deduce that the business of media is neither to promote truth nor the conscious evolution of humanity, but to simply tell whichever lie we most need to hear to keep us believing and buying.

Identifying with Success

Now that we have gained a broader understanding of the social selling environment and its prevailing climate of exploitation, we can explore some common selling techniques so that we might better defend our minds and incomes against their deployment within media.

Toward that end, let us recognize that, beyond the necessities of life, we also buy products to create a public perception of our sexual, social or economic reward potential. We do this by dressing and behaving in ways that make us appear attractive. For instance, we can draw more attention to ourselves by appearing as someone with a higher income. This requires wearing the clothes and accessories associated with being such a person. Here media advertising serves its further function by showing us which costumes to buy to appear as our chosen character on the public stage. In this way, it also teaches us how to visually bluff others into believing in our success based only on outward appearances — a *"fake it until you make it"* strategy for life.

Given the importance of mimicry to the survival of most species, we can see why we would then adopt social identities and behavioral traits that are associated with success, even just for the sakes of appearances.

This is also why we might imitate the hairstyles, clothing or language of a famous celebrity or even a fictitious film superhero in wanting to command the same level of positive attention from our society.

But while most parents have their children's best interests in mind, marketers have no such moral obligation. As a result, they will exploit this natural urge to mimic among the young and naive by enticing us to buy *the appearance of success,* be it in the form of a gold watch to appear wealthy, or designer running shoes to look like a champion.

Our mimicking of success is what also makes celebrity endorsement such an effective selling tool. Here marketers will hire a heroic public figure of sport, film or music to trick us into believing we can emulate their lifestyle by simply buying their preferred brand of shoes, lipstick, or cologne — which they may only pretend to use for the duration of that commercial or their scheduled royalty payments from a sponsor.

As a result, this is also why each generation of teenagers suffers from that ironic social condition wherein we seek to prove our individuality by imitating everybody else. Roaming the streets like herds of branded human cattle, we are products of a cookie-cutter culture whose daily fortunes are made by our predictable urge to mimic success.

Yet our societies face an even greater threat now that media has also replaced the oral storytelling tradition of our ancestors as the creator of new cultural myths, legends and future dreams. As such, it need only invent ever more appealing film or TV cartoon characters to keep us all worshipping those idols at the cash register. As an added feature attraction, our children may also be taught to solve all of their personal problems and social conflicts through the use of gun violence, fakery or sexual persuasion — just like their heroes.

The Glorious Power Pitch

Fashion models offer a prime example of mimicry's success as a selling tool. In being presented as the epitome of physical beauty, according to traits often promoted by media itself, every young girl is instructed on what she must buy to command the same level of sexual attention as her heroic stick sisters of high fashion. But what is being sold is not beauty, but power — namely, one's ability to prevail over other women in taking at will the attention and subsequent energy rewards of men.

But the power of such beauty is often just another illusion, as nature typically prevents malnourished women from ovulating to ensure that she will not bear sickly or stillborn children for lack of sufficient fat and nutritional intake. But media seems not to care about biological reality as much as it does the selling of haircare products and lipstick to teenaged girls. Instead, it misleads them about the joys of becoming a woman whose sole purpose in life is to stay silent, skinny, smiling and always sexually available, even if she cannot carry a child to term for lack of a suitable biological growing environment.

As part of this social recipe for counterfeit "girl power," we find that there are proven links between a woman's attributes and her ability to turn heads. One of them, due at least in part to media celebrity culture, is blonde hair. Let us now make use of the IPSFA sequence to write the basic behavioral script for a young women to follow in mimicking this visual aspect of the blonde "bombshell" stereotype.

I	**The Blonde** (a proven visual identity for gaining sexual attention from men in public).
P	To win positive attention and its potential rewards from sexually aroused men.
S	Purchase hair dye to conceal our natural hair color; repeat perpetually until dead or bald.
F	Being ignored; losing attention to authentic blondes or other more visually appealing women.
A	Neglecting what makes us inwardly attractive by obsessing about our outward appearance.

But young women are not the only victims of media's projections of a false identity to sell consumer goods and services. On the masculine end of media's seduction spectrum, we find boys being taught to prove their superior reward potential as a future mate through the displaying of various products associated with social dominance.

Car commercials are especially revealing in their use of manipulative marketing techniques, often becoming laughable media caricatures by way of their constant, nagging similarity. For example, to sell costly sports cars, marketers often use loud, boastful, intimidating language and imagery to inflame men's desire to win "the big race" to work each day by appealing to their competitive vanity. Now, instead of selling a mode of transport, they are offered a new weapon of social advantage to add to their arsenal in becoming the supreme leader of the roadways and tunnels leading to female arousal and conception.

Here, in bragging about a car's "performance," the word is blatantly used as a metaphor to describe a man's social and sexual performance in owning such a *powerful* car. This is also why we hear status-based phrases such as "best in its class" or "a proven leader" used to further assist men in purchasing a higher-rated mating position at their local car dealership. Ironically, this mental drama is merely the product of a marketer's imagination, as is the promise of finding unconditional love amidst a flock of hungry-eyed female opportunists seeking a free ride to material bliss.

In addition, we cannot allow our otherwise unremarkable wrist to dangle nakedly outside the open window of such an important-looking automobile. And so, we will also need one of these:

I	**Gold watch** (A symbolic means of competitive display that can also be used for telling time).
P	To gain social favor, admiration or acceptance by publicly displaying our wealth.
S	Buy an expensive gold watch; ensure its prominent display whenever in public.
F	Being identified as poor, inferior or an otherwise socially insignificant person.
A	Having to deny our competitive vanity by pretending to care about the accuracy of "Swiss time."

But all of this pedestrian parading pales in comparison to where the real power of human civilization lies, which is in the making of war and more accurately, in the war-catering industries. As such, peace is the only true enemy because no one can make any money from it.

Keeping war industries profitable in times of peace will also require the use of advertising. Aside from selling guns to private citizens for protection against rabid squirrels or governments armed with aerial bombers and nuclear weapons, there exists a far more lucrative market among world leaders clinging selfishly to the land and privileges they have stolen from their citizens. Here, advertising takes the form of alarm-calling about the imminent threat of their shameful defeat at the hands of *a better man with a bigger gun.*

I	**Alarm call** (The warning cry of birds and other animals to announce the arrival of a predator).
P	To be safely out of harm's way in having advance warning.
S	Make constant loud noise to warn others in the area of an impending attack.
F	Becoming the unsuspecting prey to a predator passing through our territory.
A	Growing careless after too many false alarm calls; a joyless life lived in constant fear.

This kind of sales pressure ensures that a buyer's spending will be commensurate with his heightened level of paranoia. As for money to finance such a costly venture, it can either be loaned at high interest from a foreign adversary, or taken out of the tax money normally used to pay for citizen healthcare and education. As such, in planning wars this way, everybody wins except those sacrificed to die in them.

Government propaganda films are another classic form of pro-war advertising that has been prevalent since film was invented. Today, we may find the war industry financing feature length films about heroic military conquests by brave young men on foreign soil. This has various affects in the public sphere: to normalize economic and moral support for war, to sell weapons to men as a symbol of power, and also to recruit a new generation of boys to fight for the glory of aging leaders under the auspices of patriotism or other variation of "good boy" behavior.

In maintaining a steady sale of human killing implements, it is also necessary for media to invent new enemies, real or imagined, against which we must continuously arm and defend our government. And once the war is over and all the dead are buried and forgotten, then we must do it all over again for lust never sleeps, and neither does greed.

I	**War** (An organized killing spree to seize the land assets and females of rival dominant males).
P	To prove our dominance and win the territory of our rivals; personal glory, parades and medals.
S	Round up young men; arm them; send them off to kill the latest "enemy"; keep buying weapons.
F	Losing a war after creating a massive national debt, thus making re-election a challenge.
A	Endless biologically-induced male rivalry; no peace; mass murder; pillaging; the orphans of rape.

In the meantime, our planet has become a military graveyard for storing unused or obsolete weapons of mass destruction, both on land and in our oceans. This could explain the massive fish kills and whale beachings of past decades. But on a more positive note, despite all this gruesome collateral damage, someone surely made a good profit.

Conditions Of Sale

We have been given much to consider in taking this long, scenic route through the sordid world of product advertising. However, this has just been a cursory overview of the selling craft and will not fully prepare us for the exploitive rigors of life in the monetary ecosystem. Yet we can now move forward with greater confidence in having learned some of its more manipulative aspects.

In concluding this exploration of the material path, we can gain added protection against the targeted mental invasions of marketers by identifying three "ambient conditions" of sale created to optimize the advertiser's chances of tempting us to buy. They are as follows:

1. The Hard And Soft Sell:
As a form of mental conditioning used to isolate women from social power in most cultures, the *Gender Wall* is also used to sell products by promoting unrealistic gender stereotypes in advertising. As such, to emulate those mythical sirens of the fashion industry, a woman must also present herself as a soft, submissive, simple-minded prey animal born to service the lustful urges of the roaming dominant male.

We find evidence for this in how woman are posed in various fashion magazines. Here she is shown insecurely looking down at the ground, shyly covering her mouth, biting her lip, or shrinking into the chest of a larger male like a frightened child. In many such images, she is being posed to signal her surrender; the most iconic of which has her raising her arms over her head to offer no resistance to being touched — or *dominated*. In stark contrast, we see men posed in "on alert" positions as though always ready for attack. In short, woman in advertising must never be seen to appear threatening to her dominant male protector and future father figure in marriage, lest he feel intimidated and scurry off back into the bushes out of fear.

These slanted social misrepresentations of the female gender can be easily discredited in the presence of any confident, socially-empowered woman. Yet media often refuses to see her, for even at the summit of political power, a male leader will be judged for his ability to project strength while his female counterpart will typically be judged for the color or fashion designer of the dress she has chosen to wear. In short, by media advertising standards, a woman's worth is not in her intellect, character or professional ambitions, but in her ability to attract men.

Men are also kept on a short leash on their side of the Gender Wall in having to wear their own gender-specific uniforms, often to convey their dominance over women. Subsequently, there is a long history of men fearing ridicule for wearing bright or light colors, including pink, due to their cultural association with femininity — and weakness.

As such, gender-based clothing often becomes a caricature of itself, as is the case if a man dresses like a cowboy, not because he raises cattle, but to visually prove his masculine identity. Coerced by culture to shop at some version of "the cowboy store," he finds there a limited selection of apparel and accessories that ultimately ensure he will always walk out of that store dressed like a cowboy, regardless of which hat or shade of leather boots he has chosen. And where cowboys do not roam, we find some other variation of that hard, calloused male stereotype who is heard loudly, boastfully reassuring his fellow uniformed workers or bar mates that no son of his would ever dare scale that wall separating the *real* men from all those "softies" on the other side.

It is this kind of purposeful cultural polarizing of the genders that also makes it easy for marketers to sell pickup trucks to men who have no actual use for such a vehicle except as a symbolic form of displaying their manhood. As such, in watching television ads for such a truck, we are given the impression that all men must surely own cattle.

2. The Sounds Of Selling:

Sound is critical to the emotional impact of the selling process, as is evident by turning down the volume during a television commercial. What we will then experience is a meaningless barrage of imagery that evokes no feeling of want or desire without the sound of spoken words and music to give our mind its emotional footing.

Like the favorite songs of our youth, sound acts as a gateway to our emotions that advertisers also exploit to their advantage. However, just as it is inappropriate to laugh at a funeral, so must the sounds of selling be appropriate for each type of commercial setting. This requires every product to have its own sonic selling strategy, including the proper emotive language, speaking tone and ambient music for the occasion.

To understand how this works, let us explore a few examples of how products and sounds are commonly matched to create a more receptive buying atmosphere:

Life Insurance (a comfort-based pitch): a deep, soothing fatherly voice is often heard over a sparse, sentimental music score. The language is meant to incite our fear or concern, then reassure us by offering the product as the solution. And now we know what we must do.

Sports Car (a glory-based pitch): A loud, boastful male voice challenges us to do battle as aggressive rock music plays in the background. The language and tone incites us to feel we must prove ourselves a winner as the short drive to work each day becomes a critical race for glory. When careening through traffic-free mountain roads, sports cars are sold with a freedom-oriented theme, using phrases such as "just you and the open road" to suggest buying our passage to unlimited social mobility.

Makeup (a comfort-based pitch): A sexy, self-assured sounding female voice is heard challenging her peers to join the fun over pulsating dance music suggesting a night club setting with loud, happy social interaction. The message conveyed is that a woman's self-confidence and social merit are something applied to one's face. The voice often has a contemptuous "what are you waiting for?" tone to intimidate women into buying that product for fear of losing out on all the fun that awaits.

Milk (a comfort-based pitch): When selling milk, a soothing, motherly voice is often heard over sentimental music, supported by visual themes associated with one's returning home to maternal love — wherein our earliest memories of breast-feeding reside.

Other Noteworthy Noises: There are many ways by which marketers weaponize words and music to target our incomes via our emotions. Here, honorable mention goes to the "happy little girl" voice inflection often used to evoke a playful, child-like atmosphere to make her selling sound like clean, innocent fun. Also noteworthy are such status-based trigger words as *exclusive* and *premium* that have us going into debt to buy luxury items designed to make us appear rich.

3. Propulsion By Repulsion
The *fear economy* utilizes fear as its prime advertising motivator to sell anything from political and religious ideologies to consumer goods. Here, various imaginary demons are summoned to close the sale by making us afraid not to buy, join or agree as the sales pitch commands.

As a result, when we hear the disembodied voice of a female in makeup commercials saying, "You deserve to look your best," it not only implies that buying this product is a defiant act of self-entitlement, but by the subtle use of reverse psychology, it also provokes our fear of rejection by implying that we could never look our "best" without it.

Fear-based advertising thrives on exploiting our want for power and autonomy. For example, as children and teenagers, we are eager to be seen as older and more independent. This creates an opportunity to sell cigarettes, makeup, alcohol and even guns as symbolic "rite of passage" products by associating them with our passage into adulthood. Later as adolescents, the shame of appearing immature can then incite us to buy those products to prove our maturity. And by exploiting this urge in their daughters, vain mothers can compete against one another by entering their children in beauty contests to mimic the kind of sexually provocative women they may have wanted to be. Here as well, the fear of losing has rewarded the cosmetics industry with unexpected sales from yet another burgeoning new demographic — six-year-olds.

And finally, the most familiar kind of fear advertising that we will encounter is the sign that warns us: "HURRY! SALE ENDS SOON." Here we are being provoked to buy — and decide — in haste based on our fear of losing. And so, rather than take time to think about what we need, we leave the store with more useless junk in succumbing to the pressure of having to make a quick decision.

"Propulsion by repulsion" is a CPJ-specific term to identify these fear-based sales techniques that propel us to buy through our repulsion for losing an opportunity. On this trajectory where fear repels us from making a wiser choice, we may buy all manner of social costumes and lifestyle accessories to become almost unrecognizable to ourselves. Perhaps such fear is also why so many ill-suited couples end up getting married — rather than waiting to find the love they need.

Keeping this in mind, let us borrow a term from media by making this our *segue* into the next program of social detoxification where we explore how the quality of our relationships with others is determined by the quality of the relationship that we maintain with ourselves.

PART THREE
The Relational Path to Joy

CHAPTER 9
A Balanced Joy Economy

Relationships connect us to what we value most in life, from the means to our survival, to the people we love and the activities we enjoy. Our quest for joyful relationships should therefore be a simple matter of deciding what makes us happy and allying ourselves to the people or circumstances that can assist us in attaining those emotional goals.

While this may seem a logical approach, it is not entirely realistic in our complex human world. For example, we cannot always choose our relationships or their circumstances, as is true with our parents or the neighborhood into which we are born. In addition, relationships are a form of economy that we maintain by trading time and energy with others and also ourselves. As a result, even with multiple choices before us, we may have to sacrifice one priority for another simply because we have not the time or energy for both. And this is what can also lead us to a state of imbalance in our joy economy.

A familiar example of such a joy imbalance is when a materialistic woman marries for wealth only to realize she must now forgo intimate companionship with a man whose social conquests keep him mentally or physically remote from her. In having made winning in one aspect of her life a priority, she now suffers an equal or greater loss in another. And this kind of trade-off is typical of many relationships.

As seekers of joy, our goal is to maintain a balanced joy economy by deciding how much we are willing to sacrifice to avoid sacrificing joy itself. Although this may sound selfishly-indulgent, it is actually quite practical when we consider how enjoyable relationships can be when in the company of people who do not feel angry or resentful in having traded their happiness for mere comfort and security.

As seekers of joy, we can also ensure a more balanced joy economy by engaging in fair practices with our relational trading partners. This means being honest about what others can expect from us so that none are left disappointed. Yet despite such lofty ambitions, the demands of daily life in a monetary ecosystem will also force us into various utility relationships to serve our highest priority, survival itself. As such, we further risk neglecting our joy in tending to the many needs of marital partners, employers and others.

In many cases, we can maintain a balanced joy economy by setting aside time for activities that trigger our spiritual joy coordinates, such as music creation, painting and other artistic endeavors. In this way, we can better ensure our continued enthusiasm for life by engaging in acts of curiosity, creativity and communion as we attend to our physical needs for comfort, convenience and control.

However, time itself can become an obstacle to joy when having to ensure our survival. For example, earning our daily income requires an average ten hour commitment, including time spent preparing for and traveling to work. Once home, we may require a further eight hours of sleep to maintain our health, which leaves us with a mere six hours to raise our children, cook and clean, and engage with our friends. In the end, there is often little "me time" to invest in ourselves.

Eventually, in struggling to maintain such a demanding relationship schedule, we may notice that the relationship between our body and spirit is beginning to suffer. Subsequently, in clearing a relational path to joy, we must give our emotional fulfillment equal high priority by ideally choosing the kinds of goals and relational partnerships that can facilitate reconnecting us to the playful, child-like essence of our being. In this way we can engage in a balanced approach to life that does not leave us in a state of spiritual poverty as we serve our biological needs. In short, we must demand more from our life than mere existence, for otherwise that is all we will get.

The Most Critical Relationship

Realistically, while not all relationships can offer us a path to joy, we can avoid many future regrets by not dismissing the importance of joy to our lives. After all, it is our joyful engagement with academic study that makes us better students, which also requires learning subjects that genuinely hold our interest rather than just showing up at school out of an obligation to our parents or teachers. Nor can that learning experience leave us mentally drained of curiosity or enthusiasm if we are to succeed in that regard. We must always feel *interested* in order to learn properly. There are no exceptions to this rule, and cheating is no substitute for achieving excellence — just ask the cheaters.

Likewise, our joyful daily engagements with a marriage partner will inspire a mutual admiration and respect that prevents that relationship from feeling like a prison sentence. Here too, we must feel a genuine interest in our relationships to ensure their own levels of excellence. As an analogy, it is not what we do to the exterior of our house but what happens *on the inside* that leads to a joyful life. Here again, joy is like an empty box that we must learn to fill for ourselves, and the same is true for joyful relationships — we cannot fake our way to a meaningful relationship; invariably, we must invest ourselves into it.

Unfortunately, our childhood experiences with joyless imbalances of power can create a bad impression of relationships and their inherent joy potential. For instance, we may be raised by a parasitic parent who treats us as an appendage by making all decisions for us, from choosing our friends and career to a marriage partner. Here, any "better life" they may claim to want for us is the life they want for themselves. As such, what we want gets in their way, so there can be no further negotiation. Subsequently, this kind of family dynamic can leave us with a reactive psychological residue that will later affect our trust and self-esteem, making it more difficult to enjoy being in any kind of relationship.

What this tragic early-life trajectory demonstrates is that we do not always enter into relationships on equal emotional footing, with many of us being at a disadvantage in negotiating a joyful balance. As such, our primary focus here on the relational path to joy will not be to "fix" other people and their problems, but to fix ourselves by becoming a more effective negotiator and most important of all, to recognize when we should not be entering into any such negotiations at all.

In that regard, most imbalances in relationships can be overcome by establishing a strong and trusting inner bond with ourselves; one that is independent of what others think of us or how they choose to react to us emotionally. In reclaiming our rightful place as the true source of love and power in our life, we are able to exert a greater command over our emotional destiny. As such, the nurturing of a genuine inner love and respect for ourselves is the first crucial step to establishing joyful relationships with others. In short, our most critical relationship in life is the one that we maintain with ourselves.

In pursuing that goal, we must begin making room for ourselves. At times, this may require us to part ways with those we care about as we work to establish a more authentic and fulfilling relationship to life itself. Such a departure may also be ideological to ensure our clearer mental passage to becoming the person we truly are rather than some wishful projection of who others would prefer us to be.

In taking this daring approach to life, others witnessing our courage may also be inspired to seek a greater share of joy in context of their own relationships. Ultimately, we need not live as trees rooted to a single location, for we are born as self-aware beings with the conscious power to affect great positive changes in our life if we keep moving forward in the direction of our joyful inner growth.

And finally, we must put our trust in what can be a slow and painful process to knowing *who we are* within any relationship, especially the one with ourselves, for it seems a general law of spirit and fate that to truly find ourselves, we must lose ourselves first.

A Measure Of Success

Even if we never lose ourselves, we are sure to encounter situations of loss that remind us of how unfair life can seem. Like the runner who loses the race by milliseconds, so might success elude us when it seems within reach. Yet no matter what happens, we must accept loss as part of life, not because it leads to happiness, but because it will make us far less emotionally volatile in relation to life itself. Let us then recall from chapter two an observation that even if we never taste victory, our life can still feel worthwhile if we are able to do what matters to us.

There will also be times where we have to struggle twice as hard to attain a mere fraction of what others acquire with ease. Moreover, most of us will not be born into households of wealth and privilege, nor will we inherit success through a hereditary bloodline. Instead, the odds favor our living an unremarkable life of comfort-seeking by default.

Luckily, most of us do not want the sole responsibility of leadership, which often leaves us to play a supportive role to those seeking some ultimate form of pleasure or glory through a quest for power. Yet what most determines our success in life is not good fortune or genetics but rather how we choose to define success itself.

Success, after all, is a *relative* term based on the activity in which we are involved. As such, even a humble life can offer many opportunities to achieve success, be it through a fulfilling career, a loving marriage, our friendships, or by pursuing meaningful goals that challenge us to rise above our current limits. This is what puts an otherwise ordinary life on equal footing with an extraordinary one, for our goal is to clear a path to joy, not wealth or social influence. For that reason, unless we are able to achieve a joyful balance of spiritual inspiration and material utility, even the most successful among us will risk sinking into despair if all we have to show for our efforts is a brand new yacht or mansion.

In taking this approach, we learn that what matters is not attaining some outwardly-directed visual indicator of our success, but to attain a state of inner contentment by our own standards of measure.

Understandably, this can create conflicts or confusion among those who expect us to meet the standards by which they gauge their own success. They may even insist that we act "normal like everybody else." But in looking closer at what being "normal" demands of us, we find a path leading to misery by fracturing the relationship we must maintain to our own unique identity. As proof, here is an IPSFA Sequence that demonstrates the process of *normalizing* ourselves:

I	**"Normal"** (A generic social identity based on widely-accepted, culture-specific behavioral traits).
P	To be accepted and rewarded as a trusted member of our society.
S	To think, behave and dress as others would expect us to do.
F	To be rejected, abandoned and persecuted for refusing to behave like a "normal" person.
A	Having to reject the truth of who we are as a means of social self-defense.

This publicly-promoted push toward normalcy confronts us early in life and is most effective during our formative years as young adults. At the same time, we are also pressured by our parents and other mentors to follow their preferred life paths. As uncertified sales representatives for our future success, what they conveniently fail to disclose are the emotional consequences for compromising our core identity to service social identities we do not wish to adopt, whether in being "normal" or taking on professional roles ill-suited to meet our spiritual needs. Only later do we realize that these are not fast, free or easy paths to joy, nor even paths we ought to consider when it means surrendering our own ambitious dreams only to flail and fail in chasing after those of others.

Once we are resolved to remain true to ourselves and travel only the relational paths of our own choosing, we may still encounter various joy-inhibiting obstacles along the way. In mentally preparing for such encounters, we are less likely to find ourselves later wondering how our identity was stolen or our life, money and spirit drained like a battery by the selfish scheming of others. As such, the more we can anticipate what can go wrong in any relationship, the better we will become at preventing the loss of our integrity as we work to develop the kind of relationships that meet our own personal standards of success.

Confusion By Design

Among the obstacles we can encounter on the relational path, some are related to relationship processes rather than people. Our earlier study of the material path revealed our complex emotional relationship to matter. Yet on the relational path an even more complex relationship exists to the means by which we access our material energy rewards.

In that regard, nature designs relationships to be intuitively simple so that even newborns can gain easy access to food and shelter. Acting as service bridges leading to the energy resources we need, our human relationships were also once as structurally simple as a fallen log across a stream in uniting families and tribal clans by our common need for food, fellowship and protection. By contrast, our present-day relational bridges more resemble those massive steel monoliths that connect distant land masses across a treacherous expanse of open sea.

Nor has money made life simpler. Rather than independence, it has bought us only an increased sense of selfish isolation and loneliness in having outgrown our need for a close-knit tribal community. And as we travel by car to buy food items grown in distant lands, we also have no need to know our neighbors, whose lives remain as much a passing blur as the scenery on our hurried way to elsewhere.

To prove how complicated our relational frameworks have become, let us consider that a young chimpanzee in the wild can still swing to a nearby tree for a banana when feeling hungry. In stark contrast, as the civilized member of any monetary ecosystem, we must first undergo a years-long process of preparation that involves the following steps:

- ☑ Submit to a lengthy school training program. (12 yrs. or more)
- ☑ Learn a marketable skill or trade. (Lasting months to years)
- ☑ Apply for a job that pays us money in exchange for our time and efforts. (Duration: unknown)
- ☑ Compete against countless others to find such a job. (Duration: unknown)
- ☑ Open a bank account to facilitate energy transactions with merchants. (1hr.)
- ☑ Pay for housing, water, electricity, etc. (Duration: unknown)

- ☑ Buy furniture, appliances, cookware, utensils, etc. (Duration: unknown)
- ☑ (And finally): Enter a grocery store to exchange our money for two bananas and a plastic bottle full of repurposed tap water. (5 min.)

Moreover, we must complete most of these preparations before we are *legally entitled* to eat our fill of bananas — and only after having first paid all applicable government taxes. And if all these obstructions are not enough, then we need only realize that a failure to comply with any of these steps could result in our dying of starvation on the street.

The irony of our self-proclaimed *superior* human way of life is that a chimpanzee retains significantly more free time to engage in the joys of curious exploration and creative play by not having to undergo this complex assimilation process to a symbolic energy trading system.

And perhaps most ironic is that our wearisome, over-worked human lifestyles may then have us paying for the mere privilege of sitting in a trance-like stupor in front of a television each night while still having to scratch ourselves like every other kind of monkey.

In presenting the chimpanzee's lifestyle for contrast, we can clearly see how unnatural our human relationship to life has become and why so many people turn to alcohol, drugs or other addictions to mentally escape a survival system in which many of us feel alienated, alone and uninspired. After all, no one likes living in a cage, including humans.

Also inherent to maintaining these complex human survival systems is our lifelong dependency on others, including strangers with whom we must share various duties and expenses. Subsequently, it becomes necessary to interrogate our relationship candidates like the primary suspect in a crime because choosing the *wrong* person, whether as our employer, marriage partner or even just a "friend," can have lifelong negative consequences in a monetary ecosystem. Subsequently, we can also expect to be cheated, exploited or betrayed by some of those we had come to trust. In the worst cases, we may become a victim of rape, murder or sexual slavery courtesy of selfish social predators who have no business being a part of any society, let alone the human race.

For this reason, a well-justified and lingering suspicion of others will often haunt our daily lives, thereby further hindering our joy potential as much as any restrictive law or social custom that dictates how or with whom we are allowed to engage in our relational quests for joy.

In short, modern human relationships are confusing, not by their nature, but by our own design. As such, we must be careful not to lose ourselves or our joy compass bearings in maintaining them.

A Fair Trade

Given what we have already considered, we may think that human life could not possibly get more complicated than having to go to school and set up a bank account just to buy some bananas — but it can, and it does. Adding further confusion to an already confusing human quest for joy is a complex array of social identities that we must now adopt to service all of these newly-defined relationships and their needs.

This will require us to take on various scripted acting roles that have us mimicking the behaviors associated with being a "student" and an "employee," as well as a "law-abiding citizen" to not only prove our value to others but also avoid being punished for any "abnormal" behavior by those already indoctrinated into the system.

As earlier revealed, this creates a complicated "Joy Bureaucracy" of borrowed identity scripts in our mind that demand the surrendering of our own unique identity. In adopting these social character roles, we are then expected to think and behave within the narrow confines of other people's externally-imposed and arbitrary mental constructs. The most common are the gender role scripts of our culture, and those of being a dutiful "patriot" — which has us defending an invisible matrix of values, beliefs and attitudes that separates our culture's reality from that of others like an imaginary wall of distinction.

In regard to patriotism, this character role offers an ironic source of pride when defending any system of government engaged in stealing our individual power to strengthen its own. As such, what is offered in return for our wholesale surrender as citizens is rarely a fair trade in the economy of this social relationship. And yet, we see in all nations how citizens obediently follow this same generic identity script to ensure their surrender to the will of any form of authoritarian government.

I	**Patriotism** (The unquestioned yielding of our personal will to that of our nation and its leaders).
P	Protection in numbers; a sense of belonging; living in a "better" system than our foreign rivals.
S	Wave our nation's flag and sing its national anthem; defend our political system of social control through acts of war and total subservience to the will of our government leaders.
F	To feel isolated, alone, vulnerable to attack, or insignificant in relation to our world.
A	Defending a potentially oppressive political system that seeks to disempower and enslave us.

Further eroding our autonomous joy-seeking is the time and effort we must invest to maintain the customs and traditions of our culture, each with its own scripted routines to learn. Here as well, we may not engage in those activities for the joy of it but to avoid being punished as a rebel or outcast. Pressure to adopt such traditional identity scripts often comes from our leaders who are better able to control a uniform mass of people who all think and behave the same. And while many do find comfort in living a culturally-prescribed "paint by numbers" lifestyle, it represents yet another obstacle to our ability to more freely express our unique identity and thereby realize our joy potential.

As an independently-minded joy seeker, we would instinctively rebel against having to become a cultural stereotype and wasting our energy to maintain such a false identity. Yet as the functioning of our societies grows ever more complex, we often have little choice but to adapt to these scripted behavioral systems, thereby leaving our minds in a kind of culturally-induced state of multiple personality disorder. Yet when our survival depends on such role-playing, our only other recourse is to live as a beggar on the streets, now that land is also no longer *free*.

At this point, we may begin to wonder: *what level of joy can we expect to attain in living our lives this way?* That question is best answered by considering how much mental freedom our society is willing to grant us in seeking our happiness. In most cases, we live like herds of human cattle contained by an invisible fence line of various political, religious or economic belief systems designed for *milking* our collective energy to serve those in power. To test this notion, let us consider whether we can avoid dying from poverty or persecution by refusing to behave as is dictated by our leaders. In many cases, we will end up in prison for "vagrancy," or tortured and killed for refusing to assume a subservient position by relinquishing control of our body, mind and soul. If we doubt this, let us only bring to mind those nations where women are still being publicly executed for their civil disobedience or disallowed an abortion even after being raped. Ultimately, some manner of threat is imposed wherever control is being exerted over people's lives — be it subtle or blatant. And predominantly, it is men who threaten us.

It is also unlikely that our leaders will accept any challenge to fight us in hand to hand combat over our right to govern ourselves. As such, most of our fighting for independence will be localized to the arena of the powerless in their struggle to gain any minor advantage over us.

In some nations we live relatively free of official interference; as long as we obey the law and pay our government *a piece of the action*, we are mostly left alone to do as we desire. In others circumstances, we may find ourselves being tormented by a mentally-unstable parent fueled by their fanatical religious or political devotion, or by an entire culture that promotes our mistreatment based on race, gender or social class. As such, we may have to make various kinds of accommodations in our approach to creating joyful relationships based on the circumstances of where, how and with whom we live.

However, as a general rule, we are most likely to engage in a more balanced joy economy by ensuring that the time and energy we offer others is a fair trade toward our living a healthier, more emotionally fulfilling life — not as a pay-off to avoid punishment. This includes all relationships, whether with family, government or greater society and justifies why our personal integrity must remain non-negotiable if we are to truly enjoy being alive — and being ourselves.

In some cases, it may be easier to die than suffer within a society that treats human life as though it has no value — a trait not altogether rare if our leaders display psychopathic tendencies. This would explain why a young man just beginning his life would choose to become a suicide bomber for his glory-seeking religious leaders. Here, his true motive is often just to escape the misery of his own existence without having to admit defeat. We find a similar sentiment among young people who commit suicide in already feeling tired of existing in a world of selfish social predators who feast upon their life energy at every turn. And if they have not the courage for such a quick escape, then they may take the slower route by way of a chronic, wasting substance addiction.

Understandably, in reading this overview of relationships, we may wonder how much worse it could possibly get. Yet it is important that we not live in denial because life is never what is being represented on television or in movies, nor does it remotely have the majesty invoked in political speeches or religious sermons. Instead, it can be downright tragic and miserable for many. As realists, we must therefore address this "rock bottom" of life's worst suffering before we can begin raising our expectations for a brighter future — both for ourselves and those who have it far worse. After all, we cannot be fully happy by leaving the rest of humankind in a joyless state of imbalance anymore than we can walk past an injured animal and not somehow feel injured ourselves.

Emotional Illiteracy

A further obstacle to achieving a balanced joy economy is what we can label *emotional illiteracy*. This is where we lack the basic education to create joy for ourselves. In that regard, schools are failing their students miserably in neglecting to offer such instruction. Instead, what we find is that many parents and teachers behave as though we can already predict our future joy potential while still in adolescence, or perhaps even worse — that they can predict it for us.

In reality, we may be forced to choose a career path for the duration of our life at an age when we know almost nothing about ourselves or life in general, let alone how to avoid making poorly thought-out and irresponsible choices. In most cases, it is simply too early to make such a serious commitment toward our future. But in a world that sees the paths to money, power and status as the only valid choices, any further consideration for our future joy is treated as a mere afterthought.

Fortunately, some of us do feel a sense of our future direction already early in life — courtesy of heeding our inner joy compass. For example, as a musician, we often know when to leave the classroom for a more harmonious internal life of artistic self-expression. Such urges guide many with early life passions, be it for mathematics, medicine, etc. But not everyone has the good fortune to *feel* their own destiny in advance. Subsequently, in later adult life, we may find ourselves trapped in some soul-stealing vocation in having believed that our financial security or winning a parent's approval would somehow ensure our happiness.

In reality, our life as a teenager is already confusing enough without having others meddle in it. Young and inexperienced, we are also more suggestible at such an uncertain time in our lives. And so it is easy to see why we may be tempted to make an impulsive career decision that later finds us wondering how to escape our miserable life trajectory. And often, there is no simple answer. Yet what we must do, regardless of our age or circumstances, is to develop a stronger relationship with ourselves so that we can better resist other people's tempting offers to sacrifice our happiness for a lifetime of unrelenting misery.

Emotional illiteracy can also result from our having been mentally degraded in childhood. This can happen if raised by parents whose emotional incompetence and abuses of trust leave us compromised in our ability to later create joyful relationships outside the family home. A further danger of such emotional abuse is that a domineering parent may deny any wrongdoing to protect their reputation. Instead, they can be so effective in promoting a false image of their supremacy that we feel ashamed in failing to meet their expectations, even if they are an undiagnosed psychotic. But most tragic about our interactions with ill-minded people is that they can leave us feeling as though we are the one who is wrong or defective, instead of the perpetrator. And sadly, looking at our world, we see that such denial of fault is common not only in our families, but also in politics, religion and business.

A further cause of *emotional illiteracy* is having to contend with the mental and physical adversities of war or poverty. Here, the constant looming threat of death limits our priorities to mere survival from day to day. At this fearful level of existence, simply finding a reliable source of income can represent a milestone achievement in our lives. For that reason, we may give little thought to more joyful pursuits when our life is a daily struggle just to survive.

In having suffered through such hardships, even the most caring of parents may impose upon us their misguided belief that joy is a luxury that we simply cannot afford. Instead, they may instruct us to adopt a more defensive lifestyle strategy whose unwavering focus on money and material security can rob us of a lifetime of emotional enrichment.

This form of emotional illiteracy explains why many people come to hoard material assets in excess of their needs while believing that joy might be found in evading death and suffering. And if we then feel an imbalance in our joy economy for neglecting our spiritual needs, we may simply look for a bigger house to store our growing stockpile of material comforts. However, we cannot expect to feel a bigger joy in a bigger house if we have yet to feel any joy in the one we currently own. Such issues of value and perspective are some of the many challenges we will face in context of our lifelong relationship with ourselves.

Reality Checks And Balances

As we come to the conclusion of this introduction to the relational path, let us consider a quote attributed to Greek philosopher, Socrates, wherein he suggests that *the unexamined life is not worth living*. This is a reasonable assessment given that even in walking we must always be aware of where to and how far we are walking, lest we thoughtlessly walk into traffic and a painful collision with our lack of self-awareness. In that regard, we must also be aware of why we are entering into any relationship and how we intend to guide it toward the fulfilling of our needs and desires — as well as those of our relational trading partner.

For that reason, our approach here has been purposely *self*-centered, for in knowing ourselves and our own needs, we are not only better equipped as candidates for all relationships, but we will also be wiser in knowing when not to enter into them. Also worth noting is that self-knowledge is not typically encouraged in societies where the focus is on keeping workers obediently serving the interests of government and economy in favor of their own spiritual betterment. As such, we are as unlikely to find a government pamphlet on seeking more joyful relationships as we are on increasing our personal freedom of choice.

Furthermore, the repetitive familiarity of our daily life routines can often make their negative features seem invisible to our eyes. Consider, for instance, an expired food container that we have yet to throw out. Likewise, the misery of an abusive relationship may also come to seem "normal" through its constant repetition. This is also why we may have to break out of our daily routines to ensure our conscious evolution; a prospect that can be just as frightening as staying where we are.

Earlier, we also described relationships as bridges that connect us to others for the purpose of trading energy. We could also see them as a kind of vehicle for steering in the direction of our future joy. Yet unlike an automobile, there are two drivers, which creates further obstacles to joy if others do not want to consult with us in choosing a destination. What we want to avoid is being a passenger to our own life's unfolding wherein we must ask: "Where are we going?" or "Are we there yet?" Moreover, we must know when to exit that vehicle if it should begin to move in the wrong direction or swerve off the road.

In meeting these many challenges, we already have various tools of introspection to help us strengthen our inner joy relationships with the outer world. For instance, using the IPSFA Sequence, we can create a visual representation of any scripted social identity or relationship that we must maintain to earn its promised rewards.

Let us consider, for example, the "button pusher" identity script that we might adopt if our only stated goal was to earn money to survive:

I	**Button Pusher** (A creatively and intellectually uninspiring occupation).
P	Allowing us to earn enough money to survive.
S	Push a button for 40 hours per week until we die or retire.
F	Poverty; losing our family life due to poverty; social shame; homelessness; death.
A	Suffering from spiritual poverty for lack of a means to stimulate our curiosity and creativity.

As we can see, the amount of time we would have to invest engaging in such a dull activity could leave us feeling emotionally malnourished. This we can verify using two other diagnostic tools with which we are now also familiar: the *Joys of Inspiration* list from the *Joy Coordinates*, as well as the C–SIX *Spiritual States of Being*.

As such, we can begin to use our deepening self-knowledge, as well as that which we will gain in upcoming chapters, to create a healthier balance between our daily working life and engaging in activities that will help to prevent our suffering from a spiritual deficit.

Reality Checks

The challenges of maintaining a balanced relationship have many of us searching for answers and we might often find better answers if we simply asked better questions of ourselves and others. For that reason, the "Reality Checks for Everyday Life" series of books that I have also authored offer many such *better questions* that can inspire us to see our various relationships and their potential imbalances in a whole new light. For example:

- ☑ Is there a means to your happiness that doesn't require others to change?
- ☑ Do you define success as being able to satisfy other people's sense of your accomplishment?
- ☑ Will you find the courage to start living it up once you are finally dead?
- ☑ Are your joy the sacrifice that has to be made in every relationship?

- ☑ What is the male equivalent of every derogatory term used to shame sexually liberated women?
- ☑ Are you failing to enjoy the taste of today's drink in worrying about tomorrow's thirst?
- ☑ Are you the kind of person that you would want to be friends with?

(For more details about *Reality Checks for Everyday Life*, see the *About The Author* section at the back of this book.)

The Relationship Ledger

Created for this book, the *Relationship Ledger* is another useful tool of introspection. It allows us to identify the joy potential of relationships by charting their purpose to our lives and categorizing their scripted expectations in relation to the *C-SIX States of Being*, such as offering us an outlet for creative self-expression. In this way we can grade any aspect of our lives, including the social identity scripts we may adopt in relation to our quests for happiness and career success.

The example below is a sample configuration with content to show how we might use the Relationship Ledger to plot the *joy potential* of any relationship we might enter, be it social, professional, romantic or even a passive relationship to food. And if we discover that nothing joyful can be plotted, then perhaps we may need to look elsewhere.

The Relationship Ledger can also list the *Joy Coordinates* associated with relationships to plot their spiritual or utilitarian purpose in our lives. The ledger can also be reconfigured to suit our needs and may be useful to therapists as a new method of joy analysis:

Relationship or ASI	Survival	Procreation	Joy	C1 comfort	C2 convenience	C3 control	C4 curiosity	C5 creativity	C6 communion
Button Pusher (ASI)	X	X		X	X	X			
Parenthood (r)	X		X			X	X	X	X
Marriage (r)	X	X	X	X	X	X	X	X	X
Friendship (r)			X	X			X	X	X

Relationship or ASI	Survival	Procreation	Joy	C-1 comfort	C-2 convenience	C-3 control	C-4 curiosity	C-5 creativity	C-6 communion
Chocolate (r)	X		X	X	X				
Cat (r)			X	X			X	X	X
Playing Guitar (r)			X	X			X	X	
Golf		Joy Coordinates:	Feeling enthusiastically committed to a personally meaningful goal?						
Etc.									

This example also demonstrates the flexibility of the Relationship Ledger in allowing us to analyze any kind of relationship we might engage in, from interpersonal to passive and from playing a guitar or communing with a family pet to eating chocolate. It is certainly unique and offers us yet another way to see ourselves and our world anew.

...

Ideally, our goal on the relational path is to achieve a state of balance wherein we neither die for want of comfort nor suffer from a joyless life for lack of spiritual nourishment. And while we each have our own unique forms of currency and modes of transaction as directed by our mind's invisible economy, there is still another way to test if we are moving in a joyfully positive direction, and that is by listening to the sound of our own *laughter*.

Does it sound like an authentic expression of joy? Or does is sound forced and listless — a noise made just to appease others, like a joyless imposter? Might it even sound cruel or menacing, as though we need to hurt someone with our laughter to compensate for a feeling of low self-esteem or other form of spiritual deficit? Listen closely.

Whatever its sound, let us make the necessary course corrections to reclaim our child-like ability to laugh out loud by choosing relational paths that allow us to remain true to ourselves, inside and out.

It really is that simple — but not always that easy.

CHAPTER 10
Trading In Illusions

Actors are those kinds of people who we admire for pretending to be someone else. And yet, they are not so unlike the rest of us in that we may also have to give an award-winning performance to earn our share of admiration upon the social stage.

In doing so, we may have to perform in a number of roles, including that of a dedicated employee, a loving parent, or a good neighbor. And when company is expected, we quickly tidy up our homes in an effort to portray someone clean and civilized. Following the directions of our various social scripts may not be so easy, nor are they always mutually compatible, but they nonetheless give each of us a purposeful role to play in life and a meaningful sense of identity in relation to our world.

Our acting talents may also be appreciated by others in reassuring them of our commitment to a relationship. For example, we might do our part to stand tall and proud for the anthem of a withering nation, or by enthusiastically applauding our child's own clumsy performance in a school play. But when the star performer is an ambitious politician offering voters false hope, or an indignant marriage partner lying to us about their sexual indiscretions, then revealed by their masquerade is a simple and often painful truth that, beyond love and shared utility, relationships are also maintained by the telling of lies.

But at what cost do we hide behind these false masks of identity? After all, lying only postpones having to face the problem whereas our accepting of responsibility hastens finding a solution. Nor does our betrayal of others inspire them to grow but often diminishes them into cowering like a frightened animal behind a protective wall of growing suspicion and distrust. And once trust erodes, the spiritual life of any relationship is effectively dead.

Unfortunately, lying also happens to be a common survival strategy in all human societies; one that is especially profitable for those trading in illusions. Consequently, there is a tremendous amount of time and effort being invested by dishonest people in business, government or even our own personal life to knowingly deceive us by any means.

Yet the most costly of all deceptions is when we ourselves become so disoriented amidst these persuasive pretensions that we can no longer be sure of our own authenticity. We may then embrace values, beliefs and attitudes that no longer belong to us but to a fictitious character we have come to portray to win our share of public applause.

Fortunately, we need not succumb to such states of self-deception if our path ahead remains illuminated by the light of our inner truth. Put more succinctly, we will not lose sight of joy if we remain honest with ourselves and others as to who we are and what we need to feel happy. As dedicated seekers of joy, this means doing all that we can to avoid relationships that could have us trading in our own illusions.

A Simple Truth

Living in a world where retailers may entice us to pay double for one item to get the second one "free," our making of wise decisions can be critical. Yet as innocent children entering this exciting new world, we can be easily entranced by the light of any false love, hope or truth that we may encounter in taking our first tentative steps forward.

Like unsuspecting moths drawn to a flame, we may then also find the wings of our trust being scorched by counterfeit friends, deceitful advertising, corrupt authority figures or predatory grifters offering us an easy passage to fame, fortune or celestial favor. In addition to those ideological and superstitious reality distortions already embedded into the collective psyche of our culture, this presents us with a confusing obstacle course to knowing what is actually real in our world and what is just another orchestrated illusion.

Unfortunately, we may not realize that we are living inside a cultural maze of mentally-projected contradictions until our thinking has long been compromised by its toxic programming. As a result, we may find ourselves defeating our own joy potential with the borrowed thoughts of guilt, shame or self-doubt that others have implanted into our mind. However, our best option for escaping this maze is not to keep moving forward hoping for the best, but to consciously rise above its deceptive theatrics to gain a more elevated perspective on the insidious nature of our mental entrapment.

We can achieve this conscious ascent by living a more honest life and challenging every oppressive illusion by which we are being governed. As an incentive to stop engaging in any further acts of self-deception, let us consider some of the spiritual rewards that await us for being a more honest and spiritually integrated human being.

The most immediate benefit of honesty is that it allows us to live a less confusing life. This is because we only have the truth to remember and not all the additional lies we must tell to conceal that truth. This also makes our pursuit of happiness more energy efficient by saving us valuable time and effort in not having to defend our lies.

Anchored in a solid foundation of truth, we also become a sincere embodiment of our authentic values. This gives us a stable, unshifting mental position from which to negotiate for a more joyfully balanced relationship with others. Conversely, we will find no joy when living in constant fear of being exposed as a liar; we will have no foundation.

It is from within such a sunken spiritual state that we learn a simple truth in that we cannot feel inwardly content if our innate humanity is being compromised by our betrayal of others or ourselves for want of money, power or personal gain. What we experience instead is our emotional exile to a lonely, superficial world of forged smiles wherein we and our fellow pretenders hide from the withering effects of our spiritual corrosion in a sanctuary of chronic denial, substance abuse, or various states of self-delusion. Yet even here, truth leads us upward.

The Power of Personal Integrity

An honest life requires that we refuse to trade in illusions, especially with ourselves. Yet in entering the socialization process of our culture, we may come out the other end in a fractured mental state wherein we may now be lying to ourselves to maintain some illusory new sense of social identity we were forced to adopt. Subsequently, we should also not expect to create joyful relationships if we no longer know who we are or what we want from life.

Whether or not we find ourselves in this compromised state of mind, we would still benefit greatly from taking a *personal values survey* to reaffirm our professed inner truths. That survey will be presented to us in the next section. Before we take that step, we must understand the technical nature of relationships as well as the differences between our *personality* and our *character*. In this way, we will be better prepared to repair any potential fracture of our authentic being brought to light by our taking that survey. Toward that end, let us consider the following:

1) A relationship is defined by our having a *physical, intellectual* or *emotional* dependence on any *life form, object, idea* or *event* — a geographic location is also just an object in relation to its surrounding space and structures.

2) Relationships facilitate our *survival, procreation* and *joy* by connecting us to the necessities and pleasures of the material world, including friendships and future mates, as well as to knowledge and ideally, the protective care of a peaceful, loving society.

3) We also use relationships as a means to winning personal glory through our *competitive interactions* with others, and to experience love and other forms of communion through *mutual cooperation* or *a shared reverence for life*.

4) Relational bonding can result from random circumstances or a purposeful choosing. In the latter case, it becomes *an outward manifestation of our inner values,* such as the personalized items that we chose to fill our homes or the friends we invite to commune with us there. In this way, relationships act as "bridges of value" by facilitating our connection to whatever we need, want, or desire most in life.

5) Relationship disputes arise from *priority conflicts* between energy-trading partners *and are always based on one or more of the C–SIX values.* When we are teenagers, for example, our innate *curiosity* for life may create a conflict with a parent's own desire for *mental comfort,* thus creating a power struggle as they fight to retain *control* over our autonomous choices in life. Even our

angry arguments over politics and religion arise to protect our predictably *comfortable* life of routine, or to retain *control* over our right to intellectual *curiosity* and unconditional *communion* with others. But also complicating matters is a paradoxical law of nature wherein we feel the simultaneous urge to seek both *control over* and *communion with* others, which can create some very confusing love/hate relationships between ourselves and others.

6) We can often become inwardly divided against ourselves in a relationship whose scripted values, beliefs or attitudes contradict those of our true inner character. This *Acquired Identity Crisis*, courtesy of our *Joy Bureaucracy*, may find us compromised in our personal integrity as an employee in being asked to lie to our customers, or as a young person having to reject our inborn sexual orientation to avoid persecution in an overtly bigoted society.

7) We can largely avoid these kinds of *Acquired Identity Conflicts* in relationships by ensuring the integrity of our personal values. This we do by reconciling the adopted values of our *social personality* with those of our *inner character* as a way to promote a greater state of *inner harmony*.

Aligning the values of our character with those of our personality is pivotal to clearing a path to joyful relationships. In this way we are able to present ourselves to others in an unwavering, confident and unified state of authenticity and personal integrity.

We can begin this process of integration by first defining *character* as the person we are when we believe that no one is watching us, whereas our *personality* is the person we may pretend to be in the presence of others. Theoretically, these aspects of our being are identical in a truly honest and integrated individual. However, dire necessity or an unruly impulse toward excessive selfishness can cause us to live in a state of hypocrisy wherein our personality projects the outward illusion that we are incapable of engaging in such acts toward which our character is secretly inclined — such as lying, stealing, or worse.

The manifestation of an Acquired Identity *Conflict* is apparent when we withhold our honest opinion from others, or worse, if we engage in vile criminal acts while hiding behind the trusted facade of our role as a police officer or religious priest. The latter can occur if society pays greater attention to our outer personality than our inner character.

In having defined the roles of character and personality within our conscious life, we can better understand why we might feel miserable in having to misrepresent ourselves to others because it forces us to live as two separate people rather than one wholly integrated human being. In short, living with a fractured identity is not a path to joy.

Furthermore, this may also leave us wondering which of the two is the keeper of our true identity and which is the impostor that has us trading in illusions with ourselves? Fortunately, we can now take the following spiritual values survey to help us find such answers:

A Reason To Live
(A Spiritual Values Survey)

As a sincere seeker of joy, we must have a vision and a plan for how we intend to achieve and maintain our feelings of joy because focussing our ambitions on survival and procreation alone is simply not enough. Yet even without a vision or plan, most of us have an idea of what kind of ideal life circumstances would make us feel truly happy and give us "a reason to live." Such beliefs are based on our values — what we value most in life beyond mere existence based on its perceived joy potential. As such, the best way to prove the merit of those ingredients we believe important to a happy life is the level of joy that we have managed to attain within our own life — are we living proof of our theory?

Beyond this, the most reliable test for assessing the joy potential of our values is whether they can also lead others toward creating a more emotionally fulfilling life for themselves. And that is also our challenge in taking this spiritual values survey: to prove *the value* of our values.

...

Toward that end, let us imagine that a beloved child or trusted friend has just confided in us their overwhelming urge to depart this world by committing suicide. Joyless without a meaningful sense of purpose, they have lost their will to live. In short, beyond our companionship, there is nothing else that makes them feel that life is worth living. As a result, death now appears to them as a better option than living.

Although determined to carry out this final act, they also feel great concern for our own emotional well-being in the aftermath of their departure. To resolve their own feelings of guilt, they have offered us an unusual opportunity: they want us to persuade them to reconsider their decision to die by providing them with a list of joyful activities or meaningful goals that will make their own life feel worth living.

In short, beyond our instinctual fear of dying, we must tell them what things of value keep us wanting to exist in this world. This gives us the opportunity to save another person's life by identifying which of our personal values might also bring greater joy and meaning to their own troubled existence.

To gain the maximum emotional impact of this exercise, let us try to imagine the overwhelming mental burden we would have to carry in being so entirely responsible for the life and future joy of someone else. Ironically, this is not so difficult once we realize that our own children, friends or younger siblings may already be engaged in watching us in our daily struggles to experience joy through the prioritizing of those same values. In fact, they may already be using those values to validate their own unwavering hope for the future — or growing cynicism.

And so, with the power to heal in our trembling hands, let us write on a sheet of paper a list of all the things we believe are worth living for. No one has to see this list or read it; however, we should get a good look at it ourselves for the purpose of our own enlightenment.

As a guideline, list at least three "reasons to live" that immediately come to mind — do not *overthink* as this suggests you have already run out of ideas. Also, an unrealized ambition for the future is just as valid because it is also informed by our existing values. And also, do take this seriously if you believe that being happy is important. Here we go:

1)

2)

3)

Hello World or Good-bye?
(Grading Our Survey)

Upon completing our *A Reason To Live* survey, we will have gained a greater awareness of the dominant currencies in our mind's invisible economy. In listing what we value most, we can now begin to apply the standards of measure that we explored in earlier chapters as a way to gauge their actual joy potential for enriching our lives.

For instance, we can use the *Relationship Ledger* from chapter 9 to chart if what we value serves more our survival or procreation than our need for joy — and whether it serves a physical or spiritual purpose based on its designation in the *C–SIX States of Being* of chapter 5. We can then determine if it is a more comfort-based value, such as buying a home, or a creative pursuit, such as learning to play an instrument. This can help us attain a more joyfully-balanced life by not sacrificing our spiritual needs for those of our physical.

We can also determine if what we value triggers the *Inspirational* and *Contentment Joy Coordinates* of chapter 4, or merely those of survival. We can even identify if what we value is a solid form of energy, such as food, or a symbolic form, such as fame or wealth. In this way, we can determine if what we seek is immediately useful in a practical sense or just a placeholder for future joy potential. We may even find that what we value is a symbolic substitute for joy, such as wanting "more money" or a seat of political power to dominate others. With each investigative step forward, we also move closer to understanding how our mind works and whether we are choosing a path that is directionally aligned with what we need to be happy.

In seeing how these varying insights converge into a unified lesson for clearing our personal paths to joy, we can revisit earlier chapters with a renewed sense of mission in having clarified what we value. As to their present context on the relational path, this survey has helped us to identify the types of social relationships we may need to enter to earn our desired energy rewards or obtain those things we value most in having clearly stated them in writing.

Toward that end, let us add some further insights to our joy seeking arsenal by identifying two additional aspects of human relationships that can help us to assess the joy potential of what we value most:

Bridges and Fences

Relationships have a dual purpose in that they act both as bridges and fences to our interactions with others. As such, building a relational bridge also creates a counterpart fence that inhibits other relationships from forming. For example, marriage acts as a bridge to a long-term partnership while creating a fence that inhibits independent behavior. Similarly, in joining an exclusive social club, we erect a barrier between ourselves and those not meeting the club's standards for entry.

While a status-hungry glory seeker may revel in separating himself from the rest of humanity, it is worth noting that our membership in any kind of a group can make access to those outside the group more difficult by limiting our joy seeking to a designated area. Moreover, this kind of separation promotes an "us versus them" duality that can lead to *Acquired Identity Conflicts* if we present ourselves to the group as a loyal insider while secretly holding the values of an outsider.

Here, the threat is to our integrity *in having to reject ourselves to gain the acceptance of others;* an act of spiritual self-mutilation for which we will not be rewarded with joy but only an enduring misery in fearing to be discovered as an imposter.

Attraction, Repulsion & Reassurance

As revealed in *The Invisible Economy*, our lives are sustained by energy and guided by our attraction for what we value most. This impacts the nature of our relationships and our choices of trading partners. We also tend to signal to others the kind of energy we seek and, just like atoms, have distinct reactions in feeling attracted to some people, yet repelled by others based on our values and their priority — or "valence."

We may notice such behavioral distinctions at a neighborhood party, where the comfort seekers huddle together for reassurance while the glory seekers and more dynamic individuals "work the room" for fun and social attention. And always, we will meet someone who appears most *attractive* to us, be it financially, sexually or otherwise.

In finding our energy niche group, we gain a sense of belonging that also feeds our spiritual need for communion (C6).

Where things go wrong is when the outward expression of our inner values surround us with a repulsive energy field. As a glory seeker, for instance, we may perceive everyone as a rival in our quest for personal power and status. We may then reflexively dominate others to disarm their potential threat. In doing so, we also prevent ourselves from being able to experience deeper levels of intimacy that arise in caring about more than our own social gains and personal triumphs.

If we find ourselves trapped within such a repulsive attitude, it will do our future joy a good service to ask: "*Who do I hope to attract with my adversarial attitude?*" A gullible and needy person — a new victim? And furthermore: "*Would I feel repulsed by meeting someone like me?*" Given that *like* charges *repel*, the latter is almost a certainty.

In terms of personal integrity, we can also be compromised by lying about our attraction to someone when it is only our repulsion for being alone that draws us to them. Yet in all interactions, we always behave like atoms as we constantly move between the energy fields of various people or relationships to seek our inner sense of balance. This is yet another way that we can consider and better understand ourselves.

...

As to assessing our final score for the survey, there is no need. This exercise was simply meant to enlighten us as to the joy potential of our values and priorities in life and give us the opportunity to think about our current relational paths — and perhaps even reconsider them.

We also need not worry if our "reasons to live" list is unremarkable because our life and values can often change instantly and without any warning. Such dramatic inner shifts can occur when we are faced with a serious illness, unbearable grief, or a spiritual transformation of our consciousness via a near death experience or kundalini awakening.

Although still not widely known or accepted, the latter two events can actually help to realign our character with the founding values of our innate humanity. These enlightening transformational events have often been documented throughout history as encounters with "God" for they can leave us in a state of increased empathy and self-awareness whose values we then express through our wholly integrated character and personality. We may even feel this in terms of an ambient aura of attractive energy around such individuals — they are more accepting.

As a result, what we can learn from all of this is that each of us is a deep mystery unfolding before our eyes, thereby giving us a reason to hope for the best and realize that life is never truly finished with us.

Breaking The Vanity Mirror

In having completed the *A Reason To Live* survey, we have a means to declare, analyze and ultimately challenge our beliefs in the inherent joy potential of our most cherished personal values. To further assist us in that process, let us also realize that in recounting *the best days of our life*, what we remember most is not the shoes we wore, but where we had worn them. This simple declaration will caution us against wasting our valuable time shopping for shoes or standing in front of a mirror when we ought to be participating in those joyful events that can enrich our lives. In short, life is not about shoes and mirrors.

Let us then also return to the metaphor of *acting* to recognize that while costumes and staging do play a role in our public performances, it is the plot in our life that matters most — for without it there is no story to tell. Here as well, we must ensure that our life is one of deeper substance and not just theatrical costumes and special effects.

We learn a similar lesson from advertising in that an attractive outer package does not guarantee a quality product. The same is true where human relationships are concerned in that we cannot afford to make conceited outward displays of our self-importance lest we want to repel those we wish to attract and attract those we wish to repel.

Central to such repulsive outward displays is vanity, a manifestation of the glory-seeking impulse to prove ourselves *dominant*. Ironically, this competitive urge also does not discriminate as to our race, gender or social class, which allows even the least qualified to put on airs of superiority. The ironic folly of such boastful displays is that *they can keep us from getting what we need because we are too busy pretending not to need it.* We may then project the false image of "having it all" while actually having a great need, be it for love, money — or a more joyful direction in life. For this reason, defensive pride will always impede the creation of honest, joyful relationships — or destroy those we have.

Another vanity-based relationship impediment is our trying to "win" every social encounter. Here, we try to steal attention away from others in any group setting while ignoring all of their contributions to any conversation. This creates a relational imbalance by preventing anyone but ourselves from being recognized or validated by the group. We also find such behavior among political dictators and tyrants who behave as though they are the only one who matters. Is this how we wish to be seen and treated? If yes, we can also expect a very lonely life.

Beneath such a facade there is typically a nagging sense of insecurity that also has us ridiculing others or "putting them down" in their status within a group — even for something trivial, like their choice of shoes. Such cruel, selfish behavior is often a vain attempt to undermine the confidence of those we perceive as our rivals for attention.

Another repulsive symptom of feeling insecure is *linguistic vanity* wherein we use long, obscure, ornamental words or foreign language clichés to impress others rather than to communicate with them. Here, our underlying motive is to prove that we are intellectually superior as opposed to worth listening to, the latter of which is the unintended outcome as others slink away from us to escape our needy auric field.

In choosing to behave this way, we also risk building walls to greater understanding rather than level bridges to promoting it. And if we then accessorize our prize-winning vocabulary with equally boastful displays of our material wealth — perhaps a pair of jewel-encrusted glasses with a matching head ornament — then we will also begin to understand why joy is rarely found in the company of those whose only goal in socializing is to keep others feeling inferior and unworthy of standing in their glorious presence.

The Blameless Society

In this chapter, we have learned how misrepresenting *who we are* to others can cause us to become as strangers to ourselves, which results in undermining our personal integrity and ability to experience greater joy in life. We then further subvert our joy potential when we actively lie to portray some fictitious character in context of any personal, social or professional relationship — be it as a husband, wife, employee, or as the leader of our nation. And when we all engage in acting this way, it creates a culture of dishonesty that undermines everything we do in that we can no longer trust anyone or their motives.

This represents a growing problem in all societies today wherein the competitive pressures of having to ensure our daily survival or wanting to attain a higher income in a money-centric system has made honesty a low priority in the lives of many. In addition, our early childhood training has taught us to expect pain and suffering for any wrongdoing, which has the unintended side effect of making us afraid to admit our guilt or take responsibility for the harm we cause others due to our ignorance or selfish inclinations. The result is an unspoken recognition among all people that telling the truth means losing our income, social status or personal freedom. And this is all true; ask any *whistleblower*.

Further complicating our quests for personal integrity is our innate status-seeking nature as human beings, which does not encourage us to humble ourselves before others. Filling us with competitive pride, it urges us instead to never back down if we want to prove ourselves the *better* man or woman in any confrontation. And so it is that we may find ourselves living in a blameless society where no one is responsible for anything that goes wrong. Yes, government systems and services may be failing us, but not by any fault of those who maintain those systems and services, according to their own faultless assessment of the situation. Instead, someone else is always to blame — even the victims themselves because the cost of admitting one's guilt is just too high.

It is a bizarre and mentally-destabilizing form of human theatre as we are told each day to disbelieve our own eyes and ears so that we can allow those unqualified for their seats of power to continue misleading us rather than bravely confessing their crimes and stepping down. And this is happening at every level of human existence, not only in the competitive worlds of politics and business, but also within our family homes, religious communities and in charitable organizations wherein the temptation to lie, cheat and steal is just as great when it means a better financial outcome for those at the top.

Altogether, this represents the greatest obstacle to attaining joyful relationships in that we cannot improve ourselves by always blaming others for our offensive behavior — or demand that everyone else must change so that we can avoid that inconvenience for ourselves.

When a brother steals from a brother, he must accept responsibility for his actions and not blame his victim for having left his possessions within tempting reach of his selfish inclinations. Nor can a man who fails to succeed blame others for his failing to make an effort. And if a woman is a chronic liar, she cannot then blame others for becoming suspicious of her every word. Yet such stories will continue to be told wherever people attempt to hide their own inadequacies behind some desperate shield of denial or threats against others rather than making the effort to consciously evolve as a human being.

Whether to avoid public humiliation or a loss of our reputation and income, many of us suffer from a tendency to point the finger of blame at others. As such, we also encounter many people who are far better at making excuses than actual progress.

Tragically, we see the same behavior in those tentative relationships between world nations as each blames the other for its own failures at home to preserve the false facade of its moral or ideological supremacy. As such, we all risk being labelled "the enemy" by someone trying to deny the true cause of their own personal failures or lack of joy in life.

Yet in taking this convenient mental detour, we also avoid investing the time, effort or money required to solve those problems we create. And this we can only do by taking a more honest approach to resolving the relational conflicts that plague us both as individuals and citizens of any nation. In short, a more joyful future of truth and integrity waits for all of us once we finally stop trading in illusions.

CHAPTER 11
The Price of Love

Like a milky-blue pearl gently drifting through the cosmos, our world is a place of hope and dreams for many, especially the young and the young at heart. But as we all soon discover, nothing is quite as it seems in this illusory place where people hide behind social masks and fear to speak the truth. We can therefore also expect that romantic illusions would abound here, with none informing our popular culture quite as dramatically as those concerning the feeling of love.

We can find proof of such illusions in the lyrics of any popular love song where there is a suspicious absence of such unromantic topics as personal hygiene or a bad credit rating. Instead, we always hear some heart-stricken crooner promising to endure any kind of hardship out of their undying love for the unnamed object of their desire.

But lest we forget, such poetic notions arise from the hearts and minds of musicians, whose creative talents often extend to living in an imaginary world whose economic instability and relentless travel can quickly erode the romantic illusions of their own love interests waiting back home. At best, they should hope not to have been replaced by a friend or neighbor who has offered their lonely lover more than just a catchy hit song about making long-term commitments.

As such, what a love song's heartfelt projections of intimacy may fail to address are the expectations inherent to human relationships. After all, we each carry with us the equivalent of an invisible suitcase that is bursting with wants, needs and desires and whose fulfillment we hope will lead to our everlasting happiness or escape from suffering. And this naturally places an impossible burden on anyone we enlist to meet all those many expectations in context of a single intimate relationship. Subsequently, we will never meet anyone as perfect as the imaginary "you" being sung about in love songs, lest we never fully unpack that suitcase for the duration of our stay. In short, the less we expect from others, the more attractive they will seem to us — and vice versa.

What also remains unsung is that sustaining romantic relationships requires dependable access to food, shelter and other kinds of daily life necessities, which requires the securing of gainful employment in any monetary ecosystem. We might therefore understand why love, as one proverb warns us, "flies out the window" when money stops coming in through the front door.

But love is not all that can make a hasty exit. Our love interests may also quickly abandon us if we should lose our promise as their path to future comforts and joy. And so, while we may enter into a romantic relationship with great expectations of unbridled passion, it is with love's painful departure that we learn a most unpleasant truth wherein our life is merely a form of negotiable currency that others shamelessly spend for their own personal gain. This crudely establishes our human value by what we can offer to elevate others in the hierarchy of their own selfish ambitions. For this reason, we must be cautiously aware of *the price of love* and what we are willing to pay for the often *conditional* affection of lovers who must pretend otherwise.

Toward that end, our hearts can benefit greatly from shattering a few more romantic illusions as we explore the true nature of love and how our unrealistic expectations might be impeding its natural flow.

What Is Love?

Ironically, despite its high profile as a long-celebrated theme in human culture, the true meaning of love still remains a mystery. This is due to the subjective nature of how we experience life, which also tempts us to define love as whatever we wish it to be — much like *reality* itself.

In addition, we are also being inundated by media advertising that promotes marital consumerism as an aspect of love. Presented to us as dream-like collages of ecstatic-looking brides at opulent weddings and happy housewives moving through an elegant home filled with shiny new appliances and fashionable furnishings, our interpretation of love in modern times is then further corrupted as being just a selfish grab for material wealth and costly comforts.

But our greatest confusion comes from the mistaken belief that love is something that is *given to us* like a gift from elsewhere and for which we must patiently wait our turn. This causes us to believe that someone else beyond ourselves is in control of how we feel — which we easily disprove each time we create our own joyful emotions by fantasizing about pleasurable activities, such as traveling, singing or being among friends. Instead, it is our selfish expectation that someone else should fulfill our emotional needs that grants them this power over our lives. Subsequently, if we had no such expectations, then others would have no influence over how we felt because it truly is our sole responsibility to make ourselves feel happy, not anyone else's. However, this is not a popular perspective, especially among those selling flowers and candy to prime the engines of a woman's self-interest during courtship.

In believing ourselves to be *separated* from love and having to await its arrival, we indulge our minds in a paradox in that we can experience profound states of loving bliss while meditating alone. In short, there is no one present to cause these blissful feelings except the contents of our creative imagination. In fact, we can choose to feel however we wish to feel using our mind's ability to generate emotionally-charged imagery at any time and in any place of our choosing. We need only become aware of our power to create love and then use it generously.

Further subverting the public's attitude are the objective materialists who claim that love is a mere byproduct of some instinctual chemical reaction, which leads to the assumption that love will soon be available at local pharmacies. Yet this clinical love sequence is reversed. Instead, our body releases "love" chemicals in response to a loving state of mind, which we can prove by meditating on thoughts of loving communion in a clinical setting where our biochemical responses can be measured. After all, we also do not release cortisol and other fear chemicals prior to becoming afraid or feeling threatened. This is just common sense.

Fortunately, love's pure emanation has as little to do with our brain chemistry as its does with buying flowers or planning a lavish wedding. Instead, it has a far more *expansive* role to play in our lives, one that we must learn to recognize in clearing a path to joyful relationships.

We can gain a more realistic perspective on love by accepting that it already resides within us as a kind of "energy reward" that we give to ourselves by ensuring its unimpeded outward flow. This reward is felt as a genuine sense of belonging to ourselves and our world; an inner feeling of safety and self-confidence that frees our spirit to explore its boundless joy potential in a state of absolute trust. That is love's ideal state and one that we can reach in bursts and increments by freeing our minds to be at peace with our existence, and with that of others.

Subsequently, we feel love most intensely when in harmony with our inner essence, as evident by the powerful emotions we can awaken through creative and transcendent mental states. Our ability to reach such higher levels of conscious feeling also requires the absence of fear. In this way, we free ourselves at the very core of our being to radiate outward and be enveloped by an aura of unconditional self-acceptance. In short, we feel love by allowing ourselves to be ourselves within an unimpeded state of authenticity.

In this light, we can see why engaging our feeling of love requires nothing more than being in a loving state of mind. As such, it does not depend on such ritualized practices as buying engagement rings, going out to eat at fancy restaurants, or casting superstitious "love spells" to make us feel this way. Instead, it only requires the courage to honestly express ourselves as the person we truly are inside. This alone is enough to make our love flow outward in almost any direction.

Clearly there is a distinction between seeking recreational pleasure through sex and seeking to "fall in love," wherein the former requires little more than a willing naked accomplice — even a total stranger or a prostitute. However, in the latter case we uncover a most compelling secret about our quest for a loving relationship is that it is merely our attempt to find someone whose own emotional courage allows us to freely express ourselves in context of a trusting mutual bond, whether it be friendship, marriage, parenthood, or a state of communion with a beloved family dog or cat. In short, *we are love,* and others simply offer us the means by which to prove it.

The Ebb And The Flow

Once we can accept that love already resides within us as part of our conscious design, we can better understand how our relationships can affect its flow. Toward that end, we can think of our love as a river of energy filled with our innate spiritual urges for *curiosity, creativity* and *communion* — the C4 to C6 *Spiritual States of Being.*

When the flowing of that river is unimpeded, we are free to enjoy life in a wondrous state of childlike awe and enthusiasm, often feeling "in love" with life itself. Yet whenever we encounter any form of mental or physical resistance to our authentic self-expression, we intuitively react as water does by diverting the flow of our love around those obstacles or withholding it like a reservoir above a dam.

Subsequently, while no external being is actually *giving* us love, our internal response to their *obstructive presence* may cause our spiritual river of joy potential to run dry or become a shallow torrent that we may choose to divert elsewhere — perhaps into an extramarital affair.

Fear is the primary cause of obstructions to our loving flow, which causes us to revert to a primal state of defensive posturing wherein we lash out in anger or cower from life instead of celebrating it. Sadly, our daily competitive social interactions ensure our encounter with many such fear-provoking situations, thereby causing us to limit the outward flow of our authentic expressions of love toward others.

As a child, for instance, we may react to the harsh criticisms of an angry parent by avoiding pleasurable thoughts or behaviors that could invite further hostility from that aggressor. In this way, our early life emotional traumas from being ridiculed, rejected or reprimanded can create lifelong insecurities about expressing ourselves in a more natural and loving way toward others. Thereafter, instead of blossoming, we may begin to wilt like a drying flower unless we regain the courage and independence of mind to allow our love to flow outward again.

By contrast, we feel infinitely lighter, freer and more expansive as a child in the company of those who sincerely encourage us to explore our inner joy potential — as we may have felt in the presence of a kind, supportive grandparent. It is the greater freedom and permissiveness inherent to such relationships that allows for our spiritual "cup" to overflow with a deep gratitude for the simple joys of being alive.

As is true for any river, we must maintain a constant outward flow of our loving spiritual essence to maintain a joyful life. This is also why we intuitively seek *unconditional* love in context of relationships so that we will feel safe enough in the presence of another to reveal our true identity. Enveloped by a secure sense of acceptance and belonging, we gain the courage to explore the wonder of our being and may even dare to risk exposing any long-hidden wounds for love to wash clean.

Here too, we will know that love is flowing by the fullness of our laughter, which will sound genuine and unrestrained, not contrived, insecure or cynical. In short, to ensure the unimpeded outward flowing of our love, we must fearlessly reveal ourselves to others, lest we also risk running dry. This is also why we must seek out relationships with those whose own love does not ebb whenever we begin to flow.

The Need For Trust

To ensure that we understand what has already been conveyed, let us restate that a loving relationship is *any meaningful emotional connection to others through which we can express our spiritual urges toward curiosity, creativity and communion*. It is through entering these elevated states of caring and sharing that we are inspired to evolve in self-awareness, thereby allowing us to more fully realize our inherent joy potential.

The need for trust is essential to this process so that we do not feel inhibited in allowing our *river of love* to flow. Unfortunately, we may experience fear at various levels due to selfishness, competitive pride or low self-esteem. This can create a divisive atmosphere of distrust in our relationships which makes it difficult to feel the kind of unconditional love so effortlessly sung about in love songs.

Aside from this, we are also beginning to realize that feelings of love are not exclusive to humans alone and can be shared with almost any self-aware sentient being. For this reason, many of us also engage in intimate states of communion with our beloved pets, who often teach us more about love than any human can. Let us therefore give some thought as to why making a heartfelt connection with a family dog or cat is often easier than making them with people.

An obvious starting point is that our four-legged family members do not have any reasons to compete against us for survival, procreation or the symbolic glories of social power and material gain. As a result, this makes them immediately more trustworthy in not being a direct threat to our social ambitions or personal interests.

In addition, the warm, welcoming demeanor and want for affection of well-socialized dogs and cats makes them easier to approach than a human who may be emotionally distant or competitively hostile. In accepting us without expectation beyond food and water, and loving us despite our flaws, we undergo a dramatic shift in attitude as we begin to behave in a kinder, more generous way toward our beloved animal friend and may even revert to a blissful state of child-like playfulness by speaking and acting as though we were young at heart again.

Another critical aspect of this relationship is that dogs and cats are better at communicating their feelings in a direct and honest manner, while their simple needs ensure that they do not harbor some hidden ulterior motive that could test the bonds of our trusting relationship with them. But most importantly, they do not care if we are poor, ugly or uneducated, seeking only our loving companionship to meet their own modest needs for physical comfort and spiritual joy.

However, the love of a pet is not entirely unconditional, for they also react to the same instinctual fears that protect all biological organisms from injury and death. Subsequently, should our behavior cause them to feel threatened, they also typically respond by cowering or fleeing from us to protect themselves. Their reaction is clear and obvious so we can respond appropriately. However, this kind of cowering and fleeing behavior is not always perceptible in people. Instead, it can manifest as the refusal to express ourselves honestly for fear of another's reprisal.

Ultimately, we cannot expect people to behave as kindly and gently as house pets, yet sharing our love with them is far easier *if we can trust them to do us no harm.* Furthermore, our trust is also easier to maintain when our expectations of love are not compromised by the conflicting values, beliefs or attitudes of our society. Instead, we must trust in the heart of our own humanity to reveal to us the next best step forward on any relational path to joy.

Family Values

The same fear of death that we share with animals also keeps us from trusting unfamiliar people or circumstances. Our immediate response is to block the flow of love as we engage our *survival mode* — which can make us excessively selfish in fearing for our lives. And if we live in constant fear, we may come to put our trust in a "higher power" for the courage to exist. Add to that our cowardly tendency to deny any responsibility for our wrongdoing and we uncover the reason for why so many people conveniently blame *God* or some other invisible force for their selfish treachery against others.

Such is the case in men's enduring holy war against women, one in which a suspiciously masculine "He-God" is the convenient scapegoat for why men alone must rule over society and all aspects of a woman's life. Under the premise of serving a higher power and purpose, men in many male-dominated cultures promote "family values" that best serve their own selfish interests. Meanwhile, that loving God's will may be deployed with such hateful force as to threaten the very existence of our family and its flowing of love therein. In short, this is hypocrisy.

Clearly, love cannot thrive in an atmosphere of distrust in our homes or on the public streets. Moreover, such a selfish, adversarial attitude actually hinders men's own spiritual development, despite any claim to the contrary of their being on a sacred path toward enlightenment.

The most blatant examples of such male-sponsored bigotry against women is embodied in the misogynistic laws of patriarchal religions that declare men superior to women. Here, a woman may be forbidden to leave her abusive husband or killed for "dishonoring" his good name by demanding a voice in her own destiny. Nor is her opinion sought in being sold like livestock into marital slavery. Instead, she may be kept from attending school or earning money to ensure that she remains ignorant and powerless to negotiate for her better treatment. Under the guise of protection, she lives as a prisoner by the rules of men.

Through this lens of social oppression, the strategy behind banning abortions is exposed as yet another way to force women into the refuge of marriage under a husband's rule. After all, in arguing that an unborn human life is sacred, we should be hearing those same men crying out against the mass-murder sprees of war with their utter disregard for all human life, including that of civilian women and children killed by these glory-seeking acts of military violence between rival males.

Nor are women allowed to have multiple sex partners in polygamist religions while her masculine He-God imposes no such restrictions upon men. Instead, in an expression of near psychopathological male selfishness, a teenage girl may be held down on a dirt floor of a remote hut while her clitoris is hacked-off to ensure that she never strays from her master's loins to seek pleasure for herself. And in more permissive societies, she is relentlessly terrorized by the marketing He-Gods of cosmetic advertising about her unsightly natural appearance; a form of psychological warfare that keeps her too distracted with her face and body to compete for power against the ruling class of men.

Even more tragic is that our lifelong exposure to systematic gender oppression has us growing up to defend such behavior as "normal." Yet there is nothing normal or spiritually virtuous about denying women power when her social responsibilities, including caring for offspring, far exceed those of men. And perhaps this is ultimately the source of the problem, for in the wild, most males have no role to play in "family" matters because there is no actual family. Instead, their only purpose is to fight for dominance against other males. And as part of this urge to dominate, we can understand why so many of these male-dominated social forces and institutions, from religion to marketers for the beauty industry, are all sending the same message — "Stay down, woman!"

Fortunately, a reasonable man of faith would never succumb to this self-serving mental fog of male entitlement. However, to clear a more joyful relational path to love, we might consider the following *Reality Check* to gain a more enlightened perspective on this problem:

> *"If God came to you as a woman, would you treat her the same as you do your wife?"*

We can only imagine how a wife might feel if she were reading this question in a culture that treats her more like a demon. Yet if anyone's loving God were to materialize in female form, would "She" want to see men showing such hateful disdain for the gender of their mothers, sisters, wives and daughters just to avoid sharing social power?

Also not surprising is that men's vengeful God is never present at any public humiliation ceremony of women; only the same angry men of mortal flesh and blood who use terror to control their increasingly fearful and loveless societies.

Fortunately, we know that the human spirit rejects captivity and this will ultimately ensure the bursting of these ideological dams to allow for a more natural flowing of power and love between the men and women of our world. Until then, we must not mistake the systematic oppression of women as an act of divine will; it is just another lie being told by selfish men to disguise their crimes against humanity.

A Perfect Union

In an upcoming section, *The Spiritual Path to Joy*, we will undertake a more forensic analysis of fear itself as well as the sometimes adversarial relationship that exists between religion and spirituality. Religion is faith-based, after all, meaning that belief in its claims does not require proof otherwise demanded in a court of law or reason. But when such claims demand that men and women behave in ways that are not only unnatural, but even cruel and sadistic, then we must wonder if this is not just another social expression of male selfishness and territorialism rather than the will of anyone's loving God.

Beyond the promoting of divisive social policies against women, God's name has also been long invoked to demand that humans must be married before engaging in sexual activity. This is an ironic moral obsession in light of "His" ambivalence toward pedophile priests or that horny old men are causing obstetric fistulas in child brides due to their bodies being too small for childbirth. And yet, for some reason, this same God cares very much about ordinary people steaming up the windows of a parked car without a valid sex license. Here again, reason suggests that this is not the management style of any supreme being but only that of mortal men seeking greater control over society.

Rather than relying on guidance from above, ancient tribal rulers needed only to behold the bloody specter of young men fighting to the death over some attractive young woman to begin plotting a diversion that, much like organized sport, would lessen the risk of lustful male violence in our communities. And so, whether it pleased anyone's God or not, *marriage* was invented as another means of controlling society.

In allotting each man a full-time woman servant to meet his needs, he could be induced to stop roaming the streets each night for random sex. Instead, his time and energy could be redirected toward clearing the land or serving his leaders in war.

In modern times, beyond giving banks, employers, governments and religions tighter control over our social behavior, marriage also sustains a lucrative wedding industry that extolls the virtues of two joining as one in a perfect union of body, mind and home furnishings. In short, there is every reason to promote marriage for countless social, political and economic reasons, regardless of how anyone's God feels about it.

What exposes this "God wants you to get married" ruse is that such monogamous pairings are rare in the wild and non-existent among chimpanzees, whose genetics and social behaviors most resemble ours.

In fact, in one documented case, a female matriarch mated with all the males in her troop in a single session, doing so without guilt, shame or fear of being dragged into the public square for execution.

Beyond nesting birds that require two full-time parental sitters, any claim that marriage is "natural" for humans is suspicious, especially if the God who decrees it mandatory seems unsure whether to endorse monogamy or polygamy — an extra perk that varies by religious sect.

However, what is true about marriage is that it justifies taking away a woman's power and forcing her into a state of child-like dependency upon men. Nor can we discount that this creates a profitable enterprise for religious clergy who charge a fee for each sexual union ceremony.

Systematically exiled from power, women are then forced to adopt a falsely "traditional" role as pleasers of men wherein she must prove her worth both as a prolific sex worker and substitute mother figure for her husband, who acts as "head" of the family. Beyond creating a moral dilemma for religions by coercing women to trade sex for survival in the guise of marriage, it also reverses natural law by forcing woman to now play the role of a colorful, strutting "bird" by displaying her sexual wares and nesting abilities to attract that most elusive of wild creatures, the well-employed and monogamous human male.

Once we compare the socially-imposed gender imbalances inherent to marriage with love's need for an *unimpeded outward flowing of our self-expression in a state of trust,* we can understand why women who are economically-liberated may avoid such an arrangement wherein her life ambitions are defined by male-dominated institutions rather than her own resident truth. In turn, her independent attitude may anger any "traditionally-minded" man who wants to keep women at a market value equal to that of goats and other livestock. And if we look around at what women can do and *have already done,* we also see the futility in any male-sponsored argument that she needs "protection" from the hardships of existence. In reality, the only protection a woman needs is from the political cages and spiritual restraints of selfish men. Globally, our challenge is to convince those men seated comfortably and waiting for their evening meal to finally get up and serve themselves.

A Natural Attraction

Stereotyping marriage is as futile as stereotyping loving relationships, for we know that from household to household there can be dramatic variations in how people behave toward one another based on personal character and other factors. Yet even the most enlightened of men can feel pressured to conform to social norms and just as every culture has its version of a Gender Wall, so does it also have expectations of how every man and woman is meant to behave in context of a marriage.

At its worst, marriage is a legalized form of prostitution if religious leaders relegate sex only to marriage and force women to enter therein for lack of having an independent choice. In such a trade agreement, she is forced to surrender her sexuality for mere survival.

In making sex her greatest trading asset, society also forces women to put an unnatural emphasis on her appearance to lure a potential suitor into her perfumed constellation of feminine charms. This invites us to consider another aspect of freeing love's flow, which is based on our inborn natural attraction to the physical beauty of others.

In forcing women to display for men — which is typically the male's role in the wild — she can also be exploited by cosmetics and fashion industries that promise her a man's attention in return for her buying costly beauty products — and using them throughout her entire life.

But while men and women are beginning to rebel against this kind of social engineering and exploitation of gender and sexuality, there is no denying that beauty serves a purpose that is far more than just skin deep. And so, to help us overcome that joy inhibiting urge to hide our flaws from public view, let us explore our worldwide human obsession with attaining a kind of beauty that rarely exists in the real world.

...

Contrary to cosmetics marketing mythology, there are no "beauty secrets" for which we must pay a queen's ransom at makeup counters. Instead, each of us is biologically programmed to feel attracted to a particular ideal arrangement of three physical characteristics that are prominent among most life forms in the natural world. These can be identified as follows:

Contrast

The coloring of flowers acts as a visual messaging system to insects that sets each species apart from its rival suppliers of food pollen and the otherwise monotonous green backdrop of the open pasture. Our own attempts to stand out as a promising relational trading partner may also require us to pose in a brightly colored dress or sports car to stand out among a similarly bland backdrop of our fellow citizens. We can also create contrast by making our eyes, lips, hair or body contours stand out in that crowd, or against the tone of our own skin. Coloring contrast is also vital. In applying makeup, for instance, a slight misstep here can transform us from a natural beauty into a circus clown. In the natural world, we will find evidence of contrast in many things, even among rocks and minerals that have no logical reason for looking their best. Yet the entirety of beauty's visual appeal is not created by contrast alone and requires the addition of yet another key element.

Symmetry

Balance is critical to all living systems and therefore also represents an important aspect of visual beauty. Just as atoms seek balance, so does a tree, whose branches do not all grow on one side, lest they bend and break. This is also why we feel insecure if our hair is higher on one side as it also makes us look *out of balance* with ourselves. Symmetry is how we create the visual perception of being balanced. This is similarly expressed in the balanced arrangement of petals on a flower wherein each one grows in compliment to the others by its shape, size, position and visual patterning. Subsequently, a blemish on our skin, a crooked tooth, or a nose that appears overly large for our face disrupts our own facial symmetry and may invite unwanted criticism for appearing out of balance in terms of our facial proportions or skin pattern. We also notice such imbalances in ourselves, which makes us fear the social consequences for not creating a perfectly aligned and evenly-weighted outward appearance for others to admire. And because none of us are visually perfect, this creates opportunities for various beauty industries to sell us ways to fool people into not seeing our imperfections.

Youth

Youth is the final ingredient in the creation of physical beauty because it signals our reproductive potential. Just as the contrast and symmetry of a flower are meant to attract insect pollinators, so is human beauty meant to attract potential mates. This is what makes *youth* a critical component of visual beauty because of its association with blossoming fertility and physical vitality. This also explains why the fertile are not sexually attracted to the elderly who are no longer able to bear or care for offspring. Yet the promise of sexual pleasure remains a potent social currency for negotiating our survival and social advancement. As such, we may be willing to undergo costly surgeries and "beauty treatments" to prolong the illusion of our youth so that we might continue reaping the many energy rewards associated with drawing other people's sexual attention to ourselves. As such, a fear of aging is common in women conditioned to rely on their appearance for their self-esteem.

...

Unlike male tomcats who can detect the scent of opportunity at a great distance, sexual attraction among humans is largely dependent on visual cues. Subsequently, beauty is how we convey to others our genetic health through the ideal arrangement of our physical features. This we can verify by our reflexive feeling of unease in seeing someone with an overt physical deformity, such as having one leg shorter than the other. As biological beings guided by natural laws, this signals to us a competitive disadvantage that our offspring could inherit. In this way, beauty is how nature *visually stereotypes* our suitability for future sexual reproduction. While this is not a flawless system to screen for good genetics, it allows us to judge at a quick glance the overall health of a potential mate. This is also why we celebrate the most physically attractive, youthful and athletic young men and women in any culture because we recognize them as being genetically "perfect" mates.

This visual promise of a perfect genetic union is also what draws the lustful gaze of men toward those flawless female forms used in media advertising. There is a natural and timeless reason why we behave this way and marketers exploit our human wants through the excessive use of sexual temptation in all forms of media. Meanwhile, we are driven by those same biological forces to create an equally powerful prejudice against "ugliness" that isolates those who are *less perfect* in meeting our standards for an ideal reproductive partner. In conjunction with our competitive urge for status, the outward expression of such a prejudice can be painfully cruel toward those who are being visually degraded.

As the recipient of people's negative reactions to our visual flaws, we may seek help from the makeup industry and plastic surgeons to create the illusion of our being near-perfect in appearance. And yet, if our children inherit these same "flaws" that we reject in ourselves, we will still manage to love them all the same. In this way, we see that love has its own perfect measure of beauty, and perhaps this is also what we ought to be obsessing over instead of the outer shell of our inner being which will soon enough leave all of us looking sexually obsolete.

…

Undoubtedly, love will always hold some mystery for us, including why it flows so effortlessly from some yet barely trickles from others. Another is when we accidentally discover our perfect partner once we stop searching. So much about love defies logic, and perhaps it is best that is remains this way. But let us make room for one last revelation about love that could also prove to be its most profound:

For whether it flows between a mother and child, a man and his dog, or young lovers in the throes of ecstasy, the true essence of our loving relationships is that they allow us to more fully experience ourselves through our intimate connections with others. In short, love gives us *the experience of experiencing ourselves.* And this is why love must flow throughout our lives if we are to know the joys of being fully alive.

Herein is revealed love's greatest irony, for it is not just the other that we seek to know more intimately, but also ourselves *through them.* This is the divine union for which our hearts have always been reaching and for which we may be willing to pay any price to hear the sound of our spirit singing its most heartfelt songs of devotion, not only for the love of our life — but also for ourselves.

CHAPTER 12
Shopping While Hungry

Desperation is a necessary human condition in maintaining a lucrative global slave trade wherein a privileged few exploit the overwhelming hunger of the masses to satisfy their own insatiable appetite for power. As host to such a master glutton, we can expect to pay an unfairly high price for our meagre survival while having to sell our lives and dreams for the future at a panic-sale discount.

But desperation has many masters, including the tyranny of a drug withdrawal that pushes many addicts to sell their bodies for an equally degrading price. And then there is the painful longing for acceptance that has many an awkward school child negotiating its own torment at the hand of sadistic peers. In short, whether it is felt as a physical, mental or spiritual yearning, a desperate hunger in any form can be an oppressive dictator in determining the course of our lives.

Luckily, many of us have convenient access to food, friends and a loving family, which largely protects us from experiencing the kind of physical or emotional starvation that can lead others to such desperate measures. Yet the insecurities and neediness that we can often display in context of our relationships proves that we are not entirely immune to various nagging strains of self-doubt. And this has inspired another lucrative slave trade wherein opportunistic people, including parents, lovers, employers and strangers, will exploit our insecurities in a selfish bid to become our ruling masters. Their secret strategy for controlling us is to make us believe that our only purpose in life is to please them and seek their approval — as though *their* happiness is the only thing that should matter to us. And so we become their willing slave.

But relationships negotiated from a position of powerlessness often lead to a joyless struggle for balance and dignity. We must therefore avoid succumbing to this insistent urge to always undervalue ourselves by understanding the energy dynamics of low self-esteem and how others can use them against us for their own selfish ends.

Ironically, our wisest instructor in that regard is our hunger for food itself, because the longer we delay eating, the more desperate we feel to replenish our body's dwindling supply of food energy. If we then go shopping while feeling hungry, this nagging inner sense of emptiness can cause use to engage in *impulsive selection behavior* wherein we waste our money on snacks and unfamiliar foods that we would never have bought had we entered the store feeling well-fed and satisfied.

Likewise, as the emotional slave to any kind of desperate hunger for love or social validation, we may also engage in wasteful relationships or social activities that are utterly devoid of spiritual nourishment. Let us therefore explore how our various fears of rejection can be exploited by others so that we are not always selling ourselves and our future happiness at a discount to the lowest bidder.

The Malnourished Spirit

Self-esteem is another word whose meaning, like that of love, seems subjective to the tongue that is speaking it. Thereupon, it could mean anything from arrogant pride or courage to unbridled selfishness. It is therefore best that we define it here for our own purposes. It will also be helpful to revisit *The Joys of Contentment* from chapter 4 for a list of specific emotional states of well-being associated with self-esteem.

That said, self-esteem is typically defined as a feeling of self-worth or self-confidence in our ability to meet the challenges of daily life. Yet such words do not identify the specific source or cause of that feeling within us. Let us therefore identify the four states of mind critical to supporting our inner feeling of self-esteem. They are as follows:

1) Feeling a deep trust in ourselves in relation to our world and others.
2) Feeling that our existence has value.
3) Feeling an enthusiasm for life itself.
4) Feeling that we deserve to experience joy.

We can now identify the symptoms associated with low self-esteem, which result from feeling entirely opposite to what we have just listed. Instead, we may now experience:

1) Feeling unsure of ourselves and insecure in our decisions.
2) Feeling inferior and undeserving of any reward.
3) Feeling apathetic or disengaged from having any sense of value for our life.
4) Feeling that we deserve unfair treatment from others; that we are somehow *guilty* or *flawed* and should be ashamed for wanting more or better.

Shame and guilt are self-esteem-crushing emotions that others may try to invoke to control our behavior, including manipulative mothers and religious cults. This reveals that our self-esteem can be tampered with not only directly, but also by way of remote mental programming from various social institutions. As such, the competitive advantages of dominating those who feel socially inferior to their leaders is obvious to anyone engaged in this kind of suppressive behavior against others.

By investigating self-esteem, we also encounter further lessons as to the physics of our psychology by understanding how "praise," which is a positive *infusion* of emotional energy into our invisible economy, can inspire us to feel more confident in our abilities. Conversely, this is also why being insulted, which is a negative *extraction* of energy, can cause us to doubt our value in whatever social role we are being judged.

As biological beings governed by atomic law, our loss of confidence is not just a convenient metaphor but a verifiable energy phenomenon. Like the nagging sensation of an empty stomach, so do we feel a kind of nagging spiritual void when losing self-esteem energy to the harsh criticism or rejection of others. Sensing this loss in energy, we then behave as any negatively-charged atom would by trying to regain our lost sense of inner balance through an infusion of positive energy from an external source. In short, we try to equalize our emotional state.

Typically, this will see us turning on our attacker to steal their own self-esteem energy in an energy-balancing act of "vengeance," or we may try to win back positive energy from our critics by doing as they say. In most cases, the latter state of willful submission is the reaction our manipulators seek, after which they can have us doing anything in our desperate attempts to please them.

Unlike the primal states of fear that ensure our survival, a feeling of low self-esteem is neither natural nor helpful to our existence. Instead, it is more a socially-induced state of spiritual malnutrition that may already have us cowering in childhood from hostile attacks against our self-confidence. This can happen if a parent who is hyper-competitive or overly-controlling uses hurtful insults to defeat our will. By making us feel inferior, they hope to gain an unfair mental advantage that will lead to our unconditional surrender to their leadership.

Ironically, in their desperation to win, we may be called "stupid" for failing to agree with the faulty logic of people ill-equipped for mental combat yet stubbornly determined to win at any cost. In reality, this is their thinly-veiled attempt to have us do what is "smart" — which is to agree with everything they say or want us to do.

Yet as children and young adults we must trust in the guidance of our parents and other authority figures and this may cause us to believe that we are at fault if we accept as truth the harsh criticisms of every parasitic abuser we encounter. Here, the only truth that matters is that anyone who truly cares about our emotional well-being would never treat us in such a cruel, selfish and psychologically-manipulative way.

Unfortunately, this kind of parasitic feeding upon our self-esteem is common wherever governments, employers or family members seek to drain our life like a battery to fuel their own selfish devices. It is also typical that such abusers suffer themselves from their own painfully low self-esteem and its energy-depleting affect. This is why we often meet people who habitually hack away at the self-esteem of others in some desperate bid to regain their own lost sense of inner balance.

To Grade And Separate

Our self-esteem can be targeted not only as unique individuals but also as groups and entire societies. For instance, our leaders will often use boastful political propaganda to elevate our self-esteem as a nation by feeding our glory-seeking hunger with claims that *our way of life is best*. Conversely, our feeling of self-esteem can be collectively diminished by treating entire groups of people as worthless or insignificant. We see the spirit-crushing manifestations of this in the systematic racism and prejudice against minority groups, which may even cause us to feel unworthy of life itself.

In patriarchal cultures, such systematic attacks are launched against the self-esteem of women to ensure their unconditional surrender to a male ruling class. Starting in early childhood, this process of spiritual degradation teaches a woman to see herself as inferior to men, often by male religious decree, so that she feels unworthy of better treatment under the prejudicial laws of this gender-based caste system. In being subjected daily to such discrimination, she also learns to accept men's exploitive behavior as "normal," thereby allowing her victimhood to even become a cultural *tradition*. In this way, the Gender Wall reveals its true purpose by keeping a woman from gaining greater control over her society — and thereby over her own life and future happiness.

A similar fate awaits victims of systematic racism or other prejudice in being forced to settle for a lesser quality of life due to their exclusion from the favored ruling group. And when attacking our self-esteem to have us settle for less, it often has the added affect of causing us to see ourselves as inferior. In this way, we actually assist our social oppressors by mentally oppressing ourselves from within — which we see being done by the downtrodden believers of religious caste systems.

Sadly, that fate also awaits many children in a monetary ecosystem as we are lured into school classrooms by cheerful young women and their promises of singing, drawing, playing and making new friends. But what we do not realize is that we have entered a human evaluation system for selecting the best future candidates to uphold our nation's economy and its hierarchal power structure.

After we stop crying for our mothers, we are subjected to a mental grading and separating process wherein our future worth as a human being will be determined by how well we follow our teachers orders and absorb their mental programming. Also, by having us compete for the teacher's approval, we will learn "the right attitude" to ensure our obedient servitude as a future employee and dutiful taxpayer. Granted, many do not see their academic journey from this perspective, but this may also be due to their being better suited for a life of conformity.

If we then fail to meet the often arbitrary academic standards of our culture, we will also be judged inferior and socially downgraded based on our poor performance. The result is that opportunities for greater financial power or social status will be largely inaccessible to us. In this way, we are marked as a reject of a factory-like schooling system that can also destroy our self-esteem for life.

Exiled to the lowest ranks of the economic caste system, we may experience a further loss of self-esteem attributed to our quality of life and the social environment in which we are forced to live. Like the state of depression that astronauts may feel in being isolated for long periods from natural organic shapes and textures, so may we feel the same sense of isolation when confined to the artificial landscape of a modern city without forests, fields, flowing rivers or clean air.

The solution, of course, is not to rely on drugs, alcohol or therapists to help us tolerate the mental anguish of living like a caged animal in a state of communal isolation and nutritional neglect. Instead, we must take bold steps to renew our ancient relationship to the natural world and one another. In re-establishing the founding community values of the tribal clans from which we arose, we might regain not only our lost sense of ecological balance, but also our inborn sense of self-esteem as worthy individuals living in a society wherein everyone truly matters.

How we manage to upgrade our human condition will depend not only on increasing women's power to lead us toward a more caring and protective human society, but also the elevating of self-esteem among all people so that we sufficiently believe in ourselves to succeed and flourish as a global community. On this path, failing is not an option.

Bad Apples

Upon graduating from the school classroom, we enter the true battle for class dominance wherein attacks upon our self-esteem define our daily struggle to survive and rise in socio-economic stature. No longer is it just parents or teachers trying to dominate us, but entire groups of people all fighting to seize control over the lives and futures of others. And all of them use the same psychological weapon against their rivals, which is to make them feel inferior.

Ironically, this also leads to some shameless paradoxes. For example, in medieval Europe, the ruling noble class referred to ordinary citizens as "commoners" to imply their own rarified status. Yet among those many commoners were such uncommonly brilliant people as Galileo, Da Vinci and Mozart, whose names and contributions to our world stand far above those of any meritless social poser of their time.

In a further paradox, we find a sexually promiscuous woman being denigrated as a "slut" while her male counterpart is celebrated for his own sexual plurality as a "playboy." In this form of social conditioning, women are shamed to deflate their self-esteem, while men are held in high regard for their outstanding groinsmanship. Clearly, the intent is to keep women lower in stature and limited in their freedoms.

But perhaps the most shameless of paradoxes is when a religious order harbors pedophiles and organized crime racketeers while boldly condemning the rest of humanity as born "sinners."

As for our daily life as a "commoner" in modern times, where once we had to compete for grades by obeying our teachers, we must now compete for our survival and status by obeying our employers. In short, we must still prove ourselves the better conformist. However, this can also lead to extreme energy imbalances in our workplace relationships if an employer abuses their position of power for the sake of their own personal glory-seeking urges — or as a form of cruel mental sport.

This reveals a further threat to our self-esteem if we are forced to cower before an employer whose own pathologically low self-esteem has them trying to prove their dominance over us at every turn. We may then be subjected to constant name-calling, threats, verbal abuse or absurd demands on our time that we fear to contest. As such, this is no longer a relationship defined by our job description but rather the sadistic tormenting of a victim by someone ill-suited for a leadership role and perhaps even mentally ill. In such cases, the abuser is trying to compensate for their own low self-esteem by displaying their power over others. Yet like hoarding wealth, such victories are never enough.

This brings to our attention a critical flaw in all systems of governing and economic control wherein the prerequisite for rising up through the ranks merely requires us to be a better conformist to the demands of those controlling our access to any higher seat of power. Referring back to the chapter, *Trading in Illusions*, we can assume that a good many ambitious social climbers are merely actors portraying the kind of person others expect them to be. And once in a higher position of power, the seeds of their mental pathology come to fruition as they transform our society into the kind of sociopathic battleground where it is no longer safe for the kind, caring and conscientious to exist.

The means to their endless rise in power also exposes a critical flaw in our school grading systems. Here, the scripted process of adopting a professional identity does not account for, nor change, a person's true character. Subsequently, any cruel-minded intellectual can become a doctor entrusted with our care by simply paying a fee and executing the "doctor" script to its certified conclusion. Consequently, while our social career training cannot imbue us with compassion, it can often help us to conceal our most serious character flaws beneath a decorum of scripted professionalism. Here is a familiar example:

I	**The Religious Charlatan** (A false healer of human suffering).
P	A convenient path to public attention, wealth and power; a useful form of social camouflage.
S	Exploit human desperation as a false prophet and healer of those suffering and in need of help.
F	Losing our easy access to power and privilege; being exposed as a fraud.
A	Having to explain how our newly acquired mansion and private jet are helping the poor.

Ultimately, we discover that the process by which we create the most educated and trusted members of society is also the means by which any sociopath or psychopath can cloak themselves in a scripted veneer of civility to prey upon others in their midst. This "fake ID" dilemma infects the entire structure of our societies and is largely automated by using the IPSFA Sequence. As such, we can literally *fake it to make it*.

What this also reveals is the often low, superficial standards to which we hold applicants in judging them a "good apple" when they may be rotten to the core. This is confirmed when a murderous psychopath infiltrates the police force or military to hunt humans for sport under the guise of being their protector. This is a far-too-common occurrence when our character is not being equally graded for its suitability in the critical social roles we often play. And in moving up the ranks, such a mentally-deranged person may hire new recruits of like mind. Herein we can understand why corrupt businessmen will vote for a corrupt politician to facilitate their predatory crimes against humanity and our natural world. In short, many of our social ills make logical sense once we understand the underlying dysfunctional relationships and mental pathologies that have helped to create them.

We can now connect all of this to a further threat to our self-esteem wherein we may be hired to work for such a sociopath or psychopath. If we consider how many world leaders have been mass-murderers of their own people, we see a disturbing pattern wherein those seeking a higher seat of social power rarely do so for the benefit of others. And likewise, we often find the most ruthlessly ambitious people displacing the kinder and gentler leaders of our society who do not have the same shameless bloodlust for power as these aspiring alpha dominators.

As a result, once in a trusted position of power, such a glory seeker may threaten to terminate our employment for being a "bad apple" unless we submit to their selfish demands. And when our survival and future retirement plans depend on having a "good apple" standing in society, then we may ultimately surrender our will to do whatever is necessary to win the approval of these bad apples that rule our society — perhaps by acting like a shameless sociopath ourselves.

And so it is that we may find our self-esteem even further depleted as we work to destroy the lives and futures of other innocent victims on behalf of some greedy social predator who has everyone convinced that he is making our world a better place — if only for himself.

The Peanut Game

Let us now turn our attention away from greater society toward our private lives at home. Here as well, we find that joyful relationships require us to maintain a healthy level of self-esteem lest we also find ourselves in the role of a compliant slave to the selfish whims of others.

As is true for all relationships, here the primary source of conflict is also our human Bio-Psychology, whose survival and procreation-based agenda causes our selfishness and competitive glory-seeking behavior. This ensures a constant underlying tension in all relationships wherein one partner may feel the urge to dominate the other or expect that all decisions side in their favor — which it does for men in any patriarchal society, or for parents demanding our surrender in return for "paying the bills." This is why arguments constantly erupt as each side seeks to assert its own interpretation of a fair settlement in any dispute.

In arguing, we find yet another venue for observing the physics of our psychology. Again, by the law of physics, any negatively-charged atom must regain its balance by taking the equal of its lost energy from another atom. In context of our highly-charged emotional collisions with others, we may feel a similar overwhelming urge to seek "revenge" against those who attack our self-esteem by way of verbal insults or status-diminishing judgments being made against us. We may then also feel a compulsive urge to reclaim what was lost to regain our own inner sense of emotional balance. As such, we can even think of our emotions as "e–motions" — or *energy in motion* — whose tiny electric charges carry with them our feelings of loss and gain.

In public life, we may witness this phenomenon in a police officer who feels the need to "equalize" by assaulting an apprehended suspect. In this way, he tries to reclaim his lost self-esteem energy and status as dominator in having been frightened or challenged by that person. In our private life, we are just as susceptible to engaging in such excessive acts of retaliation, which can cause even petty arguments to escalate into violent power struggles that endanger not only our relationships but even our lives. And this is how we fill the news with stories about a man who killed his friend over a slice of pizza, or a raging husband who beat his wife to death over her choice of words.

Luckily, we can avoid this violent descent into chaos by anticipating the progression that our relational disputes often take.

In marriages, for instance, disputes can arise if one partner feels a sense of energy loss due to the other partner's actions or inactions. This creates an internal feeling that we must correct this energy imbalance — even if only based on our misunderstanding or petty whims.

However, in accusing a partner of wrongdoing, we are also attacking those values, beliefs and attitudes by which they maintain their inner sense of identity and mental order. In short, we are also attacking their perception of reality. That is why even a legitimate grievance can often be met by that person lashing out like a panic-stricken animal fighting for its life. This often results in their aggressive shouting and posturing, fleeing the room, or some desperate attempt to distract us from the issue to avoid any further loss of their self-esteem energy.

Under these combat conditions, schoolyard rules now apply as each side engages in a selfish "eye-for-an-eye" energy-stealing competition. Herein, one partner fires a demoralizing insult or painful gesture of rejection at the other to undermine their self-confidence. In context of this heated battle, we will hear many familiar declarations that include:

- ☑ "You always…(do bad things)"
- ☑ "You never…(do good things)"
- ☑ "Everybody says (bad things about you)"

At this futile level of combat, mental conquest is the goal, with each assault meant to weaken an opponent's resolve to ensure their defeat.

We can refer to this battle as "The Peanut Game" if we imagine our verbal aggression as an attempt to steal an invisible peanut from the hand of our partner — which represents their self-esteem. Each time we snatch it away, they lose energy and must launch a retaliatory verbal assault to regain possession of that peanut and its associated feeling of emotional balance. But with only one peanut available and only one possible winner in a competition for dominance, our victory may then be accompanied by an opponent's tearful exit along with the slamming of a door as a final gesture of anger and rejection.

Sadly, in our desperate hunger to win, we often fail to consider what we stand to lose by engaging in such reckless adversarial behavior. And to further undermine the joy potential of a relationship, we may fail to resolve the underlying cause of our disputes, thus leaving both sides in a losing position — divided by the fear of addressing that issue rather than united by a bond of mutual respect in having resolved it.

Yet whether the relationship is a marriage, friendship or any kind of meaningful bond, we should not play this "Peanut Game" in naively believing that we can win it without a peaceful resolution. After all, the assaulted mind is often desperate to regain its self-esteem energy and may take any opportunity to steal it back. Who knows at whom that urge might be directed? For if not the assailant, then perhaps at those too weak to fight back, whether a child, a helpless animal, or even a classroom full of students dreaming of a joyful future.

Artificial Sweeteners

The act of "shopping while hungry" can often take a sharp turn for the worse if we find ourselves wandering through life with our self-esteem depleted in a world where social predators target the weakest and most vulnerable by pretending to be our savior. Here too, the physics of our human psychology makes this situation easier to understand.

In that regard, we can often feel the energy-depleting affect of other people's insults not only emotionally and mentally, but also physically as a discomfort in our stomach or elsewhere. This is why we may feel energetically repelled by the kind of people who gleefully insult others to boost their own self-esteem. Conversely, we may feel attracted to those who offer us praise as this causes us to feel positively charged and more confident in our approach to life.

Knowing this, some people set emotional traps to lure others into a form of slavery by seducing them with false praise. And if we are too hungry for approval to pay attention to its source, then we may also fall victim to one of these disingenuous social parasites.

To help us understand the dynamics of these exploitive relationships and our vulnerability to them, we need only look back at our early life development and upbringing. Here, as an infant, we felt attracted to our mother because she was constantly bombarding us with positive loving attention and compliments. This filled our spirits to bursting as she encouraged us to explore, learn and grow through a vital bond that nurtured our body with food and our heart with loving acceptance.

Yet as we started to develop, she began to strategically withhold that flow of positive energy to manipulate us into obeying her commands — whether to have us eat our vegetables or clean our room. And while mothers use this kind of maternal *push-pull technique* to ensure that we grow up to become healthy, independent adults, this same strategy is also used by social predators to lure us into relationships based on a counterfeit feeling of loving acceptance and trust. In such cases, that person will also first flood our life with their kindness only to later withhold it as a way to control and mentally enslave us.

"Love bombing" is a term commonly used to describe this emotional recruitment technique used by religious cults who literally "bomb" our minds with positive attention and acceptance. This is our first clue that something is wrong because most strangers do not act this way toward others unless they are selling a product — or themselves. Yet as a naive new recruit, we are meant to associate our sudden surge in self-esteem with our newfound connection to the group. In this way, we will fear to lose our newfound privileged access to their emotional support and may choose to join them so that they will continue to invest their time and energy into making us feel both appreciated and "special."

In reality, they do not care about us at all. In fact, their behavior is a form of *artificial sweetener* that will soon leave a bitter aftertaste in our lives. For shortly after joining, group members will begin threatening to withhold their "love" unless we agree to earn it. In most cases, this means sacrificing our body, mind or income to their cause — which is typically to serve their leader, who derives the benefits of exploiting a devoted group of gullible followers. And like an infant suddenly cut off from the flow of love, so may we also fear losing our future emotional energy rewards for disobeying. In this confused and vulnerable state, we might then ignore our better judgment and wind up as yet another discarded human toy in the mental playground of some self-deluded sociopath. And after spending too much time in their alternate reality, we may also feel terrified of leaving our life of slavery for a better one because of the lies we have been told about "the outside."

Ironically, a similar kind of cultish *love bombing* occurs in context of marital courtship. Here, the candidate enters into early negotiations with an equally suspicious display of generosity and kindness to create an unrealistically favorable impression of their future reward potential. Having bloated our self-esteem with various strategic acts of positive reinforcement, they may then threaten to withhold the further flow of their "love" energy unless we surrender to their demands — whether by signing a lifelong contract to share our assets, or performing various sexual services in return for a free dinner and car ride home.

In a further irony, this process is reversed in military training where new recruits are *hate-bombed* to destroy their self-esteem, and then reconditioned to associate their newfound feelings of self-worth with being an obedient soldier. And in another ironic twist, instead of going to prison for murder, we will be *love-bombed* for getting our "first kill."

Love bombing is also used in advertising where we may hear a cheery voice declaring that "Smart shoppers choose [this brand]" to trick us into buying that product to earn its attributed praise.

Consequently, the use of false praise to artificially sweeten human relationships is not a well-guarded secret, while selfishness on our part often ensures our complicity in any state of victimhood.

The Fruits Of Our Labor

As earlier stated, the merits of food need not be advertised to the hungry. Likewise, the abundant rewards of relationships need not be listed here in clearing the obstacles to a more joyful communion with others. However, in concluding this part of our journey, we should not forget the many rewards to be gained by establishing a more honest and loving relationship with ourselves. And that includes our creating fewer impediments for others to find their own harmonious sense of inner balance. In this way, we make room for joy in every relationship. To further assist us in that regard, let us consider some further critical aspects of creating an enlightened union so that we might bring even more joy to our individual quests for a life together:

Transience: Relationships change as a reflection of our changing needs and life circumstances. We may therefore discover that a once pivotal relationship can take us no further in our personal evolution. A prime example is our departure from the controlling influence of our parents in transitioning to adulthood. We must accept that relationships are not nearly as enduring as is our lifelong need of them. Let us therefore embrace those changes necessary to our life's continued unfolding and not hold it against others for also wanting to experience more of the awe and wonder of their own unfolding relationship to life itself.

Slavery: Relationships involve a constant negotiation for energy. As such, by keeping us low in stature and expectation, our oppressors can more easily demand our time, energy or surrender for little more than stale bread and dirty water. Worldwide, our enslavement of human and animal species betrays a selfish imbalance in our overall relationship to life itself; one that hinders us from attaining a more joyfully-balanced and democratic state of communion within all global relationships.

Debt-Counting: People who are overly-generous toward us may be secretly tracking "all they have done for us" to later negotiate a desired payback. This is why desperation should not be our reason for entering any relationship, lest we trade our future joy for a temporary reprieve from suffering. A truly generous person will never remind us of their generosity — only selfish manipulators do this to invoke our guilt. As such, the integrity test for love is that the person will still treat us with equal kindness despite our not conceding to their demands.

"Bad" People: As a general rule, people may label us a "bad" person for failing to do as they want. Their goal is to have us wanting to reinstate our "good" reputation by pleasing them. A clearer path to joy is to avoid playing their rigged mental games and generate instead our own inner sense of self-worth. This we do by engaging in personally meaningful pursuits that incorporate the "Joys of Inspiration" as listed earlier. For those who have never chosen a path to emotional success of their own, this can be a spiritually-liberating experience in finally being able to do something that we feel is *important to us* rather than only to those who want to reap the benefits of our obedient servitude.

Our Emotional Legacy: As a biological entity, our death is inevitable, as is the ritual gathering of family, friends and anyone affected by our departure from their lives. Subsequently, to hear someone give a eulogy that describes us as "a hard worker" or "dedicated employee" betrays that they have nothing joyful to remember about us. Let us therefore consider our emotional legacy — the emotionally-charged residue that we have been leaving on the memories of those we will eventually leave behind. How do we wish to be remembered by them? And if it matters at all to us, then let us act to create a legacy that also ensures our own fond memories of ourselves in the years of our decline. Bitter or sweet, the only enduring fruits of our life's labor are these memories we create for ourselves and others. Let us therefore work to plant and nurture a bountiful orchard of goodwill in the hearts of those with whom we have shared any kind of meaningful relationship.

And finally, let us be reminded once again that the memories we will one day value most will not be of the shoes we had worn but of where we had worn them. In that regard, let us now change to a more suitable form of mental footwear for our oncoming journey to a sacred place within where our minds may never have thought to travel before.

PART FOUR
The Spiritual Path to Joy

CHAPTER 13
The Silent Partner

Born into this hectic human world of constant demands and endless expectations, we may have little time left to think about anything more than our next scheduled task. Yet for many of us there will come that inevitable moment of reckoning as we are struck by the futility of our struggles to succeed if we are destined only to die and be forgotten.

It is in that moment that we join a long list of puzzled seekers as to why we should exist at all — an oppressive cosmic riddle that can nag at us from the day we become aware of an impending tomorrow when there will be no more tomorrows to come.

For many, this unsettling encounter with reality initiates a lifelong quest for inner peace that may find us sitting in silent contemplation or singing raucous songs of salvation in a crowded house of worship. Yet no matter the route we take, it represents an irreversible first step inward and upward on the spiritual path to joy.

Spirituality is a natural and necessary aspect of human life, yet like politics and food production, it has also been largely corrupted by the selfish quest for power. As a result, we must now be more suspicious of any religion or self-proclaimed spokesman for God seeking to exploit our instinctual fear of death to control our lives. And if we should fall into their trap, then we might also become so possessed with paying and praying to enter their promised afterworld that we may look more forward to our dying than living a more joyful life here in the present.

Aside from selling dubious tickets to paradise, religions can also be hijacked by male glory seekers who will then turn our inner quest for wisdom into a violent global war for territorial dominance. This has further condemned spirituality to be misrepresented as a tool of social oppression or a flimsy overcoat of sheepish behavior worn by wolves. In short, the corruption of religion has given spirituality such a bad reputation that many now view nihilism as a more enlightened option for understanding their place within the world.

Fortunately, the kind of spirituality we will be exploring here is not a culture-specific form of mind-control made for mass consumption. Instead, it emanates from the core of our being as an insistent hunger to know ourselves as a limitless and loving expression of joy.

At its heart, spirituality is an inner quest for a comprehensive state of wisdom that allows us to make the most balanced, inclusive and harmonious decision in any life circumstance. This highly alert state of mind is also known as *self-awareness*. By contrast, we are spirituality asleep if our life becomes an automated sequence of mental routines and rituals. Herein, like "the selfish sleeper" of chapter 7, our decisions are largely informed by impulsive gut reactions prejudiced by outdated fears and obstructive beliefs rather than a thoughtful presence of mind. As such, it is the role of any *legitimate* spiritual practice to awaken us from such an unconscious life by introducing us to *the silent partner within* — a wiser, happier, more contented version of ourselves waiting to guide us toward the realization of our greater joy potential.

The Journey Inward

In earlier chapters, we learned how the convenience-oriented urges of our conservative biology can affect our attitude toward thinking itself. This explains why we often cling so stubbornly to our beliefs, including those concerning religion and its promised afterlife rewards — which seem suspiciously easy to attain, even by the worst of career criminals.

Yet we should be realistic about such beliefs, given that there are a multitude of religious groups all claiming to be the keepers of the truth and the preferred religion of God. As such, we must be discerning in our approach to spiritual wisdom lest we accidentally join the wrong group in haste. Our inborn biological selfishness also makes us an easy target for predatory religious cults who take possession of our wallets and minds by way of our want for personal gain. This further proves why we must be skeptical of any promise of future joy that requires surrendering our time, money or mental freedom in exchange for what sounds too good to be true and can only be confirmed once we die.

Truthfully, we cannot live in a house built by another's imagination, nor gain inner wisdom by looking out toward others. Instead, we must travel the spiritual path as an active participant, not an idle spectator.

To engage us in the unfolding of our conscious evolution, we also need a more objective and inspiring definition of spirituality. Here is a CPJ-specific definition of the inner quest for enlightenment:

> THE ROLE OF SPIRITUAL PRACTICE IS TO FACILITATE OUR RETURN TO AN ORIGINAL STATE OF CHILD-LIKE AWE AND WONDER, BUT MUCH THE WISER IN HAVING LIVED A UNIQUELY CHALLENGING LIFE. AS WE BEGAN, SO MUST WE RETURN IN A JOURNEY MADE NECESSARY TO RID OURSELVES OF THE FEARS, PREJUDICES AND FALSE IDENTITIES WE MAY HAVE ADOPTED TO WIN ACCEPTANCE IN ADULT SOCIETY. OUR GOAL NOW IS TO REVEAL OURSELVES TO OURSELVES AS WE ARE, NOT AS WE OR OTHERS WISH US TO BE.
>
> THE CUMULATIVE LAYERS OF IDENTITY AND MENTAL SCRIPTING THAT NEGATED OUR CHILDLIKE ESSENCE MAY STILL BE BINDING OUR SPIRIT TODAY. THE SPIRITUAL JOURNEY IS THE PROCESS OF RETURNING TO OUR RIGHTFUL PLACE AS THE SOURCE OF LOVE AND POWER IN OUR LIFE. WE DO THIS BY BREAKING DOWN ANY REMAINING MENTAL BARRIERS THAT MAY STILL BE KEEPING OUR AUTHENTIC INNER SELF CONFINED TO SOME LIMITED RANGE OF ITS FORMERLY BOUNDLESS AND JOYFUL EXPRESSION. AND THEN WE MAY NEED TO CRY, NOT ONLY FOR ALL THAT WAS LOST, BUT FOR ALL THESE NEW WONDERS WE HAVE FOUND.

...

Before we proceed, let us reflect on what is missing from this new definition of spirituality. For one, fear plays no part in it, nor is there a promise of an afterlife or the promoting of hatred for specific groups of people, including homosexuals or rival religions. Instead, we find a simple explanation for what we are seeking that is consistent with all that has been conveyed since the first chapter. In short, it has integrity in the message that it imparts. Again, we have nothing to fear, hate or avoid — only the goal to seek greater inner knowledge of ourselves.

In this definition, the spiritual journey is more like an inward-bound archeological expedition to reclaim ourselves at the core of our being. As we do, we begin to penetrate the layers of our conscious corruption, beneath which we will rediscover an astounding person awaiting us; an innately-empowered *silent partner* to guide us through the rest of our lives and — as may ultimately be proven to the reluctance of many a skeptical mind — perhaps even longer still.

What we each ultimately learn from experience is that the spiritual journey is a form of personal death and rebirth that occurs while we are still alive and whose purpose is to serve our conscious evolution rather than ensure us a better seat at God's table.

The Inverse Reality Principle

To further demystify the spiritual journey, let us consider that when trees grow too close together, they cannot reach their full potential as individuals. This is because the lifelong development of each tree is being unduly influenced by its proximity to neighboring trees. As a result, each tree will typically grow to be undersized and poorly fruited due to an overwhelming demand to share limited resources, whether sunlight, space to grow; soil nutrients or rainwater. And then there is the threat of diseases and parasites spread by their close proximity.

The negative impact of overcrowding on tree growth offers a useful analogy for our own spiritual journey because, unlike our externalized quest for social success, we must turn inward to become successful at being ourselves. This is also why the spiritual journey is not a public event or group activity but a solitary pursuit; one whose fruits will also grow best by not allowing others in close proximity to weaken our inner resolve to reach the summit of our authentic self-expression.

Spiritual development works in reverse order to what we experience on the outer life paths. Using *The Inverse Reality Principle,* we build our identity from the inside-out guided by our internal sense of reality. We can understand the significance of this approach by considering who we might have been had we not assimilated to the collective external reality of society by adopting its prescribed identities and lifestyles. In taking a more inward-seeking approach, we also ensure our authentic self-expression in acting from an attitude of self-acceptance ("I Am") rather than one of self-denial. Here too, the IPSFA Sequence makes this inward-seeking process clearly visible and easy to understand:

I	**Self-Acceptance** (A positive, self-affirming state of mind based on accepting who we are).
P	To find joy on our own terms; to be guided by our own intuition and reasoning.
S	"I am as I am." — remaining true to our inner essence.
F	To lose our power of self-determination to the will of others; to be an impostor.
A	Enduring public scorn or suspicion for not adopting a recognized or "normal" social identity.

There is an innocent simplicity to this way of thinking because it places no conditions on us to be anything more than who we are. Yes, we still require instruction on how to survive like the offspring of most species, but what we avoid with this attitude is having others tell us who we are or who we *ought* to be. It may seem absurd to give someone administrative control over our consciousness, but this is what happens if we fail to defend our identity from corruption. It is therefore little wonder why we would feel compelled to find our way back to who we truly are and often struggle to do so. In contrast to self-acceptance is self-denial, an outward-seeking attitude that leads to such corruption of our authentic identity, as demonstrated in the following example:

I	**Self-Denial** (An oppressive, self-negating state of mind often caused by low self-esteem).
P	To find joy according to the terms and conditions of others in return for their acceptance.
S	"I am as you say that I am"; concealing our true identity to please others and avoid conflict or guilt.
F	To lose the social rewards associated with gaining the acceptance of others; to be abandoned.
A	Constant longing; never knowing our true identity out of fear of being punished for exploring it.

As we can see, by seeking to be who others want us to be, we must abandon the authentic aspects of ourselves, thereby also contradicting the purpose of the spiritual quest. In short, we cannot return home by traveling in the opposite direction. And if we do decide to turn around and return, then our journey will be longer and more treacherous than had we stayed nearer and truer to the person we are and know best.

Learning From The Masters

Our spiritual development is a subjective process that unfolds inwardly according to its own unique terms and schedule. As the captain of our conscious vessel, this means that we cannot forcibly bring the horizon closer to us but must patiently travel toward it at whatever speed is best suited for our own personal craft.

This transition toward becoming a more authentic and enlightened version of ourselves can be sudden and include profound altered states of mind or mystical epiphanies. Conversely, it can also be such a slow and subtle process that we may neither detect nor fully appreciate our genuine progress toward conscious mastery. The deeply personal and intimate nature of our spiritual unfolding also proves that there can be no "one-size-fits-all" approach to personal enlightenment. As such, the external imposing of generic mental control systems upon our spiritual development is not only an invasion of our mental privacy but can also do us great psychological harm by derailing our internal process rather than accelerating it. As a seeker of joy, we are therefore best to choose our own spiritual path and avoid any superstition-tainted or outwardly focussed detour being offered by those with questionable motives. Our independent seeker's attitude may be unpopular with those who have been indoctrinated by various existing "spiritual" systems, but as we shall see, our attitude also has a long and celebrated pedigree, one to which no serious aspirant can close their eyes — or their mind.

Our need for mental sovereignty on the spiritual path also forces us to address two paradoxical behaviors exhibited by members of many organized religions. The first is one of pure logic wherein we are told that an all-powerful God is observing our every thought and immoral act to judge our worth for eternal life. Yet for reasons unknown, instead of recruiting us by direct mental contact while already on the premises, that all-powerful deity instead takes the longer route by sending mere mortals to invite us to join that religion. Ironically, it is their nagging insistence on meddling in our private spiritual affairs that may deter some of us from joining. In reality, their invasive trespassing upon our mental territory may have ulterior motives, including a recruiter's own need for mental comfort by having us mimic their predictable lifestyle. At worst, there is no concern at all for our spiritual development but only an insistence that we surrender our body, mind and income to the false prophets of some cultish theocratic empire ruled by men.

The second paradox concerning religion puts an ironic twist in the promoting of institutionalized spiritual development once we consider that those spiritual prophets we are being encouraged to imitate were themselves not *followers* of others. This revealing piece of wisdom is also included in every religion's scripture wherein the revered spiritual masters to whom its insights are attributed were in fact renegades and outcasts of their own societies; original thinkers who refused to follow in the footsteps of others, nor conform to their beliefs and lifestyles. Instead, they each exercised their individual right to mental freedom by walking their own spiritual path as a freethinking individual. As such, maintaining one's independence of mind is part of their sacred teaching — if not by direct word, then surely by their living example.

Moreover, they defiantly challenged any conventional teaching that offended their sensibilities while also breaking new mental frontiers as opposed to repeating what others had told them to think. And just as the lone oak grows tall and strong, so did their own spiritual identity come to fruition during long periods of self-imposed isolation far away from the meddling influence of their traditionally-minded societies.

As such, when a religious recruiter claims that the scripture of their religion is a true account of human history or "the word of God," then they must also accept as truth that enlightenment is best attained by finding our own way through life, just as their prophets had done.

The ultimate revelation here is that in trying to imitate our masters, we may actually be negating the most sacred aspect of their teaching, which is to always remain true to ourselves. Moreover, how are we to ever hear God speak to us when others are constantly talking?

In reality, not all followers of religion are spiritual seekers. Instead, they treat religion more as a social club that allows them to avoid the kind of social isolation and mental solitude wherein the great masters, once lost in their own confusion, had ultimately found themselves.

Tools Of The Spiritual Trade

As one might expect, the convergence of old world superstition and new world economics has inspired a new age of consumerism wherein its merchants of magical thinking offer a heavenly assortment of goods and services to hasten our journey within, or at least to their checkout counters. Fortunately, the only tools of the spiritual trade that we will ever need are the innate gifts of consciousness, intuition and emotion with which we are born. These are all that any serious spiritual explorer will require to find their way inward and upward.

However, as a convenience-oriented species, we may seek shortcuts to uncovering life's greater mysteries, including our own. Meanwhile, our fear-based mental intolerance for uncertainty urges us to fill any void in our understanding with a convenient myth that allows us to regain our sense of comfort and control over life. For this reason, we must be careful not to obstruct our spiritual journey with restrictive beliefs or superstitious rituals that make a mockery of our intelligence instead of helping us to solve those greater mysteries.

In this regard, two beliefs currently dominate the conscious human landscape — "creationism" and "evolution." Yet whether it soothes our mind to believe that an unseen "God" has created all that we see or that life's brilliant complexity arose from a great nothingness that has relied entirely on "dumb luck," either belief reveals our preference for taking mental shortcuts that place a greater importance on arriving at our chosen destination — some preferred answer or explanation — rather than on the journey toward wisdom itself.

This attitude is akin to wanting a degree in medicine without having to attend school. It is why many devout followers of both science and religion now blur the line between logic and fantasy to maintain their cherished beliefs — while conveniently ignoring evidence that might test their faith or even convert them to other ways of thinking.

But most of all, what this reveals is that we cannot legitimately call ourselves a seeker if we already believe that we know the answers, or at least feel that we know what the answer *cannot* be. This is not only a problem that creationists and evolutionists face, but anyone who has a prejudiced interpretation of reality from being *mentally conditioned* to ignore all other realms of possibility. And that is neither scientific, nor a sign of faith in what we believe if we fear to let our beliefs be tested for their durability in any court of truth or reason.

In contrast to any such defensive mental attitude, our most valuable tool on the journey of enlightenment is an honest, open-minded and humble approach to life, for anything less is a lifelong invitation to be humiliated by the truth and reality itself. As such, while we may never know the origin of life, we nonetheless remain the most reliable source of wisdom for solving our own life's mysteries. And yet, as we begin to explore our inner selves and experience our own spiritual revelations, we may discover that we now share a common set of values with other spiritual aspirants, regardless of the path they have taken to come to the same realizations. For this reason, we all will ultimately discover that this shared wisdom is the essence of our humanity; the expression of our highest virtues as a pure, unblemished soul as seen through the eyes of our awakening mind. Yet how we find our way to such states of revelation may be entirely different from how others arrived there.

In this sense, spiritual enlightenment is like a city to which we each can travel by many roads, including that of religion, yoga, meditation, holistic body therapies, near death experiences, kundalini awakenings, grief, PTSD and other emotional trauma, or even through the use of mind-altering chemicals. As such, this further justifies why we must remain humble on our journey inward, for those who announce too boldly their plans to travel to some exclusive spiritual destination tend to be more interested in their footwear than in taking that first critical step inward on the journey of a thousand miles.

The Method Of The Healer

Using the previous analogy, there are many roads by which we could travel to the city of inner wisdom. And if we walk them intentionally, we may experience profound states of joy and wonder in exploring the uncharted dimensions of our being. In short, knowing ourselves better can make us a happier person.

Yet even those who are reluctant to explore their inner life may still find themselves on a profound spiritual journey through the gateway of *crisis*. Here, the death of a family member, beloved pet or other form of agonizing loss can be a trigger for our spiritual evolution by leaving us sufficiently weakened to surrender our pride and the stoic facade of strength and certainty we may be projecting to others. Metaphorically speaking, the darkest soil is often the most fertile for these spiritual transformations, which also explains why religious recruiters can find a more receptive audience among the grief-stricken residents inside a hospital or prison. In short, emotional suffering can provide a perfect medium for inner growth, albeit an uninvited and often painful one.

As an aspect of our conscious design, there is a brilliant natural logic to using traumatic events to inspire our spiritual development in that they may be the only force powerful enough to break our stubborn resolve in clinging to values, beliefs or attitudes that no longer serve our future growth. In bypassing our intellect, these transformational events fuse their spiritual lessons into our inner being using the searing heat of our inflamed emotions, without which enlightenment would be more like an intellectual meal served to us cold and flavorless and thereby without a lasting sensory impact upon our lives. This is why emotions are a critical tool in our enlightenment because they allow us to strongly feel and thereby remember such important events.

While our encounters with traumatizing events can initially leave us cowering in agonizing pain, fear and self-pity, our raw psychic wound may later become the very vehicle that delivers us to a more fulfilling life wherein we might take uncharacteristic risks or break free of our restrictive thinking habits to learn, grow and often find joy in serving the needs of others.

We can find many examples of such profound life transformations through the gateway of crisis, including the mother who has lost her child to a preventable accident and then uses her newfound insights to help others avoid the same needless tragedy. By extending her broken inner being outward, her wound becomes the vehicle of her salvation wherein she uses the oppressive force of grief as the righteous fuel for her personal healing and conscious evolution instead of allowing it to push her into spiritual decline. In this way, she often finds her greater purpose in life and eventually, a newfound source of joy that she could otherwise never have claimed without enduring such a tragedy.

This reveals a common trait among those who ease the suffering of others in that *the method of the healer betrays their deepest wound*. In short, we heal in others the pain we know best within ourselves. And therein lies not only a meaningful spiritual goal, but a broader path to joy that encompasses with integrity all the aspects of our inner being.

The Unspeakable Word

As we each travel our unique spiritual path toward enlightenment, one of the more frustrating aspects of this journey is our inability to share the dramatic and exciting details of our interior life with others. Like anyone experiencing something new for the first time, we want to tell others about it. However, there is no way to effectively communicate such information for various reasons, including the subjective nature of our internal spiritual development.

Raising our voice will not help us because the problem is not one of others being deaf or lazy-minded. The issue is with language itself, whose symbolic sounds and markings we use to externalize our inner experience of the outer world for sharing with others. Words are the foundation of whole languages and thus our conscious relationship to sequential thought itself. Strung together into a cohesive sentence, words allow us to create a mental image or emotional impression of our life experiences so that we can convey them to others.

Subsequently, if no word exists to define an experience, then it can also not be properly communicated to others. In this way, the absence of certain words and word sequences in our language can create an obstruction to mutual understanding — which may even be the goal of leaders and social institutions that want to censor our thinking.

In addition, unless the listener has had a similar experience, they will have no personal point of reference in their memory banks to interpret our words. As such, these limits within their own understanding can make us appear to them like an incoherent tourist who is lost in some foreign country. Instead, they may try to explain our situation in terms of what they can understand — which is a gateway to prejudice as they retreat to what is most familiar to their own minds.

Frustrating encounters such as these give us an opportunity to give some consideration to the relationship between thought and language. In many respects, language controls human consciousness by giving us the mental construction materials to build our thoughts and express ourselves. As a result, our thoughts and actions can also be controlled or censored by limiting our vocabulary in any culture or institution.

As part of a broader topic, this introduces us to the idea that others, including governments, religions and industries, can control our minds by denying us the linguistic reference points to identify those kinds of realities or experiences that they wish to deny us. In short, we cannot have free speech when our language is being imprisoned.

As an example, people in government, industry and science are now debating over whether our planet is heating up as a result of human interference. Here, the end goal of the accusers is to introduce a more responsible level of environmental stewardship by all concerned. And yet, by simply renaming "Global Warming" to "Global Poisoning" we not only give the problem a more accurate name, but also make it easy to prove with an endless trail of evidence from industrial poisons that are undermining the biological health and reproductive ability of every species on our planet. "Exhibit A" would be a worldwide blood test.

But instead we are led far off course from solving the problem as we fight over how to measure earth's ambient temperature — while oil spills, radiation and toxic chemicals continue to destroy our planet. It is both a clever and dangerous distraction. It also proves how language can be used to confuse our minds and keep us from communicating a problem that others want us to ignore so that they might continue in making their obscene profits by creating that very problem.

Book burning is the best-known expression of this top-down urge to control our behavior by censoring our thoughts. A further aspect of linguistic censorship is when we are conditioned to attribute positive emotions to some words yet negative values to others. This is why we might feel positive emotions for a politician who uses words such as "freedom" or "patriotic" yet feel an urge to dismiss those who speak to us about "racial inequality," or "UFOs" in our skies. In this way, we can be trained to internally censor even the most legitimate ideas and life experiences by disallowing their entry into our mental culture.

In behaving like scientists who have abandoned their objectivity, we also hinder our conscious evolution by avoiding all mental threats to our feeling of certainty for which we have neither words nor internal points of reference. "Out of sight, out of mind" as is often said, and that is also how the conscious evolution of our world is being suppressed.

Subsequently, if we then experience a profound spiritual event that we want to communicate to others, instead of being met by a person's wide-eyed curiosity and joyful enthusiasm, we may find them fearfully closing their mental doors and trying to diminish our experience as something either more familiar or comfortable for them to talk about.

Consequently, a spiritual awakening that fills us with indescribable joy may be interpreted by others as a state of demonic possession or undiagnosed mental illness. This is further ensured when we are being taught to believe what is both possible *and* impossible. As such, when encountering anything that we believe should not exist, our mind may impulsively dismiss it out of mental self-defense. This also shows us the limited value of language when faced with another's fearful lack of mental receptivity. For this reason, it is often easier to demonstrate the gifts of our spiritual journey by way of our actions, which always speak louder than any words we may be struggling to find. Moreover, this is often the only evidence we can offer to others for the existence of a better future world that truly is within everyone's enlightened reach.

Ultimately, such experiences also remind us of the deeply intimate nature of a spiritual transformation, which occurs for our sole benefit and must therefore not be treated as a team sport or an opportunity to monetize our journey. And most certainly, it must not become infused with our selfish biological urges lest we continue to form marauding armies of fanatical religious warriors lusting for world domination.

In having gained some understanding of the high points and pitfalls of the Spiritual Path To Joy, we can now better anticipate the various mental distractions that can cause our conscious evolution to veer off its own path toward enlightenment. In that regard, one of our most daunting challenges is to find a sense of inner peace in societies that are awash with the fear of both living and dying.

And so, let us take yet another step toward a deeper understanding of ourselves by studying fear as an obstacle to our spiritual maturation and lifetime quest for inner peace.

CHAPTER 14
A Peaceful Mind

Logically speaking, once we are dead, we will have nothing left to fear because we cannot die twice. But until that day comes, fear will remain a powerful guiding force in our lives, as evident by our lifelong seeking of mental and physical comfort. In short, we must learn to accept fear's presence as it will undoubtedly not be leaving us anytime soon.

As the unbiased protector of life, fear instinctively repels us from any threat of death or injury we may encounter in its effort to keep us alive. Subsequently, this also creates an opportunity for others to use our fear of dying against us by making us too afraid to challenge them in any competition for mates or territory. As such, they may win by default of our desire to avoid an early grave — even if they are the weaker one.

In human societies, our social dominators employ this same strategy to keep us cowering in submission to their demands. Using physical violence and mental terrorism, their goal is to keep us feeling weak so that we never gain the courage to become self-empowered individuals acting of our own freewill — or to dare make our own selfish demands. Subsequently, a natural instinct that is meant to protect us can also be used against us as a weapon of intimidation to ensure our surrender to those in power. And should we protest this arrangement, armed police and prisons are always standing by to assist us with our grievances.

Knowing the advantages of keeping the public in fear, many social leaders use intimidation as a preemptive mental strike to ensure our lifelong obedience. A familiar example is our fear of being punished by invisible Gods or demons to keep us submitting to religious tyranny. Meanwhile, the shock value of witnessing public executions sends a chilling message to never challenge our government's dominance over our lives. Elsewhere, our fear of dying from poverty has us fighting to defend a way of life that is killing us as we insist on more jobs instead of an escape from these industrially-polluted wastelands by which we measure human progress. In this way, fear's live-preserving impulse to protect us from death is now causing us to live in misery in countless new ways by our submission to joyless or even deadly circumstances.

In the previous chapter, we defined the role of the spiritual journey as returning us in wisdom to a joyful state of childlike awe and wonder. If we accept this definition, then it also stands to reason that we must free our mind from fear's relentless grasp if we are to re-engage with the playful essence of our founding childhood innocence.

Admittedly, it would be difficult for anyone to cheerfully sing a song with a gun pointed at their head. Yet, using this gun metaphor, our aim is to identify which guns are real and which are only harmless replicas that we need not fear. By freeing our minds in this way, we may one day be rewarded with the serene gaze of a learned spiritual master in having realized that a peaceful mind does not arise from building up our defenses, but from conquering our needless fears. Let us therefore embark on a courageous inner quest for mental peace by exploring our ancient human relationship to fear itself.

Cages Within Cages

Earlier we learned how our fear of suffering can create "comfort traps" that keep us from fully engaging in the joys of being alive. Meanwhile, the fear of rejection can have us wasting precious time criticizing our reflection in the mirror rather than celebrating the genuine miracle of our existence. In this way, fear turns from protector into oppressor as our efforts to control every negative outcome causes this natural ally to start behaving more like *the enemy within* as it relentlessly attacks our self-esteem.

In countering such self-directed attacks upon our peace of mind, we must first make a more realistic assessment of our human condition. To begin, we have never been true "predators" except in our own heroic imagination. Clawless, fangless, thin-skinned and highly vulnerable to attack by anything from mosquitos to roaming lions, we instinctively seek safety in numbers from the hostile threats of the wild by forming tribal societies to protect ourselves.

The progress of human civilization is also largely due to our shared desire for greater comfort, convenience and control in relation to the circumstances we fear most to encounter. This has transformed once small, isolated tribes of nomadic hunters and gatherers into swarming masses of wage-earners who now hunt and gather money to survive in our crowded city habitats.

Yet in entering these protective sanctuaries of human civility, we also inadvertently increase our fears rather than diminish them. Moreover, while no longer tormented by wild beasts, we remain just as vulnerable to the threat of hunger, disease, injury and random violent attack as we were before — as demonstrated by continuing poverty, rape and war.

In addition to our oldest fears, we have also created a host of newly invented dangers to avoid in context of our monetary ecosystems. They include unemployment, eviction, failing in school and being killed by motorized vehicles. Less critical but equally terrifying are such fears as failing to use underarm deodorant or not brushing our teeth, to which we may also respond with various forms of inhibiting paranoia.

In managing our growing list of fears, we tend to find comfort in the certainty of living a structured life. Subsequently, what began as small tribes wanting to organize their daily survival strategies into cultural traditions has now led to our collective "box world" containment under the control of various political and religious institutions. And common to all of them is their use of fear to keep us inside our boxes.

This intuitive human impulse to create organized structures is also a natural extension of atomic behavior, which informs the creation of all organized structures, from human bodies to solar systems. This same urge to organize also informs the creation of social identities based on the structure of the IPSFA Sequence, which also mimics the push-pull mechanism inherent to atoms. The benefit of imposing structure upon our lives is that we can save time and energy in following a predictable, seemingly unchanging survival routine. But when each fear demands its own scripted routine to control it, we quickly become imprisoned within a complex mental framework of fear-managing systems whose exclusive focus on our physical and mental comfort leaves little room for our joy in their design.

As a result, we may live a comfortably miserable life maintained by the fear of losing control over whatever threats our secure lifestyle was meant to contain. And with each new fear we adopt, its added need for containment increasingly drains our time away from engaging in more joyful activities. And so, we come to live like frightened rabbits in our cages within cages of conditioned fear wherein escape may either seem impossible or too frightening to consider. And yet, many of the threats against which we are defending ourselves may not even be genuine but only the frightful shadows of an overactive imagination.

An Education In Horror

Our obsession with fear is not surprising. After all, with survival being the main priority of every living organism, we are instinctively attuned to pay more attention to potential threats than potential sources of joy. Simply put, defending our life is more important than defending our happiness. Furthermore, many fears, including those of facing loss or the unknown, are also linked to our fear of dying, which increases their intimidation potency. Thankfully, we can quiet at least some of those fears just by learning to understand them better.

In that regard, horror movies offer us a highly educational classroom in that their storytelling technique relies almost entirely on assaulting our mind with violent, fear-provoking thoughts, sounds and imagery. This allows us to create a list of common human fears based on our own fight or flight reactions to watching them.

Our typical reaction to a horror film feels like riding an emotional roller coaster of shocking anxiety wherein our body reacts in sympathy to every threat encountered by its unsuspecting victims. Such anxiety is predictable given that we can barely outrun a swarm of determined mosquitos, let alone an angry poodle. In reality, we are near the bottom in nature's hierarchy of predators, which is why we often react more in proportion to our feelings of vulnerability than the actual danger posed by a threat — crushing a harmless spider, for example. This is also why we hunt large predators for "sport" to compensate for our feelings of vulnerability. Without fear, hunters would not feel compelled to defeat superior predators in the wild, lest they could also be eaten as food.

Aside from deadly predators, we can also experience anxiety from any number of threats including invisible bacteria or "immigrants" from a foreign nation. The same feeling of vulnerability is also what drives our leaders to seek some ultimate weapon of doom to match the enormity of their private fears of being publicly overthrown and humiliated. As such, all these themes find their way into our fear-based entertainment.

Horror films further torment our minds by creating blood-lusting villains that seemingly cannot die, which denies us the ability to subdue our attacker. This is why murderous criminals must always rise for that one last attempt to kill after we assume they are dead; a limitation easily overcome by just creating undead zombies hungering for our flesh.

Our human fear reactions are highly predictable, thus giving horror storytellers an endless list of ways to provoke our cowering response to their cinematic offerings of mental terrorism. Among the lowest fruits hanging on their tree of horrors is to simply turn the lights off and let our fearful imagination stumble around blindly in the dark.

Nor should it surprise us that the fears being exploited in horror films are many of those that we share with other species. This includes our need to run from danger, which explains why "cornered" animals are so dangerous in their desperation to flee. This is also why horror films often depict victims being trapped, typically in a dark cellar or all alone on some remote planetary outpost with alien beasts stalking them.

Knowing our inherent susceptibility to countless fears, it will help us to identify them as an itemized list of mental and physical threats to our existence. The bracketed contents reveal how we might encounter them in horror films or even real life situations.

Mental threats, including:

- ☑ Darkness and isolation
  (being lost at night; being alone; unfamiliar places; solitary confinement).
- ☑ Being trapped, restrained or held against our will
  (alien abduction; kidnapping; marooned in outer space; imprisonment).
- ☑ Chaotic, irrational or insane behavior
  (the domain of psychopaths; behaviors causing uncertainty; religious cults).
- ☑ Unexpected attacks by unseen predators
  (home intruders; sharks in deep water; stalkers).
- ☑ Strangers who show signs of "ugliness"
  (villains with hideous scars; deformities; broken, rotting teeth).
- ☑ Loud, unfamiliar, aggressive or distressing sounds
  (screaming; growling; police sirens; distressed, high-pitched squealing).
- ☑ Confusing and intrusive sounds
  (disembodied whispers; sounds only heard at close range; breathing).
- ☑ Aggressors undeterred by empathy or fear for their own survival
  (fanatical terrorists; zombies; alien predators; the demons of religion).

Physical threats, including:

- ☑ Any natural cause of biological death
  (falling from heights; drowning in deep water; suffocating inside a coffin).
- ☑ Weapons causing agonizing injury and death
  (Saws, knives, hooks, spears, axes; spikes; crucifixion with nails).
- ☑ Hazardous environmental conditions
  (earthquakes; hurricanes, thunderstorms; floods; tornadoes).
- ☑ Bodily assault by disease or parasites
  (viral pandemics; flesh-eating organisms; mind-controlling brain implants).
- ☑ Animals stereotyped as being dangerous for various reasons
  (spiders, snakes, wolves; wild animals with rabies; dinosaurs; sharks).

In reality, our exposure to most natural threats is now greatly limited due to the sheltered lives that most of us live. Yet we continue to react to them because they remain embedded within our psyche as part of a broader survival instinct. As such, we make an easy target for any social dominator who wants to see us scurrying off into a dark corner where we pose no threat to their selfish aims. This explains much of what we see in actual life, as governments, religions and media use mental and physical threats to control our lives. And given that staying alive is our highest priority, the inducing of fear has become an effective political tool to ensure worldwide our cowering submission to those in power.

As an example, let us consider various kinds of mental terrorism that are commonly being inflicted upon our human species:

- ☑ Military intelligence terrorism: *water-boarding* (the fear of drowning).
- ☑ Legal terrorism: *imprisonment* (fear of being trapped; cornered).
- ☑ Political terrorism: warnings of *enemy attacks* (fear of loss; death; rape).
- ☑ Ideological terrorism: warnings of *socialism* (fear of being held captive).
- ☑ Religious terrorism: *the devil* (fear of predators; endless suffering; burning).
- ☑ Relationship terrorism: *divorce* (fear of loss, abandonment and infidelity).

Fear makes us easy prey to anyone using it to their advantage. In some cases, as when crimes are committed, a reasonable use of threat may be justified for gaining a confession. However, in the case of religion, we must wonder why mental terrorism is so often being used to teach us *how to love one another*. Surely there are better ways.

Death: The Final Insult

Many religions have justifiably earned a poor reputation for exploiting our fear of death — and eternal torture. However, this kind of mental terrorism has a long lineage dating back to Egypt's *Cult of Osiris*. Here, according to some historians, it was claimed that twenty seven demons awaited us upon dying to determine our soul's worthiness for paradise.

This inspired a form of religious racketeering among the priesthood wherein wealthy believers were tricked into buying a custom-scribed "Book of the Dead" that would secure their safe passage to immortality, despite any moral shortcomings. Still active during Roman times, the influence of this cult explains why offshoot religions have borrowed its demons to scare us into filling the seats and donation bowls in their modern temples of worship. This does not disprove life after death, but should warn us against the kind of *spiritual* leaders who want to charge us a fee to get into the afterlife — or a better seat at God's table.

As to death itself, we can understand why it remains a powerful tool of mental intimidation given that every biological organism spends its life running from it. And this is also why we remain on alert for danger — even when it lurks only inside our imagination.

Welcome or not, dying is our final obligation to the young and the one task that even the habitual procrastinator is sure to complete. But while the dead seem oddly at peace with it, we the living are often mortified by the prospect of our future non-existence.

This fear of dying is understandable. After all, we spend our entire lives working to perfect our way of living, which includes amassing the best material goods we can afford while developing deep emotional bonds with friends, family and others we love. And we invest all of this time and effort for what — to be covered in dirt and abandoned, or burned beyond recognition like a forgotten roast in the oven?

Yes, death is cold and unfeeling; it does not care if we still want to live or how dearly we are loved or needed by those we leave behind. It seems especially insulting to human beings, for we believe ourselves to be the better species in having learned to read, write and set our alarm clocks — it just seems so unfair to have to give it all up in the end.

As a consequence, we have translated our fear of dying into a desire to live forever — a reward also promised by most religions. But fear alone does not make for an ambitious career in the afterlife and so it may be useful to question our true motives with a reality check:

"If you could live forever,
what reason do you have for wanting to?"

Ironically, in answering this loaded question, some of us may even realize that we want to live forever yet already feel bored with life for lack of inspiration. In short, what have we to lose in dying if our life lacks a joyful purpose? This presents us with an ironic dilemma that we may want to contemplate further — an eternity of boredom.

In reality, it is our instinctual feeling of vulnerability and desire for control that accounts for much of our emotional attachment to this physical world. This leads to our dread in knowing that a day will come when we must face the ultimate fear of losing control over everything, from our bowel movements to our bank account. And naturally, this scares us to death — at least in a figurative sense.

Fortunately, the experience of dying is for many people nothing like the terrifying exits depicted in horror films. In fact, if we can trust the testimony of those who have died and lived to tell about it, death is a joyful transition into another dimension of conscious existence that we will greet with a profound sense of awe and wonder rather than dread.

What is most ironic about the testimony of near-death experiencers is that not only do they lose their fear of dying, but some actually look forward to dying again in having had a preview of what is to come.

Regardless of how we will ultimately experience our own demise, we must make peace with death before it arrives, lest our joyful childlike spirit enter a premature state of rigor mortis from always living in fear.

Eyes To The Ground

Our obsession with fear is understandable, yet it can sometimes get out of hand if we become overly anxious about dying. We may then suffer from various kinds of neuroses and phobias that have us defending a territory for which there may be no intruder. As a result, we may live a life of misery in guarding against some impending threat that may only exist in our imagination or as a highly unlikely potential risk.

The irony of such a morbid fascination with doom and gloom is that we can meet people who are physically disfigured from birth defects or injury who have a far more cheerful outlook and enthusiasm for life than those of us living in the shadow of fear. Given their lofty spirits, we might wonder why religions waste our shame on sexuality rather than directing it at the refusal of able-bodied people to explore their own unlimited joy potential. Their mental immersion in the worst that life has to offer reveals yet another insight into human consciousness that can help to keep our own attention on more joyful pursuits.

As a quick thought experiment, let us read from this book while also engaged in a meaningful discussion. What we will notice is that we can only maintain our focus on one activity or the other because our thinking is *unidirectional*. In short, we have a one-tracked mind. This means that we must constantly switch our focus, thereby diminishing our emotional experience of both due to a lack of undivided attention, much like when a student does homework while listening to music.

We face the same limitation when our mind becomes distracted by fearful thoughts that push other more joyful thoughts aside. As such, we can either take a fearful or a trusting approach to life, but not both simultaneously. We must therefore choose wisely what to think about lest we sabotage our ability to contemplate more joyful activities.

However, an unavoidable problem with owning a one-tracked mind in that our quest for survival has a higher priority than our quest for joy. As such, our mind inherently prioritizes focussing on fear-based concerns for our physical comfort, convenience or control over those related to our curiosity, creativity or desire for communion. And if our mind is then constantly bombarded by threats to keep us running from danger, real or imagined, we may become too distracted to make our pursuit of happiness an equal priority in our emotional life.

As seekers of joy, we must avoid the obsessions of looking for danger in all things or justifying our suspicions by only *seeing what we believe* rather than *believing what we see*. And if we fail in that regard, we may leave ourselves with insufficient time for positive thinking to counter our mind's negative bias — as evident in those who suffer from chronic cynicism or shyness. The result is not unlike walking with our eyes cast down toward the ground in that it makes us unable to see the wealth of joy that awaits us above our limited low perspective on life.

When Good News Is Bad

Clearly, our fear of death has us running from danger in every form, be it hunger, pain or other threats of suffering. For this reason, many of us are working to attain a more peaceful and optimistic state of mind. Yet we may also engage in an ironic contradiction to such behavior by purposely provoking our fear of death as a form of entertainment.

Among such activities, watching the news is the most popular. Here, the sun could be shining, the birds singing, and the whole world could be locked in a loving embrace, yet the news media must continue to broadcast only the most horrific aspects of life to ensure its ongoing success. In short — good news is bad for the news business.

Measured by this perverse reverse standard, an ordinary childbirth is "bad" news, whereas the death of thousands in a catastrophic event is the best news one could ever hope for as a news programmer.

As viewers of this morbid media spectacle, we are being engaged in a mutually-rewarding conspiracy of negative emotional gratification. Here, the newscaster feeds our lust for "fear pornography" by arousing our primal impulse to fight or flee through the presentation of largely contrived sources of fear. As a result, each day we can invite a host of entertaining new horrors to assail our minds in the safety of our living rooms — instead of having to go skydiving or swimming with sharks.

In recognizing our fearful nature and that news is rarely informative or relevant to our personal life, it seems spiritually careless to subject ourselves to such a constant stream of negativity. And yet, like those thrill seekers who feel most alive when nearest to death, so might we become addicted to the fear chemicals released by our body if our life lacks sufficient excitement to stimulate our emotions. And this is the role that news plays in acting as a *surrogate emotional experience.*

Frightening news stories feed this chemical addiction by acting like a terrifying mental amusement park ride that causes us to feel equally alive and exhilarated. We prove this with our sympathetic response to boxing matches and other sporting events wherein our body feels like it is involved in the struggle. The same occurs when watching the news as we react viscerally by imagining ourselves in those circumstances.

For this reason, the evening news or any kind of fear programming, including horror movies, would be boring to watch without our having this kind of an emotional investment in the struggles being depicted.

And this explains why we may sit in front of our televisions crying out "Oh my God, how terrible!" over and over until some suspiciously cheerful weatherperson signals the end of another day's mental assault on our peace of mind. Yet we cannot behave like nicotine addicts who rationalize their addiction by claiming to enjoy it. Instead, to absolve us of guilt, our co-conspirators at the news station dress up this horror show to appear as something other than a fix for mental thrill-seekers. And so we hear authoritative male voices offering honorable slogans such as "The news that matters" to make us feel better for watching.

And yet, if the news failed to offer us the blood-soaked tension we crave, then we may not sit through its endless barrage of commercials that pay for our ghoulish nightly infusion of shock entertainment.

Admittedly, this is not a cheerful interpretation of news media, but its intentional use of fear-provoking language only further confirms these suspicions. As an experiment, we could list how often the words *shocking* and *disturbing* are used by news anchors, or if any news story fails to incorporate such ominous keywords as *horrific, violent, tragic, fatal, bloody, victim, assault, murder, police* or *crime*. Not surprisingly, all such words are psychologically linked to our *fear of death*.

Ironically, what is missing from these fear-centric broadcasts is the language of joy, including any cheerful adjectives such as *wonderful, glorious, delightful* or *beautiful*. Even more revealing is that on the most serene days when all seems well in our world, newscasters are forced to scavenge the tragedies of foreign nations for bad news, whether the mass drowning of people on ferry boats, violent ethnic clashes, deadly viruses, or any other evidence of the worst that life has to offer.

Sadly, by saturating our minds with fear, we are also denied a more honest and realistic portrayal of life beyond that being depicted in the one-tracked mind of news reporting. In this way, we may also be led to see only the fears we believe in rather than believing in the joy we can see beyond news media's own limited low perspective on life.

The Endlessly Barking Dog

This unflattering exploration of news media has brought us full circle in the use of mental terrorism to control human social behavior. As a gentle reminder, we are still working to identify the obstacles to joy on the spiritual path, of which fear is the primary obstructor. As such, we might then ask what greater good does it serve society to have endless portrayals of human suffering broadcast into our minds via media?

Objectively speaking, newscasts serve the same function as does the "alarm signaling" of animals in the wild. Heard as the loud, repetitive chirping of chipmunks or squirrels, it alerts other animals of intruders in their midst — the loud barking of a dog serves the same function. But what if that alarm signal never stops? Does it not then become just a worthless form of communication; just background noise? And how might our positive outlook on life be affected by a never-ending stream of daily negative affirmations about the dangers of our existence? Are chronic fear and hopelessness some of the potential side-effects?

Moreover, newscasts do not involve us in solving the problems that they present, treating us only as helpless bystanders to the smoldering wreckage of other people's misfortune. In this way, we are exposed to a form of spiritual rape in being tormented by events to which we are unable to respond in a supportive way, as our innate humanity would urge us to do. And given that this is more the role of family, friends and neighbors: why involve the anonymous public in other people's private suffering? Yet underneath it all, we humans have a morbid fascination for death and newscasts are in the business of selling advertising space for products. Hence, this is just another symptom of profiteering in a monetary ecosystem; a gossip tabloid dressed in formal attire.

What is missing from media newscasts is a balanced portrayal of our human reality, for we are more than the sum of our worst atrocities but also lovers of life, defiers of the impossible and creators of hopeful new tomorrows. Yet in utter defiance of that reality, good news only gets a passing mention, often to signal the end of yet another day's emotional holocaust. Ironically, even good news topics typically feature a "happy ending" story about animal suffering or the like, lest we fail to feel our anticipated share of emotional agony from the experience.

Sadly, our human hunger for conflict is evident in all forms of media entertainment, wherein there is little interest in watching people being joyful or at peace. Instead, they must be conflicted and suffering or we lose interest in the telling of their stories. Today, distressing police and medical dramas, hostile talk shows and tension-filled competitions of elimination are the media's primary fear drug to feed our addiction to strong emotions that keep us feeling alive when our repetitious life of routine comforts leaves us feeling little to nothing at all.

Yet the darkest aspect of fear-programming is its potential use by those in power to keep us in a constant state of mental terror. After all, in feeling weak and vulnerable, we also feel too inhibited to step out into the world to boldly live a courageous life of self-determination; one that requires challenging those in authority if they resist our want for greater autonomy and social freedom. Subsequently, those with the most controlling power to lose may find it useful to monopolize media to broadcast both information *and* misinformation. This can then be used to keep us looking away from the legitimate problems of society; or to divide us in fear so that we refuse to work together to protect our world and future existence from the threats of the insatiably greedy.

And yet, all we need to do to counter such bad news is to get up from our couches and look outside our front door. This will confirm that we still live in a world where the sun shines, the birds sing, and we are free to love our neighbors if we can overcome our fear of them. And in the distance, we may even hear a dog noisily barking at a squirrel for taking bird seeds from a feeder — still, nothing to get alarmed about.

CHAPTER 15
A Reverence for Life

Crystal amulets, hypnotic angel music and tantalizing tales of miracle cures define the carnival-like atmosphere of a *New Age* trade show as it follows a time-honored "spiritual" tradition that is less a calling to serve humanity than a profitable enterprise to enrich its merchant gurus. And like their snake-oil-selling predecessors, these peddlers of magic elixirs and mystical beliefs also need not prove their claims when faith alone is enough to lead their enchanted flocks to the nearest cash register.

Bewildered by this barrage of advertising appeals, we may begin to wonder if the only purpose of the spiritual journey is to light scented candles or get a *shamanic* foot massage. But while their baubles and trinkets might cheer us up for awhile, what none of these hawkers of faith-based goods and services can do is ignite within us that sacred fire of a genuine spiritual awakening — an event to which no amount of scented candles can bring the least flicker of illumination.

Yet under their relentless sales pressure — or out of our own want for convenience — we may then settle as many do for merely replacing our outdated superstitious rituals with newer ones, thus keeping yet another time-honored tradition alive by surrendering our power to some force beyond ourselves — be it to Gods and angels, or a piece of polished quartz dangling from a hand-crafted leather necklace.

Aside from its commercial distractions, spirituality also need not be a somber affair as though we are attending God's private funeral. There are far more lively and entertaining ways to inspire us to wisdom and goodwill than by provoking our fear of eternal damnation. In fact, we can find these alternative acts of worship in some unexpected places, including in the daily ritual of people who brave inclement weather and sacrifice their personal comfort to bring food, water and shelter to a colony of feral cats. Giving freely of their time, energy and love, they engage in a life-enriching form of cross-species communion that is an expression of their reverence for life.

In transcending their own inborn tendency toward selfishness, these devoted caregivers engage in a spiritual joy economy wherein giving to others feels like giving to themselves. What motivates their generosity is an innate wisdom more felt than understood. Yet we can all make ourselves available to this reverent way of knowing with the tools of an open heart, an open mind, and the courage to invite the world into our loving temple of worship by opening our doors to both.

And herein we celebrate one another, not as masters and slaves, nor as humans and animals, but as equal beings sharing the bounty of our existence in a magnificent living world. In this way, we revere not only in the greatest but also in the least that mysterious spark of God-like consciousness that resides within all of us.

But such tender wisdom can seem illogical if we have yet to feel that sacred spark glowing within ourselves. And so, let us work to ignite it.

Relevant Revelations
(The Kundalini Awakening)

Legends, myths and creative story-telling have inspired some familiar spiritual stereotypes wherein the enlightened person is not only seen as infinitely wise but also exceptionally kind-hearted. This latter trait is an expression of their reverence for life, which involves the valuing of others as equal to one's self and thereby deserving equal respect.

Such an attitude stands out in our midst because — despite our fear of death — we tend to show a high disregard for life itself, including our own. This we prove with our deadly addictions and other high-risk thrill-seeking behavior; the reckless looting of our natural resources by industry leaders, and even our summer-long crusade against "nuisance" plants and insects with lawnmowers and chemical killers. As such, any visitor from another world would find a species at war with everything in its path and showing a particular cruelty toward animals. In regard to the latter, we even trap, poison and kill them just for living in our midst, while needlessly tormenting captive creatures in the food and medical industries in having placed a higher value on profit than on treating other sentient beings with dignity and respect. We even hunt and kill animals *just for the fun of it*. In short, we are a serious threat to all life, including our own.

War-like and ruthlessly selfish, we then make a big show of holding our wisest peacemakers in high regard, as long as they stay out of our way. This is also why we find far fewer of these genuinely "good" people in positions of power than in our political prisons and cemeteries.

Admittedly, there is no easy solution for our widespread selfishness and indifference to the suffering of others, but we can begin to develop a more reverential state of mind by considering how the kinder and gentler aspects of our human nature can be undermined through our culture-specific socialization processes.

In that regard, our social mentors teach us to memorize information relevant to our culture and learn various rules of conduct to ensure our civil obedience. As this is occurring, our competitive aggressions are being channeled into various contests for athletic, academic, economic or military dominance. In preparing for such combat, we must adopt various social identities along with their values, beliefs or attitudes via an IPSFA Sequence. This mentally separates us from our rivals, which creates an adversarial "us versus them" or "me against the world" state of mind. We are then separated even more by the pretext of various political, religious and class distinctions. At the end of this process, we are no longer the person who entered it, if not ideologically, then at least emotionally. In short, we are no longer *natural*, nor is our way of life, which often separates us from contact with nature itself. Thus, we stand alone in a tribal workforce society of strangers in an environment that can make us oblivious and apathetic to what exists beyond it.

Further to this and as earlier noted, our adopting of scripted social identities does not change our true character but only masks the most unsavory aspects of our human nature to ensure a more orderly society. As such, we cannot know who is hiding beneath that scripted veneer of civility because anyone can learn to act like a "good" person in public life — at least until their own hypocrisy unmasks them.

And this is where our topic takes an unexpected turn. For in taking all of these conditions into account, we can understand why competing to survive in societies where falsehood and fakery run rampant can be a stressful ordeal for anyone. As such, many people have sought refuge in drinking alcohol, where under its influence they become almost too eager to shed their social armor and reveal themselves to others.

This is due to alcohol's chemical affect of eroding the acquired fears that bind us to our scripted layers of social pretense. As such, drinking alcohol may not only cause us to discard important social inhibitions, such as not having sex in public, but also those that protect the illusion of our separateness from others. While in some people this may expose a distraught person hiding behind a mask of suppressed emotions, it can also imbue others with the courage to leave their mental fortresses of conditioned fear to engage in a more open, honest way with others. In short, not only does alcohol help us to be more authentic but it can also facilitate our spiritual communion with greater humanity.

Aptly named a "spirit," alcohol offers us a temporary path to spiritual surrender to facilitate a more reverential kinship with others. However, our selfish attachment to remaining in this chemically-induced state of bliss can destroy our body and relationships if we become addicted to drinking our way to mental freedom each day at any cost.

The earlier mentioned "unexpected turn" is that we now understand the process of spiritual awakening by having referenced an experience familiar within all cultures — the act of getting *drunk* as someone who feels socially-inhibited. Fortunately, our bodies are naturally-equipped with a far more potent yet infinitely less hazardous vehicle for spiritual transformation by way of a "Kundalini awakening." While still not a well-documented aspect of human conscious evolution and potential, once activated in the spine, Kundalini energy can initiate an internal process of *acquired identity and fear deconstruction* that can leave our entire lives changed forever. As such, it must also not be treated lightly as yet another form of mental status-seeking by glory seekers.

At the summit of the Kundalini experience, we are awash with an indescribable feeling of love more powerful than we have ever known and a genuine sense of "being at one with everything" that is no longer just a tired spiritual cliché. The term Kundalini itself derives from the yogic tradition, whose intent was to prepare spiritual initiates for its powerful internal surges of energy which, like a cosmic lightning bolt, can even do harm if endured too long. Unfortunately, as the Kundalini energy recedes, so does our access to its inner-worldly dimensions of unlimited spiritual insights. Thereafter, as one popular enlightenment idiom confirms, we return to the humble task of "carrying water and chopping wood" as once again we resume our everyday lives.

Whether triggered by meditation, a near-death experience, ingesting psychedelic plants, or emotional trauma, Kundalini's divine spark has a lasting impact on our life as it pierces the core of our inner being to reveal an aspect of ourselves once lost but now found. And with its discovery comes a feeling of our being reborn with a renewed sense of enthusiasm for life and connection to our world. This is the "light" of which religions speak, even if many have lost their own. Yet those who manage to reach this inner summit of spiritual enlightenment will feel a greater reverence for life in seeing themselves as part of all that exists, *including a colony of feral cats*. In short, we no longer feel separated by divisive thinking or fearful of being wholly ourselves. Instead, we feel as one with all things — or a great conscious stride nearer to it.

Kundalini Simulation 1
(Remembering The Ocean)

Religious scripture is a mystery at best, often documenting events long after they have occurred by people who did not witness them. Yet there is evidence to suggest that the founders of those early religions were attempting to document their own spiritual revelations arising from a kundalini awakening. We can even suggest that the original intent of religion was to impart the wisdom of their enlightenment experiences upon novice seekers by communicating the insights gained from these powerful episodes of self-illumination. This may help to explain why many religions share the same spiritual core values, if little else.

Unfortunately, the language and intent of such information can also be altered in passing through the hands of people whose agendas are not aligned with matters of the spirit. Today, their editorial meddling has created a conflict of interest where religious texts may still convey some of their founding truths while also acting as vehicles for political propaganda and cultish mind control. Fortunately, we can gain some sense of the original wisdom imparted during a Kundalini Awakening through a mental exercise that simulates one of its best known aspects, which is the feeling of boundless unity with all of existence.

As earlier stated, a Kundalini awakening typically envelopes us in an overwhelming feeling of love. This makes us far more receptive to new wisdom and profound inner transformations in feeling both euphoric and somehow "protected" from harm. Unfortunately, we do not have the benefit of feeling this way in our everyday lives where our existence is largely defined by boundaries and barriers of fearful selfishness. Nor is our stubbornly certain mind known for its willingness to surrender control of our perception of reality. As such, it may be helpful to begin this process by recognizing that the institutions of science and religion both generally agree that life arose from a single cause. But while no moral code or gender has been attributed to this cause by scientists, its affect is self-evident in that we are each a part of its living legacy.

This popular "unity" model of life's origin confirms the underlying connection we share with one another, regardless of how we choose to interpret that original event. Yet the dominance of our physical senses keeps us focussed on the objective reality of the material realm, thereby promoting a sense our being separate from everything else. Further complicating matters is that we have mentally separated from others into opposing teams based on politics, religion, intellect, race, gender and other traits. However, using our all-powerful imagination, we can transcend these illusions of separateness by envisioning that original source of all life as a cosmic ocean filled with conscious energy.

NOTE: Read the following passage, then use it later as the basis for a meditative visualization to help you increase your feeling of connectedness.

...

In the beginning, there was a cosmic ocean teaming with life energy. Like any body of water, our cosmic ocean also expanded its reach by separating into smaller aspects of itself and forming the equivalent of rivers, streams, bogs or short-lived rain puddles from which passing birds can drink. Yet, no matter its location or incarnation, each of those aspects remains an expression of the whole from which it arose.

Likewise, no matter how small or insignificant our life may seem to us, we have not lost our founding identity as part of that which created us. In this way, this temporary human form we take is just a convincing outward illusion assisted by the perceptual limitations imposed upon our minds by our five physical senses. Yet inwardly we remain as we always were — an expression of that one unified source of energy from which we all have grown toward conscious maturity.

And just as each raindrop remains a part of the first great ocean from which it arose, so do we remain as part of that founding cosmic whole. We can refer to this as "God" or whatever we wish, yet without its being we would also not exist to contemplate the boundless mysteries of life as this eternal spark of consciousness cloaked in human form.

Moreover, the widely-accepted belief that we all arose from a single unified source gives each of us a valid reason to recognize that *everyone* in our world, whether human or animal, is also a part of us, just as we are a part of them, and will forever remain, given energy's lifespan.

As such, we are like the members of a single cosmic family, whether in love or at war, bound forever by our indivisible pedigree as roaming little sparks of self-awareness trying to find our way back home.

...

Kundalini Simulation 2
(The Grateful Embrace)

As noted, Kundalini Awakenings can trigger intense feelings of loving reverence for all things as we awaken to our interconnectedness to the essence of life itself. This inner sense of knowing and its attributed powerful emotions then propels us to reach out and reconnect to that greater whole in feeling it as a part of ourselves.

Although a profoundly personal experience, we can simulate it here using another mental exercise. This allows us to temporarily transcend the illusion of our separateness created by our social conditioning and the social identities we adopt from society.

NOTE: Here again, read the exercise first, then use it as the basis for a future meditative visualization to increase your loving reverence for life.

...

We begin by closing our eyes and imagining someone or something that evokes our deepest feelings of love and devotion. This emotional attachment can be to a marriage partner, child, parent, a beloved family pet, or even a cherished place in the wilderness. Let us then imagine ourselves embracing what we love as a heartfelt gesture of gratitude for its existence and for bringing so much joy into our lives.

In feeling our loving gratitude flow out from the core of our being, we may even cry or laugh out loud for joy; an emotional response that will serve us well for what comes next.

In having reached the summit of emotional intensity in focussing on what we love, let us then imagine opening our eyes to find that what we are embracing is not just one person, place or thing, but the entire world, including even those we dislike or disagree with. In short, let us imagine embracing everyone and everything in our loving arms.

Although nothing can compare to the actual experience, this can help us to understand how spiritual reverence is felt by those receiving this gift of worldly wisdom in context of a genuine mystical epiphany.

In this transcendent state of mind, we see our entire world through the peaceful eyes of an all-encompassing appreciation for the existence of all things. Forgiving faults and failures, our mind is free to care for the well-being of others as our fearful impulses recede and the core of our authentic being emerges as the essence of love itself.

...

Understandably, the struggles of living in a competitive society and coping with the selfishness of others can offer us more reasons to push the world away than to lovingly embrace it. We may therefore find this exercise useful in offering us a momentary reprieve from the stresses of daily life by using our imagination to rise above our human dramas and drift awhile in a silent, starlit expanse of the cosmic sea where the artificial boundaries of mind and body dissolve to reveal a magnificent unified "us" awaiting our future return.

The Illusion of Independence

Maintaining a reverent and inclusive state of mind is not easy when even our own body is pulling us in the opposite direction. Yet we have reached a critical point with our war-making, agricultural and lifestyle proliferation technologies that we need to find a sustainable balance for our future survival lest we destroy the very world upon which our continued existence depends.

One of the factors that keeps us from seeing the light in this regard is the illusion of independence, wherein our five senses and physical body conspire to make us believe that we are somehow separate from everything else in our world. At one level, this is true, because we are a unique biological entity negotiating life from a subjective state of mind. But for the most part, our independence is a perceptual fallacy.

That illusion is now creating serious problems in our interdependent world as our intelligence allows the fruits of our selfishness to grow unchecked to where they can endanger the lives of all species on a large scale, including our own. At the root of this problem is our quest for dominance and our subsequent condemning of weakness in all forms. Here, under the influence of our Bio-Psychology, we attempt to prove ourselves the top candidate for mating in ways that range from flexing our muscles and driving fast cars to cruising nuclear-armed warships along the coastal waters of our alpha male rivals in foreign nations. In short, the once simple matter of ensuring that our sperm is destined to fertilize the most eggs in our village has now metastasized into a global quest for dominance by men who are pathologically stuck in a selfishly aggressive mode of consciousness. And what they least feel in beating us into submission is a reverence for life — ours, or even their own.

Further inciting men's lust for power is their associating the state of "dependency" with childhood weakness. This propels some men toward tragic extremes in proving their independence. Yet their futile attempts to deny reality are easily dismissed by simple truths, such as leadership being dependent on followers, or wealth on having paying customers.

Simply breathing defies this illusion because we cannot live without oxygen — nor food, water and shelter. Yet the way some glory-seeking men carry on, they would claim their independence from the sun just to avoid sharing the spotlight with someone else. However, in grasping for power on such a massive scale, their failures also cannot simply be remedied by declaring bankruptcy and moving on.

Such is the case for men drilling thousands of underwater oil wells in our oceans without having the technology to prevent a catastrophic loss of sea life and habitat from their imminent spills. Ironically, aside from cutting into profits, perhaps they also see *the protection of life* as somehow being "women's work." Sadly, this same reckless attitude is threatening life wherever men have mentally separated their want for power from all other concerns including their own need to live on a planet that can sustain their future lives and sperm count.

This pattern of male apathy is seen in all facets of industrialized life, as businessmen dump industrial waste or even human excrement from entire cities into our oceans, while carelessly spraying herbicides and pesticides on anything that threatens a singular plant type from which their own existence is sustained. And now, women have joined them.

We can already predict the final tragic outcome of our story in failing to plan for nothing more than our economic success, while recklessly looting and polluting our planet so that it also winds up being just one more lifeless piece of stone drifting in the cosmic darkness.

In contrast to our destructive illusion of separation from reality and its consequences, we would be wiser to see our world through the eyes of a farmer growing apples in a natural outdoor setting.

As that grower, we have no choice but to be reverential and inclusive in our relationship to the natural world; we cannot only favor the apple but must also value in equal measure the soil in which it grows, as well as the rain, the sun and all that contributes to nurturing our fruit. Here we embody a reverential lifestyle by embracing the interconnectedness of all things in life's delicate web of existence. And we do so knowing that the removal of a single element may cause everything to collapse.

In reverence, we seed a path through life that avoids a future harvest of death. As such, we must see our world not only through the eyes of a grower of apples, but as the seed itself in recognizing that our future success depends on the equal success of many others beyond ourselves. And so, rather than stumbling our way toward extinction, let us adopt a more enlightened approach by rejecting all such irreverent behavior.

Throwing Water At The Wind

We can strengthen the case for reverential thinking even further if we remind ourselves of the old adage: "What goes around, comes around." After all, it is not only orbiting planets that make cyclical returns, but also our behavior towards others. As such, it is not just a mere tenet of religion that *what we do unto others will return in equal measure* but also a warning to the wise that is supported by the laws of physics.

Returning to the physics of our human psychology, let us recall that if we steal the "self esteem energy" of others, it causes in them a need to win back that energy to regain their lost sense of balance. In most cases, they will replenish it by exacting their revenge against us.

However, if we are too strong or important to retaliate against, then they may choose to redirect their need for vengeance against a weaker human or animal victim who acts as a symbolic proxy for us — their intended target. Yet by attacking the innocent, they may also set off a chain-reaction of vengeful side-affects if those victims redirect their own want for revenge on other unsuspecting strangers. In this way, our initial attack may be avenged by countless proxies "infected" by our own victim's attack against them. And if we consider how many people in our world are unable to exact revenge upon their attacker, then this may explain why so many random attacks occur against the innocent who become unwitting links in an endless chain of vengeance.

We can find evidence for this everywhere, including among *middle managers* victimized by high level bosses but having only the power to reclaim their lost self-esteem by attacking employees below them. And while some will dull their pain with addictions, others feel a need to conquer others to escape this feeling of being a "loser" in life. In the extreme, we hear about them on the news for having committed mass murders against innocent strangers who also act as proxies for those who made these energy depleted individuals feel equally victimized.

In acting out this way, such people are trying to ensure that everyone *feels their pain* or that they are recognized as the "winner" in having had the last word — often before killing themselves to avoid losing further to society's legal revenge system. As these examples show, negotiating a fair balance with others proves a wise choice, not only to maintain a peaceful society, but also to prevent acts of terrorism by those who feel the need to avenge their emotional losses. In short, our selfishness will always catch up with us eventually, from one direction or another.

This situation is akin to throwing water at the wind, where a portion of it will always return to land on us. Likewise, we must be thoughtful in how we act toward others lest we create a kind of energy-deprived social environment wherein we must live in fear of complete strangers who may secretly be plotting to exact revenge against us for someone else's psychic debt — even one they could have inherited from our own original acts of vengeance — "What goes around, comes around."

Ultimately, it is not wishful thinking but reality itself that forces us to accept that having a reverence for life is the most logical approach to organizing our societies. In short, we need not live in constant fear if we choose victory for all wherever possible. Only this can ensure a more balanced and joyful world for all of us to live in.

I Am You

A reverential attitude is a natural outward expression of being aware of our interconnectedness to the greater web of life. In seeing our world in a more inclusive light, we are inspired to express our respect and innate goodwill in a much broader and far-reaching manner.

This intuitive sense of concern for others is often a residual spiritual gift left in the wake of a Kundalini Awakening, yet we need not have such an experience to benefit from the wisdom it imparts.

Among its other valuable insights is that our world acts as a mirror reflecting back our attitude. As such, some will see their love reflected back to them, others their selfishness or hatred. In short, the loving are not to blame for any lack of love in our world. Nor the joyful.

This mirroring affect can also act as a powerful teaching tool to show others how to treat us by how we treat them. Subsequently, we cannot expect mercy from those we abuse, nor words of praise from those we condemn. As such, we must approach others with kindness and respect to better ensure living in a world that mirrors these same virtues.

Ultimately, we can inspire a more reverential world just by seeing ourselves in others and treating them as we would want to be treated. We can even plot this inclusive attitude using an IPSFA Sequence:

I	**I Am You** (An attitude for treating ourselves kindly through others).
P	To ensure that we get the best treatment, in whatever form we encounter ourselves.
S	Treat others like an *independent* extension of ourselves — be kind to ourselves in any form.
F	To cause the suffering of others as a result of our inconsiderate treatment of them.
A	Having to share our time and energy; not always focussing only on our selfish needs and wants.

In expressing a reverence for life, we are no longer all that matters; an attitude that can bring us greater joy in redefining our relationship to life itself. We may then, for instance, no longer lie, cheat, steal, or take unfair advantage of others. We may also stop killing insects out of a higher regard for other lifeforms. In exuding a reverential attitude, we allow all living things to tend to their survival and even attempt to ensure their safety should our needs endanger their existence. This may mean relocating spiders or opening a window for a fly to escape rather than mercilessly crushing it — knowing that, but for a twist of cosmic fate, we could well have been born a fly at the mercy of our attitude.

And in meeting a stranger, we see not a lesser or greater person, but a reflection of ourselves; a fellow spiritual traveller also hoping to live a joyful life without needless suffering at another's hand. Subsequently, we must extend our kindness to ourselves in every form we encounter, be it human, animal or plant, for that is how we would also want to be treated in return. Admittedly, things do not always work out as we may desire, nor will this approach endear us to mosquitos or crocodiles. Yet the overall message is clear in that showing a reverence for the life of all sentient beings is a direct reflection of our conscious evolution as a human being — an ethical act of spiritual communion.

The opportunities for showing a reverence for life are endless once we recognize how much life is all around us and seeking to live its own version of a joyful existence. For instance, our lawn is a living entity, as is the soil in which it grows. We should therefore avoid mistreating the soil because it is the life support system not only for our lawn, but also for countless creatures existing in an interconnected system of energy trading of which we may be completely unaware. In this way, showing respect for the soil benefits every life depending on it, including ours.

Ultimately, our goal is not to obsess about "doing no harm," but to ensure that we are acting with the highest regard in our treatment of other life forms by never intentionally leaving *victims* in our wake. In this way, we act as living proof for the existence of something greater within ourselves than only biological selfishness and fear. It also shows us that spirituality is not about wielding magic powers, making psychic predictions or praying our way to a better seat in heaven. Instead, it is about a simple change in our attitude that could change everything.

CHAPTER 16
Playing with God

In each chapter, we have seen examples of how our *Bio-Psychology* can unconsciously direct our social behavior in countless ways. Under the influence of our instinctual glory-seeking impulse, for instance, we feel inwardly compelled to draw attention to ourselves as a top candidate for mating. This is why young men can feel driven to buy a radiant red sports car, and young women to wear an equally radiant red dress to attract a potential mate from among that procession of lustful drivers.

In ironic contrast, our fear-based comfort-seeking impulse acts as an equally powerful counterforce that may compel us to avoid standing out as a competitive threat. This may cause us to buy a bland-looking automobile instead and dress to blend into a crowd to avoid detection by the more aggressive of social dominators and recreational bullies.

To say that we are inwardly conflicted would be an understatement. However, the net result of all this outward strutting for attention and dutiful trimming of our lawns to avoid upsetting our neighbors is that such activities can keep us admirably busy for decades without offering us any emotional nourishment in return. For this reason, we may begin to feel that something important is missing from our lives.

That *something*, as already identified in *The Invisible Economy*, is an emotionally meaningful pursuit to fill our spiritual cup; some means by which to actualize who we are instead of existing as an anonymous expression of various biological urges and socially-scripted demands. Let us therefore consider another of life's open secrets in that creative self-expression is vital to the lifelong process of our self-actualization; our conscious evolution depends on our being an *original* thinker.

Yet many of us are unfamiliar with this notion and may see creativity as just another form of monetized social competition for which we must be sufficiently "talented" to qualify. Moreover, even as we admire the artful self-expressions of others, the act of creative thinking itself may be discouraged in our culture because it causes us to become more individualized and self-governing; a trait for which innovative artists can be equally famous. In short, creativity inspires individuality.

Subsequently, to promote mass conformity, leaders must defeat our inborn urge toward individual self-expression. In this way, we can be kept marching in thoughtless unison as a regimented mass of obedient workers dutifully serving our nation's economy. As a result, many of us now exist as frustrated creators, having become spiritually inhibited in our ability to know the life-affirming joys of creative self-expression.

In reclaiming our creative birthright, we may also discover, as many artists do, that the very act of creating is like "playing with God" in that it also involves the constant unfolding of mysteries and miracles as we venture into the unknown. Ultimately, we are never fully in control of our creative process. Instead, we act more as a conduit for subconscious mental content and various *unseen forces* that seem to conspire with us in having declared our intention to create.

For example, we may experience sudden flashes of critical insight, immaculately-timed instructional dreams and other such unplanned conscious events without which we might never have attained such a level of excellence as we often surprisingly do. These "happy accidents" not only bring a child-like sense of awe and wonder to the creative process, but also make it an incredibly joyful and inspirational activity that we can engage in throughout our entire lives.

Let us therefore consider the act of creation and those obstacles we may encounter in collaborating with our creator within to actualize the limitless imaginings of our inner being in the outer world.

A Spiritual Reality Check

Creative self-expression is vital to a joyful life because it stimulates our conscious evolution and allows us to experience our very own inherent "superpowers" as an individual by materializing the spiritual contents of our creative imagination. Conversely, to demonstrate how the process of being culturally socialized can undermine our inborn urge to create, let us answer a question that may already be familiar to our minds:

"What would you buy if you won the lottery?"

To make this more interesting, we can pretend that our winnings are limitless. In this way, our decision-making will not be inhibited by our fear of running out of money — we can just keep on spending.

And now, invest some time into writing a list of impulsive purchases that you might make if given a chance to spend an unlimited amount of money on anything you desire.

NOTE: Do not continue reading until you have made at least a partial list as this exercise may be critical to your future joy.

Your Lottery Win Wishlist:

1) (Example) Buy a really expensive car.
2) (Example) Eat at a really expensive restaurant.
3) (Example) Buy a house for somebody else, just to be "nice."

In making this list, our mind may regurgitate the symbolic trophies of a ready-made path to joy that was pre-programmed for us by our culture and media. As with our *A Reason To Live* exercise, this may reveal underlying motives that we may not express in words but only through symbolic purchases — such as buying that radiant red sports car. For many, an expensive yacht or private jet may top the list, thereby revealing a glory-seeking desire to draw attention to ourselves and our newfound economic status. However, the true purpose of this exercise is to establish *what is missing* from our list of potential purchases.

Typically absent are items such as a musical instrument, art and craft supplies; tools for sculpting, or ingredients for experimental cooking. In short: *the tools of the creative trade.* In a broader context, this may expose a psychological bias in our culture that trains us to seek our joy outside of ourselves instead of inward and to invest our imagination in dreams of heroic material conquests — "Someday, I'm going to buy myself a really nice…[insert name of desired product here]."

Obviously this will not be true for everyone, including those already engaged in artistic hobbies or creatively-oriented careers. However, it does give us the opportunity to question if we are perhaps missing out on an important part of our lives by not making use of our creative imagination as a means to greater joy and personal empowerment.

As may be evident from our list, commercial media helps to promote our mass diversion away from creativity and towards consumerism by offering us *symbolic joy substitutes* to keep us dutifully spending. This is also why we can predict so easily what will appear on the lottery win wishlist of most people. But while spending our way to joy may serve the greater good of bankers and business owners, it can also leave us sitting atop a mountain of meaningless joy decoys wondering why we still feel so incomplete after having bought "all the right things."

To better understand how our creative desires can be suppressed or redirected under the influence of our culture, let us retrace a common path of social indoctrination that may reveal where we might also have abandoned our own spiritual urge to become a creator.

Artists In Exile

Artistic self-expression requires not only an inspired imagination, but also a sense of spontaneity. Unfortunately, these vital aspects of the creative mind are of minimal use in pursuing a scripted life of material comfort. And that is also the kind of life we are being prepared for in school classrooms — the repetition of accepted thoughts and routines.

Here, we are taught to live each day by clocks and calendars as we follow a predefined cultural recipe for living a predictably "normal" life as future adults. Beyond basic academic skills, we are also being taught when to eat, even if not hungry; when to wake up, even if still tired, and when to buy gifts, even if not feeling generous on that scheduled buying day. In short, we are being trained to *avoid* spontaneity. In this way, we are being culturally "brainwashed" to accept a simple-minded existence of lackluster social conformity that makes us *predictable*.

But teachers are not to blame, for they must live by the same clocks and calendars and can teach only what is prescribed by their overseers in government, business or religion. And this is how all of us are being systematically enticed to surrender our unique sense of identity and creative potential for a life of servitude not unlike that of a worker bee in the economic hives of our society.

As a child entering school, our developing mind has but two choices: we can either become an obedient conformist, or risk a life of poverty by clearing a path to joy guided by our own conscious authority. We can therefore empathize with any child who hates school, not only for forcing us into mental combat for *class dominance,* but also for causing us to abandon any self-seeking, creatively-inspired path to joy that fails to have commerce as its primary focus. As a result, many young adults will flounder as anonymous specks forced to buy their daily ration of substitute joy at a shopping mall while watching others succeed on creative paths they had long abandoned. That is our tragic plight when our creator within has been forced to live in exile.

To be fair to our culture and its dedicated educators, some of us find comfort in having others tell us how to live and who to be in that it offers us a sense of certainty while delegating responsibility for our life decisions to someone else. In addition, a higher education can propel us into a rewarding career that may even allow us to be creative in ways not directed toward consumer predation. Yet it must be said that such regimented mental programming stimulates development largely in one sector of the brain at the cost of negating others that could lead us toward a more emotionally-fulfilling life of creative self-exploration.

This assertion is supported by MRI scans of musicians who show an increase in their brain growth from a lifetime of playing an instrument.

In other words, our creative activities have the potential to not only expand our conscious horizons and actualize our greater joy potential, but also trigger the development of new brain structures. As such, we must wonder what heights of joy we ourselves might be failing to reach by not engaging with this creative aspect of our conscious lives.

Our inborn need to create is robustly supported throughout history, including by those ancient humans who invented paint so they could also express on the walls of caves the thoughts, images and emotions that defined their own life experiences. In later years, people engaged in basket weaving and other hands-on crafts wherein their minds were constantly tasked to invent new designs and improvements. Today, this kind of individualized inventive thinking is less critical as automated machines churn out masses of flawlessly identical products, leaving us with little more to do than buy them.

Our human urge to be involved in the creative process is further validated by an anecdote from the early days of food marketing. Here, one company was struggling to sell its ready-made cake baking mix to housewives who felt they were *cheating* by not making it themselves. The company solved both these problems by instructing women to add an egg to the mix to keep them involved. And so, many broken eggs later, that cake mix went on to become a top-selling favorite.

What this anecdote reveals, aside from the guilt that women of that era may have felt for cutting culinary corners in the kitchen, is that our personal involvement in the creative process is still important to us.

Obviously, the obstacles we face to living in more creatively-vibrant and self-expressive cultures cannot be solved by simply adding an egg. Yet all along the path of human history, we find evidence of our feeling the need to engage in the creative process as an outward expression of the process of creating ourselves. And so it seems reasonable to assume that our trajectory forward in any culture is to look back and see if we did not accidentally leave something important behind. Yet in doing so, it is equally important not to leave such retrospection to those only interested in art and culture for its resale value. Instead, what we must work toward is *a species-wide rebirthing of the creative spirit.*

Capturing The Spirit

The Material Path to Joy introduced us to the *C–SIX States of Being* and in particular, the *Spiritual States of Being*. Here on the *Spiritual Path to Joy*, we can further call upon their wisdom to guide our way. For instance, *Creativity* (C5) is directly opposed by *Convenience* (C2), which means that being creative is a biological inconvenience and that our body may even fight our impulse to create. However, this assertion is more theoretical in that most dedicated artists feel they have little choice but to create because it feels spiritually akin to breathing. Yet it does suggest that a more comfort-oriented person may avoid exploring their creative potential because — beyond the obvious investment in time and energy that it requires — it may cause them to feel physically, mentally or emotionally uncomfortable for being so demanding.

This reveals yet another helpful way to use the *C–SIX* by comparing how biases in our own life priorities may be affecting our creative joy potential. For instance, by examining our daily activities, we can see if we spend more time engaged in satisfying our lower, material-based biological urges (C1 – C3) than those of the spirit in the upper-levels (C4 – C6). We can be even more precise by identifying which activities feed our spiritual desire for creativity. In this way, we can increase our creative joy potential by correcting any imbalance showing in how we choose to experience life. Ultimately, this can prevent us from losing years of joyful activity to having made the quest for physical comfort and personal security our only ambition in life.

Harkening back to the *Relationship Ledger* from the *Relational Path to Joy*, this also reveals how critical the *Spiritual States of Being* are to ensuring our overall joy on all of the four life paths.

To help us better understand how the priorities of the *C–SIX* states apply at a more practical level, we can use the activity of *gardening* as an example. Here, if we engage in gardening as exercise to relieve stress or boredom, then our concern for the outcome of our creative efforts would be secondary to our want for comfort. Conversely, if we were to use gardening as a creative pursuit, then this would lead to a change in our attitude and the quality of the outcome. Suddenly, our every action would take on greater significance than being mere "yard work," which then inspires us to take a more thoughtful and relaxed approach. The result will be a more artistically-sculpted landscape that also leaves us feeling more emotionally fulfilled than had we shown no interest in what we were doing or in the final outcome of our efforts.

The same applies to cooking when we treat it as a vehicle for creative self-expression rather than just a means to our survival. Ultimately, no matter what activities we engage in, there is a great spiritual advantage in taking a more creative approach. We can further confirm this by taking a stroll through the streets of any inner city landscape.

Here we will see how architecture can also prioritize our quest for material comfort — as evident by the sullen, box-like look of utility in many buildings we encounter. By contrast, we will also find that some buildings were designed to capture their architect's spirit in solid form or the vibrant character of the community that it serves. Visually, this can also alter our mood by playfully lifting our spirits in passing by.

In becoming aware of such opportunities for creative self-expression and recognizing their importance to both our individual and collective mental well-being, we can begin to lay the cultural foundation for a far richer emotional life for all people by balancing our social priorities to meet not only our basic material needs, but also those of our spirit.

The Reluctant Creator

We all have the capacity to be creators by virtue of our imagination. Yet as we have seen, this tool of self-expression may be suppressed to control our minds and priorities as a nation for political and economic reasons. We may also divert our attention away from creative thinking due to personal inclinations or life priorities. In all such circumstances, we lose a significant path to joy that can inspire, enrich and entertain us throughout our entire lives. A further obstacle to unleashing the power of our personal creativity is when we feel intimidated by those more advanced in their creative skills and expression, which can make us feel inferior and thereby diminish our self-esteem.

This internal struggle is the result of our being conditioned to view creativity as a form of competition rather than a path to joy. This is yet another example of how our interpretation of reality can become the victim of cultural stereotyping.

Based on our earlier evaluations, stereotyping has already proven itself to be the enemy of individuality, curiosity and our understanding of spirituality. And naturally, it has also infected our understanding of the purpose of creativity in many cultures. Yet this corruption began by promoting another stereotype, which is that competition is good for society. Yes, but what kind? We will later consider this notion in detail, but we can already predict its flaws by expecting a 100% human infant mortality rate if mothers start *competing* against their babies for food and shelter instead of sharing with them, as nature intended. However, given that the males of most species are not biologically attuned for infant care, we can understand why the need to rebalance our social priorities is easily overlooked by those pathological male glory seekers who infect our societies with a belief in that competition is the essence of humanity. As such, they will treat all social activities as a contest to display their dominance, including our creative endeavors.

Here again, the primary facilitator of this mass indoctrination is the school classroom in teaching us to compete for academic and physical dominance. We then bring this adversarial attitude into the monetary ecosystem, wherein it infuses everything with a glory-seeking ethic. As a result, creative self-expression has been transformed into a popularity contest for fame and fortune not unlike race car driving or marketing soft drinks. This mindset is best illustrated by "pop" music, wherein the music is often treated as secondary by promoting an artist's sex appeal or fashion sense, which audiences then mimic in competing for their own share of public attention. This is also why so many bands sound identical in trying to mimic the top-selling artists of the day rather than daring to express their own unique sonic individuality.

This market-driven *outward* focus on economic exploitation ignores the spiritual function of creativity as a path to facilitate our conscious evolution through the quest for excellence. Instead, it becomes another extension of our *Bio-Psychological* glory-seeking urge as we compete to be "number one" at the top of the charts.

As a result, by seeing the creative process as a form of competition, we may become a reluctant creator in wanting to avoid the emotional stresses related to competition itself — including being judged and ridiculed for our creative efforts. Many of us understand this feeling in having been intimidated in childhood for not demonstrating the same skills as a fellow classmate, whether in drawing a horse, singing a song, or playing a piano. Subsequently, we may today feel intimidated by any form of creative activity that threatens to make us feel as foolish as a nervous child under the scrutiny of our parents, teachers and peers.

Yet we can overcome our artistic performance anxiety by realizing that this inborn urge to create and express ourselves was not intended for evaluating our human market value based on quarterly earnings. Instead, aside from its obvious utility in problem-solving, our creative ingenuity acts as a spiritual conduit to a greater inner dialogue with ourselves. As such, we need not feel intimidated or envious if someone is more talented or popular because we are each engaged in the same act of opening up new frontiers of creative expression within ourselves. We can instead see one another as sources of inspiration that allow our inner child to better explore, create and play as it was always meant to do — for the pure joy of it. It is not important what some competitive art collector or reseller thinks of our work because their game is one of exclusion for the sake of individual glory and profiteering.

And as we take our first brave steps to opening a dialogue with our creator within, we should also keep in mind that even the very best had to start *at the beginning* — where all things are made possible.

Three Ways To Play

Whether improvising in a jazz quartet, a comedy troupe or on a piece of sketch paper, we are engaged in a form of playing. This is why we can open ourselves to vast new horizons of pleasure-seeking when we invite creative self-expression into our lives. We may even be inspired to invent innovative new products or ideas to improve our society.

As stated earlier, we can assist this evolutionary process by becoming aware of how the *C–SIX States of Being* can influence our choices of activity and social behavior. It may also be useful to investigate the act of playing itself in relation to our joy-seeking activities on the spiritual path. In this way, we can not only fine-tune our approach to creatively expressing ourselves, but also determine if we are playing on the right field to score our desired emotional victories.

In that regard, categorized below are three popular ways to play and explanations as to how they relate to our lifelong quest for joy:

1. **Physical combat against others:** This is the means by which most animals compete for survival and territorial dominance; we express this through our participation in competitive sports and visually through beauty contests or status-based displays of materialism. Although the idea of being selected as the winner makes us feel happy or relieved to not have lost, it is nonetheless an activity that relies on engaging with others to defeat them, be it symbolically or by physical force.

2. **Mental combat against others:** Here we use our minds to elevate our social status by dominating others with displays of our superior memory retention, strategic thinking or mental trickery. This is done through academic testing, games of skill, public debates or committing masterful crimes to compete against the minds of law enforcers. Here as well, the essence of such activity is a competition against others to defeat them; *a creatively-enhanced variation on the theme of war.*

3. **Creative combat against ourselves:** Here we engage our mind in creative activities to accelerate our conscious evolution as a spiritual pursuit. We do this through a lifetime of quests for personal excellence in self-expression channeled through subjectively meaningful activities including songwriting, painting, scientific exploration, fashion and

other forms of creative design work. In this arena, we have no rivals to exceed but only *the less-awakened creator we had been yesterday*.

Here as well, we must be cautious not to stereotype creative pursuits as being the only worthwhile activity. After all, we can feel a profound sense of joy and communion with our team members in playing sports, although at the cost of creating tribal divisions and a vast number of "losers" being left behind. Skillful playing can also be highly creative, as well as the innovative strategies used for winning. It is these aspects of physical combat that also make sporting events so widely appealing.

Meanwhile, children feel intuitively compelled to engage in physical challenges to develop their bodily coordination and self-confidence, just as most young animals do. But building up a sweat is not enough to live a happy life. We must therefore also engage in solitary acts of creative self-expression to promote our spiritual development, which has the added benefit of leaving us with fewer injuries to contend with.

In creatively challenging our mind to rise to ever-greater heights of self-expression, we also fulfill our spiritual mandate to become a wiser, more self-empowered version of our authentic selves. And when we direct our competitive energies inward, we also help to promote a more peaceful world by relying on ourselves as the source of our joy rather than engaging in conflicts wherein our defeating of others determines how happy we will feel on any given day.

Killing The Messenger

Taking a longer scenic route, our purpose herein has been to highlight creativity as a tool for our spiritual development; one that can both replenish our self-esteem and lead us further along our path toward self-awareness and enlightenment. For those seeking technical advice, there is always a fellow creator or group nearby, ready to share their artistic knowledge with newcomers and offer good advice.

Yet as we come to the end of this section on spirituality and prepare to consider more wide-ranging global topics in the chapters ahead, it may be helpful to revisit an earlier statement about the threat posed to our creative self-expression by those in power.

In that regard, to gain control over society, an ambitious leader must enforce a predictable, repetitious survival routine for others to follow, which is the antithesis of any *creative* thinking process. Subsequently, the spontaneity and evolving nature of our creative mind poses its own threat to those forcing such a restrictive lifestyle on others. This has led to the creation of laws and cultural traditions to impose a regimented way of life on each new generation to ensure that it remains as easy to control as those that had come before it. Here is that mental script:

I	**Tradition** (A pattern of behavior typically repeated to prove our cultural or social identity).	
P	To feel certain in who we are; to control the uncertain future by endlessly repeating the past.	
S	Repeat what was done yesterday; avoid new approaches to life and unfamiliar ways of thinking.	
F	To feel disoriented and powerless within our existence; to lose our identity; to feel uncertain.	
A	Suppressing our spiritual, intellectual and social progress by shunning innovation.	

In addition, people are hostile to ideas that threaten their traditional ways of life. While the natural course of the creative mind is to evolve, innovate and improve itself, we may find instead an anti-progressive mindset among those who want to maintain their hold on power or avoid making any kind of social change for fear of the unknown:

I	**The Fundamentalist** (A staunch defender of any traditional means of controlling their society.)	
P	Maintaining absolute control over our life by controlling the lives of others; a scripted certainty.	
S	Discourage curiosity, creativity, freethinking; defend against the threat of change; burn books.	
F	Losing our means of control over our life and that of others; uncertainty; loss of identity.	
A	Spiritual stagnation from inertia; constant inner fear directed as anger against others.	

Such oppression may be popular among leaders, but not always their followers. And so, based on the laws of nature and physics, whenever a government attempts to impose some predictable life of dull-minded routine on its citizens, it is met by an equally predictable retaliation. This may take the form of public displays of civil disobedience wherein various kinds of freethinkers seek to gain attention and support for protecting our freedoms of choice. But this kind of anti-establishment posturing is often little more than street theatre because any genuine threat to those in power is quickly met with a show of force in an effort to "kill the messenger" who dares to seed doubt in the public's mind.

Since ancient times, killing dissenters or "enemies of the state" has been done as a public relations campaign to show us what awaits if we stray from our traditional role as obedient servants to those in power. Today, the media carries out these public executions by destroying the reputations of truth tellers and whistleblowers, perhaps by portraying them in ways that shame us into dismissing their ideas. Ironically, this creates a mental paradox in many cultures wherein the truth is treated as a lie to protect those lies masquerading as truth. In this way, the rule of the powerful is maintained over their misguided followers below.

We find evidence for this whenever innovative ideas to improve our society or reverse our planet's ecological decline are *publicly executed* in media to protect the economic interests of those who control the more traditional ways of making food, energy, medicine or armed warfare.

Similarly, too many religions have turned spirituality into a stagnant pool of superstitious rituals and storybook fantasies to prevent us from becoming wise enough to escape a substitute reality wherein we may never know the soulful joys of mental and bodily freedom.

Subsequently, as we engage in playing with God, others are engaged in trying to play our God, which acts as a fitting introduction to where we are going to venture next.

Let us now bring forward the many insights gained in traveling the material, relational and spiritual paths as we continue on our journey of self-discovery along *The Global Path to Joy*.

PART FIVE
The Global Path to Joy

CHAPTER 17
Empires of the Mind

A Trojan Horse, by broader definition, is any outwardly attractive gift whose inner contents are meant to harm or exploit us. Looking back on the history of commercial television, we see a medium that has also gained its power and influence over the public by acting in a similarly sneaky fashion.

Attracting millions of hapless viewers with the promise of being entertained, few of us knew of the strategic boardroom negotiations taking place to rent our collective mental attention to the makers of laundry soaps, automobiles and other consumer products in return for their financing of our favorite shows. Such unflattering matters are not shared with viewers even today. In this way, television acts like a Trojan Horse in disguising its want to control how we think and spend our money behind the illusory facade of keeping us "entertained."

Beyond instructing viewers on what fashions and accessories to buy to mimic its latest crop of media-generated pop idols, television also exposes us to various tools of mental persuasion. Among them is the "laugh track," which alerts us when to laugh during a comedy show, lest we fail to see the humor in it for ourselves. But what is never broadcast is the intelligence gathered by human behavior researchers who found that we are more likely to laugh if surrounded by a group of laughing people — which the laugh track simulates for those of us watching at home alone. In this way, our minds are being tricked into believing that a show is more entertaining than it may actually be.

Now let us move beyond the economic motivations of commercial media to consider how our minds are being similarly conditioned with the public broadcasting of values, beliefs and attitudes by the systems that govern our societies.

Trained since childhood to conform to behaviors that best serve our rulers, we are subject to a form of mind control so effective that it has us believing that we are the ones making the decision to act, whether it be to sing a national anthem, serve an invisible God, or surrender our income to anonymous tax collectors. Yet our social indoctrination may also be a Trojan Horse if presented as a path to hope that only leads to a lifetime of servitude in one of many parasitic empires of the mind.

In clearing a global path to joy, let us explore the mental architecture of these exploitive human control systems so that we can design future societies that would allow all of us to thrive in greater peace, prosperity and freedom instead of always just a privileged few.

The Political Paradox

As global citizens, our collective quest for a joyful life would be far less complicated if every exploiter of the masses would openly confess their self-serving motives to us in advance. In this way, we could deny them that privilege or at least negotiate a more equitable settlement. But as political speech-making has long demonstrated, honesty is always the first casualty in any war for social domination.

Instead, our manipulators will deliberately create obstacles to our knowing their true intentions. One such infamous example occurred when tobacco executives and marketers promoted nicotine addiction to teenagers by declaring that smoking was a cool, sexy way to prove their maturity and social independence. And clearly, they succeeded by recruiting generations of young people to an addiction that gave them cancer and other wasting diseases. But measured by the values and standards of economics, our growing global addiction to a deadly poison represented a glorious victory for those in the tobacco industry and their grateful shareholders. In those circles, it is called "winning."

What this suggests is that money is more important than human life and that our only obligation as a willing betrayer of the public's trust is to find a way to conceal the truth from our victims.

As the unwitting public being preyed upon by such social predators, what makes us more susceptible to their devious trickery is a bias in our thinking that has us projecting outcomes in our favor. In short, we tend to be hopeful, at least where it concerns our own future success. This also makes it very easy for unscrupulous groups and individuals to deceive us for financial or political gain by simply claiming that their actions are meant to serve our best interests. In short, they are utilizing the now familiar "Promise of Joy" from our CPJ lexicon.

What motivates others to descend to such depths of depravity is that now equally familiar behavior of "glory seeking," wherein the winning combatant of a species — typically the dominant male — is awarded preferred access to prime territory and females. But whereas wild male chimpanzees and other primates must still rely on physical strength to intimidate their rivals into submission, we humans now rely on mass mind control as a bloodless substitute for dominating our own kind.

An example of such mind control is achieved by yet another familiar belief in the power of money, which allows any weakling to dominate society by our consensual agreement in the illusion of their *economic* might. In reality, all they own is a lot of hand-signed paper. Yet today, even the strongest must bow before these invisible masters of our global destiny, thus giving absolute power to those in control of what are essentially *make-believe* monetary trading systems.

Yet money is just one of many mentally-projected realities that our minds have embraced in the shared hope that good fortune will favor us someday. Among others are the imaginary borders surrounding our imaginary nations, where the power of our imagination controls most aspect of our lives, from housing prices to the laws that govern us. As with product marketing, we are also not educated as to how these mental containment systems induce the surrendering of our individual power to those who benefit from our submission to their will, be they pampered monarchs, religious clergy, or mass-murdering dictators.

Yet without public education or debate on such matters, we cannot address a glaring political paradox wherein we, as voting citizens, must trust in the "good intentions" of these self-serving alpha dominators to lead us toward a future state of genuine democracy and shared access to power. But all the evidence based on Bio-Psychology, natural law, human history and reality itself suggests that we would be foolish to expect our oppressors to bring us the keys to our freedom, for their empires can only exist by keeping us trapped in this needful state of child-like dependence on their supreme guidance and authority. And that is exactly why we, as ordinary citizens, must take the initiative to not only educate ourselves about our condition, but also mature to a higher level of self-determination by acknowledging what has been done to our minds for *thousands* of years by our rulers. It begins by exposing the most common form of mind control being administered to harvest our collective energy within any empire of the mind.

Promissory Mind Control

Whoever controls our mind, controls our actions. This one simple truth explains why we have all been subjected to a promissory form of mind control since childhood wherein we are offered a future reward for our obedient submission to others in the present.

As earlier revealed, our first experience of this kind is typically with our parents, who may promise us a reward in return for our achieving higher grades in school. Yet most parents have the integrity to deliver on such promises, not only because they care about us, but also because they face direct consequences for lying to us, including the loss of our trust and favor. Conversely, a person's immunity from direct retribution may embolden them to cheat us. That is why we may be targeted by foreign swindlers against whom we have little legal recourse. Similarly, the social and economic remoteness of political leaders can embolden them to lie to voters in also believing themselves immune from future punishment. In short, our remoteness from a social predator may give them the necessary courage to promise us anything.

Childhood is also the time when we are first exposed to promissory mind control on a social scale. In some cultures, this involves our being told about "Saint Nicholas," a bearded old man who brings gifts only to *well-behaved* children. The result is that we might obediently behave ourselves all year long in waiting for that day when our reward is said to be coming. This trains us early in life to delay our own satisfaction for the sake of a future reward. It also conditions us to trust that others will deliver on their promises. Yet far too often we find our trust being betrayed by people making promises that they never intend to keep.

Among them are religious charlatans who promise to deliver us to a prestigious future paradise in return for our lifelong yielding to their demands for money. Others include political candidates who steal our votes by promising to initiate social improvements that never come to fruition. Today, entire nations of citizens are being shamelessly misled by disingenuous rulers who have us believing that by serving their best interests, we will be serving ours in some glorious future paradise that never seems to materialize; a problem that would never arise in a *direct* democracy wherein citizens vote for social initiatives, not politicians.

Meanwhile, in convincing us to wait for our share of the prize, these social predators can enjoy the rewards of our faithful servitude and escape punishment before their crimes can be discovered. After all, we cannot demand a refund from a religious charlatan who has died, nor hold a lying politician to account once they have accepted a lucrative position with the company in whose interests they had been legislating while in office. Instead, we are often left with nothing but our bitter disappointment in return for having invested our time, money and trust into some unscrupulous social parasite.

As alluded to in *The Promise of Joy*, this form of mind control can have dire consequences for our future joy as global citizens. Once we are governed by a collective faith in the empty promises of our leaders, we may also be kept from questioning the integrity of their promises by laws that forbid such discussion or intelligence agencies that patrol our minds and behavior to ensure that we do not infect others with the truth of our dire predicament. Assisting those forces of oppression are angry mobs of "true believers" who will denounce us as a traitor if we dare to question our complicity in this blatant act of spiritual rape.

As a consequence, we may find ourselves trapped for generations in the exploitive mental empire of some deluded madman, held in place by a false hope that our future joy and prosperity must surely be on the way at the supreme guiding hand of our glorious leader.

All For One

In chapter four, we learned the importance of promissory mind control to sustaining our global economies. This is evident in the many kinds of products being sold under false pretenses, from openly fraudulent "anti-aging" creams to costly medical treatments that sicken more than they heal. Beyond product sales, promissory mind control is also used by grifters who promise to lead us to success in any form we desire by masquerading as a legitimate authority figure in that field.

Among them are fake modeling agents who promise young women a glamorous future career in return for an endless demand for fees to secure modeling work that never materializes. Also on that list is every unscrupulous government official who promises us a better future yet spends our tax money on personal luxury items and female escorts while awarding lucrative public contracts to their wealthy donors.

Beyond proving that human selfishness knows no bounds, this also reveals a common pattern of social behavior wherein people try to take advantage of us by pretending to be an authority figure without having any actual experience or proven success in that field. We will find them in all walks of life, including as politicians in high seats of power who have no history of ensuring anyone's future well-being but their own.

Today, we are inundated with advertisements from people promising to work miracles on our behalf, whether disguised as politicians, stock brokers, life coaches or spiritual gurus. And all it takes for them to lure us into their parasitic lairs is a little bit of creative lying about all the wonderful things they can do for us — *sometime* in the future.

Yet despite its effectiveness, promissory mind control is not a long term solution for those seeking to exploit others for a lifetime of selfish gain. Many of us need only be fooled once by a liar to never trust them again. Naturally, this creates a problem for grifters who cannot rely on repeat business from customers they have already betrayed. The same predicament confronts those charlatans claiming to foresee the future; how many false predictions can they make before losing all credibility with their followers, and with it all that free money, sex and labor? And so, as a means to prevent reality from constantly infringing upon their lucrative illusions, a more enduring form of mind control was needed. Hence, *the Mental Empire* came into being as a means to turn human slavery and unquestioning servitude into a way of life.

Looking back upon human history, we find that the more masterful social predators were first to create various "mental empires" — a more invasive form of mind control that allowed leaders to exploit others in perpetuity by offering them a lifetime of empty promises in return. We may then see a connection between this parasitical exploitation of the public and any social group wherein a single person benefits most from the combined efforts of others. Political dictatorships offer us another prime example, as do religious cults.

Here, the trick to ensuring our mass surrender under a single ruler is to create a shared belief system and homogenous sense of group identity among followers. This identity must fulfill our *C–SIX* needs for *comfort, convenience, control,* as well as *communion* — an emotional reward inherent to being part of a group. In more cultish groups, our curiosity (C5) is redirected toward learning only about the empire and little beyond it. This demonstrates that *ignorance* is a primary key to holding human minds captive — the less we know, the better for those seeking to exploit our trust under their supreme guidance.

Designed as systems to remotely control our social behavior, mental empires are based on an IPSFA Sequence to maintain both our sense of group identity and the empires hierarchal leadership structure, be it a political, theological, economic, hereditary or gender-based control system. In regard to gender, the Gender Wall is also a form of mental empire in that it promises us some implied reward in return for our adopting an idealized version of the masculine or feminine identity stereotype specific to our society. Yet with so many variations of those gender ideals from culture to culture, it proves that this is yet another illusion perpetrated by the builders of invisible mental walls. And like all such empires, their influence is meant to spread as a reflection of their glory-seeking leader's own increasing want for power and control over the lives and fortunes of others.

Our mental emperor will typically be a domineering "alpha" male who controls a servile mass of obedient followers by our belief in his promises of joy or our fear of being punished for not obeying his every command. That leader can also be a women, yet the more selfish traits of male biology ensure that men are most likely to exploit us this way in competing for dominance — as demonstrated by the predominance of male leaders in all global seats of political, religious and economic power. It is through their mental empires that our collective energy can then be harvested in its various forms, including money, labor, sex or military service against some rival foreign empire.

Monarchy typifies the power of the mental empire's illusion over the lives of others. Here is a system of governing designed to protect one family's dynastic monopoly over the land and its people by spreading a belief in that family possessing a *supreme leadership trait* inherited by way of an ancestral *bloodline.* And while no blood test exists to confirm their claims of a royalty-based human exceptionalism, it is nonetheless an effective superstitious belief system that has allowed many a king to feed his insatiable lust for power through a global conquest of foreign lands and their indigenous people. It is for this reason that we now also speak the language of our conquerors and uphold their values systems — until such time as other dominant males within society attempt to declare their independence to form their own mental empires, as often seen by the creation of anti-government militias and religious cults.

This also exposes an ironic condition existing within these kinds of parasitic relationships wherein the conquered are forced to pay for the means of their captivity. In political empires, for instance, our taxes pay to employ police officers and other government agencies to ensure our collective submission to the control of the empire and its value system. As such, under the rule of any selfish dictator, we will find ourselves in an "all for one" support system wherein that *one* is only for himself.

This is proven by the elevated lifestyles of leaders who dedicate their lives only to serving their own selfish interests — at our expense.

My Friend, The Enemy

A "Mental Empire" is a consensual illusion that we make to appear real by our collective participation in its theatre. In short, it exists only by the power of our collective imagination. Yet under the influence of our emotions, we can easily forget that even our nation is just an imaginary construct that cannot exist unless we believe it does — as wild animals demonstrate by their oblivion to the imaginary national borders that surround them. For that reason, the power of any government lies not in its hallowed halls but within our minds as a list of values, beliefs and attitudes that we adopt to ensure its continued power over us.

Naturally, this poses a threat to our leaders if we should ever decide to stop pretending that their mental empires exist. To help counteract such a threat, they also employ another technique to control our minds by creating a repulsion for "the outside world" that dissuades us from leaving their mental containment system. And as we look at the many kinds of mental empires in our world, whether a nation, religious cult, or even the beauty industry, we will notice that each empire has created some fearful enemy whose menacing presence keeps us from straying beyond the perimeter of our mental captivity.

We can now refer back to insights from previous chapters to better understand the obstacles to joy inherent to our present circumstances on the global path. For instance, we explored our feeling of physical vulnerability as a species and how it causes us to seek safety in numbers to guard against the dangers of the wild. This survival reflex does not leave us, whether we live in high rise buildings or grass huts. As such, in times of crisis, we instinctively seek comfort by forming groups and engaging in group behavior.

Such a crisis can take many forms, giving our social manipulators a long list of fear-provoking threats to trigger our flight response and have us forming defensive cluster groups. A common human fear is of our being attacked by an intruder. This fear has most of us running like a frightened child for its mother's protection, now represented by our group's leader — the mental emperor. This kind of predictable group behavior also allows skillful political manipulators to maintain lifelong control over our society by keeping us in a constant state of fear. In this way, tyrannical governments behave not unlike a terrorist organization in reverse by directing fear inward to keep their captive citizenry from wanting to escape their controlling influence.

We will also recall that creating an enemy is part of the *fear fencing* strategy to divide both our thinking and our world into a two-tiered hierarchy of "good versus evil" where ours is always the *good* side. This self-serving stereotype of belonging to a superior group is then used to attract new recruits and prevent the disenchanted from leaving its influence, thereby keeping us herded like obedient human cattle.

As group members, we are often forced to engage in bonding rituals wherein we "shout down" our enemies while declaring our own group's superiority to generate a false sense of tribal self-esteem.

Many of us are now familiar with the term "virtue-signaling," which refers to displaying our virtues to gain approval from others. But since virtues are subjective to a group, this means that murdering our enemy could potentially also be considered virtuous by its members. We also assert our loyalty or want for approval by using heroic banter. This may involve yelling insults at vulnerable outsiders from within the safety of our roaming gangs or, as racists may do, by speaking lowly of those excluded from our group while praising the virtues of "our own kind." Regardless of what is being said or done, the intent is to always enforce a belief in that we are superior to those we condemn. In short, this is a glory-seeking behavior designed for the gullible masses. Yet beneath all such posturing is the transparent motive to keep everyone under the controlling influence of the group's privileged leader.

Today, countless leaders use this "divide and conquer" manipulation technique on their members, whether soldiers in the military, voters in an election, or athletes facing a rival sports team. This reveals a familiar pattern of behavior among all groups, be they the citizens of a nation or members of a drug-running street gang, wherein the alpha leader protects his territory by keeping others seeing themselves as superior to those groups or entities identified as "the enemy." In this way, that leader gains not only the group's constant protection from outsiders, but also the energy rewards associated with their loyalty and surrender to his authority. Again, typically in the form of money, sex, or labor.

Among the many *enemies* being so condemned we find: communists, capitalists, terrorists, liberals, conservatives, feminists, blacks, whites, Jews, Muslims, homosexuals, sinners, non-believers, satan, aliens, tax collectors, rival gangs or greedy businessmen. Subsequently, having a common enemy creates lucrative opportunities for others to exploit us as a group by keeping us fearfully working to defeat that threat. The same ploy is used by controversial talk show personalities who pretend to side against the common enemy of any militant group to exploit them for financial gain. Unleashing hateful tirades against an opposing political party, invisible cabals of *elites*, or parents not wanting their children to be shot at school, they create an environment wherein their listeners feel emotionally-charged and superior to those who are being so enthusiastically condemned. In return, that charlatan is rewarded for his feigned loyalty by sitting atop a lucrative pyramid of advertising revenue and products sales designed to protect "us" against "them."

Branding The Herd

In studying mental empires, it is apparent that they are all somehow the same. For instance, every group, be it a neighborhood street gang or a nation state, uses a graphic insignia to mark both its territory and members. Subsequently, the national flags that we are taught to salute in school classrooms are but the symbolic equivalent of the urine scent left by wild animals to mark their own territory. But while emblems, flags and uniforms are outward manifestations of *branding* the human herd, the most significant territorial marking occurs inside our minds. Herein, a scripted group identity is created whose elements can keep us feeling proud, hopeful and motivated to serve our leader.

In this regard, every mental empire imposes a list of values, beliefs and attitudes on its followers to alter their interpretation of life or even reality itself. Familiar examples include religious and political groups who use the power of an almighty God or a governing ideology to rule over our lives from above. Here again, groups prove their similarity by using a customized IPSFA Sequence to create a mental containment system through which the thinking and social behavior of every group member can be remotely controlled by its leader. For example:

I	**The Chosen Ones** (A group believing itself of higher value in relation to all other groups).
P	To be the dominant rulers of society; to gain more privileges for ourselves; to find eternal joy.
S	Submit to and follow our leader; obey the rules; denounce our enemies to show our allegiance.
F	To be treated as "the enemy" or exiled; to be kept from reaching paradise or "the promised land."
A	Having to pretend that all other groups making such grandiose claims are lying, except our own.

Having reviewed *promissory mind control* and *fear fencing*, we can also anticipate why *the promise of joy* is used as a recruitment tool by those atop the mental empire. Meanwhile, shouting down our enemy as a bonding ritual while provoking our fear of punishment all work in tandem to keep us from breaching those imaginary walls that keep us contained and ready to exploit. In this way, any leader sitting atop this pyramid of social advantage can easily harvest our collective energy for their own continued personal gain and glory.

In having identified those features common to mental empires and their scripted identity groups, it is then ironic to hear any nation boast of its being *different* from others when they all share the same mind control system by which a privileged few can dominate and exploit a disempowered majority. This is also why we find similar conditions of poverty, slavery or the suppression of intellect, individuality and the female gender to ensure a constant upward flowing of energy toward those in power. Again, they are typically always men.

Mental empires are maintained by a belief system that controls the thoughts and behaviors of its members. However, these belief systems are susceptible to corruption by new generations of leaders who may alter those beliefs or rules of conduct to serve their own ends. As such, a charitable organization or religious institution founded with good intentions can easily transform over time into a kind of Trojan horse by masquerading as an entity that serves the greater good while harboring selfish motives that defile its founding values. And unless we remain vigilant and speak out against their hypocrisy, the sinister intentions of such corrupted group entities may never be exposed to their victims.

Sacred Illusions

All nations are mental empires in that they impose their belief systems upon us to control our behavior. This belief system is transferable by way of mental recruitment so that our children learn "the system" from us just as we had learned it from our parents and teachers.

Religions also work in the same manner, but are often a sub-mental empire of our nation's greater political containment system. Yet they may exert an equally powerful influence on our thinking and behavior and thus undermine our nation's complete control over us. As a result, religion may be forbidden in nations that worship a "deified" leader or political ideology because their recruitment methods are too similar.

Likewise, the scientific establishment is a sub-mental empire whose own values, beliefs and attitudes may defy those enforced by our rulers, especially in a theocracy. As such, if these mental control systems are ideologically opposed, they can create internal and social conflicts in attempting to stake their claims on our mental territory. That is why choosing one system over any other makes life easier for most. Such Acquired Identity Conflicts add to our Joy Bureaucracy and can leave us feeling ever more divided against ourselves as a member of various adversarial identity groups. For that reason, it is essential that we now resolve these widespread mental conflicts to clear a more joyful path to inner peace and sanity for all global citizens.

However, this is problematic on many fronts. To start, no one in any high position of power who is exploiting us through "the system" cares what we think or feel as long as they can keep reaping their rewards — as dictated by our biological selfishness and glory-seeking impulses. And if our leader is a greedy man, then his nurturing instincts will be cropped from his priorities as a matter of competitive convenience. Instead, it will always be our fault for being a victim, or so we will be told by those preying upon us from above.

As such, our lives become highly complicated under the control of a harmful system whose rulers refuse to help us. Classic examples of this behavior include the ignoring of sexual predation by religious clergy to protect the sacred illusion of their institution's moral authority.

Today, we face many obstacles to personal and global joy from these empires of the mind. Among the more disturbing is when our rulers exhibit the predatory behavior of psychopaths or legislate too harshly under the influence of their selfish paranoia in fearing to lose control of their empire's free-flowing fortunes. As such, that leader or council of elders may rule over us with a remorseless iron fist to ensure that we continue to obediently service the means to their glorious excesses of power, glory and obscene wealth.

Here again, this is why dissidents and government whistleblowers are condemned as "enemies of the state" in their attempts to enlighten us about our captivity within these parasitic systems of exploitation.

For that reason, we are challenged worldwide as citizens and nations to find a resolution to our ongoing human entrapment wherein entire nations are being held hostage or dying in rivalries between what are essentially little more than oversized, nuclear-armed street gangs ruled by demented thugs and wealthy men with impoverished hearts.

CHAPTER 18
The Captive Society

The natural world offers an endless resource for understanding human behavior that is demonstrated by other animals. The *slave-making* ant, for instance, steals the larvae of other ant species so that they can be born in their underground prison colonies. In this way, the abducted newborns believe themselves to be ordinary citizens of a society that has actually enslaved them.

As human beings, we are subject to a similarly rude awakening when born into social control systems that others have created to exploit us. After all, we did not invent the concept of nationhood, politics, religion or banking. Instead, we had to reinvent ourselves to accommodate their intrusion into our unadulterated perception of reality.

In doing so, we also became inadvertent participants in a form of mind control that ensures the survival of those systems by having us conform to their scripted regimen of thinking and behavior. Whether we label it brainwashing, social engineering or public education, the socialization process is meant to ensure our conformity to the various control systems inherent to our culture.

Yet in assimilating to this scripted way of life, we may find ourselves having to support institutions that promote militarized mass murder, class warfare or ecological suicide, while their territorial disputes with rival empires makes us the sworn enemy of people we have never even met before. In short, someone at the top is really messing things up for the rest of us and we need to get to the bottom of it.

As a peace-loving and fair-minded human being, we may have our own ideas as to how we can better manage the affairs of our nation. Yet in wanting to discuss such improvements with upper management, we will encounter a mind-numbing maze of bureaucratic diversions that are designed to keep us from ever gaining the kind of high level access that only bribery, celebrity status or prostitution can buy.

And should we protest too loudly, we will be met by a solid black wall of militarized guards who will sweep us like unsightly debris from the steps of public institutions that behave more like a private men's club of which we are not a welcome member.

Nor can we expect commercial media to portray our heroic struggles for justice and equality in a favorable light, for they are the public voice of the wealthy stakeholders and advertisers who also want to protect their privileged status within a rigged system. Instead, they may depict us as radicals, fanatics or an "enemy of the state" for disturbing a peace as illusory as the empire itself.

And as each new generation of glory seekers battles for control over these social exploitation systems to feast on the enslaved below, we come to realize that our nation may not be as altruistic or fair-minded as its public relations media campaigns would have us believe.

Instead, it may be more like a prison colony wherein we only exist to serve the interests of self-absorbed narcissists and power-hungry sociopaths. Let us therefore examine the means by which our nations can be imprisoned in the event that we might someday want to set ourselves free from having to live in a captive society.

A History Of Plunder

Marketing campaigns can make almost anything appear worthy of our time, money and respect. As such, a well-crafted brochure could make the desert seem like an inviting tourist destination, or a violent dictator appear to be a kind, gentle father figure of his nation. Such obfuscation of reality is part of the propaganda process, which attempts to make people or ideas more attractive by concealing their unsavory traits.

This same public relations strategy also hides the fact that governing is not an act of charitable kindness but one of conquest over the land and people. After all, when a coalition of lions enters the territory of a resident male, it is not with the intention of creating a benevolent future lion society but to have sex with his pride of females. And that requires unseating that current ruler and defending this new territory from other males with the same intentions. Here too, the natural world reveals the truth of our human behavior where history books may fail.

And so, whenever men travel to foreign lands to claim the territory of their own rivals for power, we must not pretend that they are doing so for the sake of anyone but themselves. It is simply an ancient male domination ritual that gets more destructive with each passing war. As such, hidden beneath their polished veneer of diplomatic civility, most nations share a violent history of plunder wherein their founders set forth to capture, contain and exploit our once free-roaming ancestors.

Violent conquest was often necessary to defeat our instinctual urge to be free. After all, like any animal, we also do not want to be cornered or caged. And so we naturally resist being enslaved by others. Nor were we eager to surrender our crops or labor to those contributing nothing to our lives yet demanding a share of our earnings. This natural human defiance to tyranny has long complicated the efforts of our conquerors who sought to profit from our collective submission to their demands.

In response, aside from prisons and torture, they also came to invent mental empires for harvesting our collective energy by promoting the kinds of beliefs that could enslave our minds. And while armies of eager young soldiers guard its outer perimeter, a lethal battery of law enforcers work from within to keep us bound to a consensual reality that defines our national identity and its culture of truth and justice.

Today, we still live in such mental empires wherein freedom is but a longer chain that only the wealthy or deceased can afford. However, in having been born into those systems, we see our entrapped condition as being "normal." Meanwhile, basic provisions for our survival and shallow entertainment keep us thoughtlessly distracted and ignorant of our situation — a combination referred to in ancient Roman times as "bread and circuses." Nor can the voices of our individual suffering be heard over the din of commercial media as it celebrates the glorious economic and territorial victories of our modern day rulers or those famous celebrities who offer us a glimmer of hope that we might also one day escape our bondage to a life of anonymous servitude. In short, the stage has long been set; the play and its plots long written.

This may seem an unflattering perspective on nationhood and other forms of mental empire, but it serves as a realistic counterweight to the sugar-coated propaganda to which we may be subjected to ensure our submission to these social control systems and their operators. In this way, we can make a more enlightened appraisal of our present human condition and any improvements we must make in clearing a global path to joy for all currently enslaved nations.

Follow The Leader

In assessing our global obstacles to joy, among the most annoying is how easily we allow ourselves to be led by others, whether as groups or individuals. This inclination to *follow the leader* is an inherent aspect of our human design in forming a dependent bond with our mothers at birth. Our submissive role during childhood later allows for a seamless transfer of parental power and authority to our tribal chiefs, who may now only be a remote, faceless government bureaucracy conveying the demands of its equally remote leaders.

This creates the misconception that we are born to be "parented" by others; that having our life overseen by authority figures is beneficial. However, history has already shown us the downside of such behavior wherein our surrendering of personal power and will has caused entire nations to collapse in following some mentally deranged dictator on a murderous path of global conquest or sectarian extermination. And then there are those suicide cults led by demented sex-offenders whose notion of spirituality is to ingest poison to escape reality and the legal repercussions for their crimes. And sadly, these clichéd uses of mind control continue to be just as effective today in herding the gullible to an early grave or a life of slavery in some remote, cultish compound.

But there is also a valid reason for our human herding impulse based on biology and physics. This is seen by how intuitively we form social groups the same way that atoms form molecules. Understandably, we each have needs that may only be met by joining with others, or some weakness that can only be offset by their strength. Here again, we see the physics of our psychology in action by the transferring of energy from a stronger to a weaker source in a shared quest for balance, as is done between a mother and her child.

In the wild, this herding instinct offers vulnerable grazing species greater strength in numbers by allowing them to present a united front against aggressive predators. For chimpanzees and elephants, there is a further need to create a protective communal learning environment because their offspring are slow to mature toward independence. At all times, adults are in charge of what is often a *shared parenting* process.

As human beings, we are even more vulnerable and slow to mature. This is further complicated by our growing dependence on technology while being collectively governed within unnaturally complex social control systems. Herein, freedom is a wishful paradise attainable to us only by way of death or wielding an uncommon power over everyone else. And this explains the motive of many leaders in seeking their own independent path to greater personal freedom.

As children, our human herding impulse has us joining sports teams and clubs or forming schoolyard alliances based on age, appearance, intellect, gender, or even a shared distinction of being an outcast of all other groups. It is within these group settings that we also first become aware that some members of our group feel compelled to dominate others by displaying their superior skill and strength or by posing as an authority figure. This also reveals how early our glory-seeking impulse rouses us to proclaim our dominance as a mating candidate by naively demanding the submission of our rivals in any group setting. We are essentially practicing for our selfish future rise to power.

From here, each aspiring dominator must decide how to exploit our natural inclination to form groups to serve their own selfish ambitions. Today, human civilization is a reflection of this same dynamic between leaders and followers in forming political regimes or religious cults for the purpose of conquering other groups on a social or global scale. And whether our numbers are few or many, we each must follow the leader, for better or worse, lest we lose the privileges of group membership, or even our right to exist for second-guessing our group affiliation.

I	**The Follower** (A subordinate guided by a dominant individual).
P	To achieve success under the guiding authority of others.
S	Follow the leader; always do as instructed; always seek top-down approval.
F	To be shunned or persecuted by our group; living by our own inner guidance.
A	Being misled; being discarded once we are no longer of value to our leader.

The Company Store

Slavery is an oppressive energy imbalance in human relationships that we seem unwilling to correct, even in more enlightened times. After all, what could be more convenient than having someone else tend to our survival while we use our free time for horse jumping or terrorizing foxes? Moreover, slavery satisfies our social status-seeking impulse by allowing us to play a dominant role over the enslaved — a welcome boost for any glory seeker's self-esteem. And so, with each progression of human civilization, we find new ways to incorporate slavery into our systems for organizing human social behavior. Overtaxing the working class, for instance, ensures that no one can afford a house bigger than their master's, while long hours for little pay ensure that no one has the free time to participate in public protests for greater equality. That such exploitation occurs on a global scale proves it to be a species-wide trait that also hinders our collective quest for balance and joy.

Slavery is enforced by our isolation from power to disrupt our ability to be self-sufficient. In this way, by taking our land or money, we can be kept in a child-like state of dependency upon our exploiters.

One example of isolation slavery is practiced by those unscrupulous resource companies who hire men to work in a remote location where they are utterly dependent on their employer for their daily survival. In having been tempted to relocate by promises of higher wages, they now discover that the cost of food and other necessities exceeds their income. In this way, the company can recover its costs by overcharging workers at "the company store." As a result, those men cannot escape their isolation or poverty in a system designed to enslave them until the work is done. And each time the company store raises its *price of living*, they must pay it or die — a condition that is common in cities where our daily survival is also dependent on the goodwill of others.

Another variation of the *Company Store* enslavement strategy is used by foreign colonial empires to loot the land resources of indigenous tribes by destroying their culture and means to survive.

Here, the process often begins by offering gifts to establish contact with tribal leaders and assess their weaknesses. As the invader, we may then destroy their natural food supply — by killing most of the wild buffalo in one case — or relocating the tribe to a desolate land ghetto where their survival is utterly dependent on their captors. In this way, the conqueror now rules over their fate and whether they live or die.

Children are then isolated from their tribal customs and language to undermine their traditional survival skills and cultural identity. The fear aspect of religion is often imposed to frighten the conquered into submission — as was done in ancient Rome by using the fear of angry gods and demons to help police the public. The final result is a state of alienation that leads to cultural extinction from suicide or addiction as the captured seek any means to escape their hopeless confinement.

Not surprisingly, we find a similar tactic aimed at the inhabitants of many cities wherein minority groups may be isolated from economic and academic opportunities to decrease their social power and ability to be self-sufficient. This is also why those in positions of higher power and privilege have no incentive for correcting these social imbalances because it would help the enslaved to compete on a level playing field against their ruling masters. Instead, their loss is rigged into the system so that "the house always wins" in perpetuity, as expected.

Dolphin City

Isolation is a reliable hunting strategy because it better ensures success for predators, whether a pack of wolves isolating a young deer from the herd, or a pedophile isolating a child from its parents. This strategy is also employed by religious cults and "slave nations" who isolate their members from access to external cultures, media or academic study. In this way, they can create a devoted army of captive slaves who believe they are living a privileged life because they have no means to compare their own circumstances with those of others in our world.

Not surprisingly, we also enslave animals by isolating them to create a similar dependency. For example, let us imagine a dolphin swimming in the ocean, free to eat anything or go anywhere until she is abducted by human predators from the sea-life entertainment industry.

Held captive and unable to escape her small concrete holding tank, she is then trained to adopt a new method of survival requiring her to perform "tricks" for paying customers to earn her daily wage of dead fish. As time goes by, her ocean home and freedom become a distant memory while her traditional survival skills weaken from neglect — as may her dorsal fin and free spirit. As for her offspring, they will never know that a limitless ocean paradise exists. Instead, like ants born into a slave colony, they will also think that the water park is their natural home. Like any prisoner, our captive dolphin now also becomes utterly dependent upon her captors for her daily survival and would die if left on her own. This may even cause her to fear leaving the marine park prison if escape was possible. The same ironic condition arises among prison inmates who may yearn for the familiarity of prison life once forced to fend for themselves "on the outside" after decades of living in a caged state of dependency.

Today, our lives in any modern city mirror that of trained dolphins living in a marine amusement park. Like them, we are also forced to perform for the public each day from inside small enclosures devoid of natural resources. Here, instead of dead fish, we earn a daily ration of money upon which our life now depends while hoping to buy back increments of our former freedom from what little remains after we have paid our taxes and other expenses. Moreover, despite living in a toxic landscape that fosters feelings of anxiety and isolation, few of us would choose to return to the wild in also having forgotten our ancient ancestral ways of survival. And each time our cost of living rises, we must also pay "the company store" its asking price lest we suffer the dreaded consequences of starvation, eviction and social rejection that await us upon joining the ranks of the needy poor.

Ironically, any attempt to improve our lives may require increasing our financial debts, which further increases our bondage to the system holding us captive. Systematically contained, restrained and financially drained, it is difficult not to equate our present human condition with an evolved form of human slavery. If this were not true, then we would have some degree of freedom to choose alternative and more natural ways to live beyond lifelong economic servitude or a slow, agonizing death from poverty and homelessness.

Cages Of Comfort

As seekers of joy on the global path, we face many obstacles to getting our world on a more enlightened track. In that regard, let us recall that famous proclamation of monarchy: "The King is dead — long live the King!" This paradoxical statement announces that the old leader has simply been replaced by a newer one. In short, nothing has changed and the system for maintaining control over our society remains intact, which this declaration seems to suggest is all that really matters.

This exposes us to a further unpleasant fact that our lives are merely moving parts in the lifeless, automated machinery of our government as it perpetually consumes and excretes our lives like meaningless units of spent fuel energy. Yet we helped to create that machinery through a culture-wide conspiracy of wanting ever-greater levels of comfort. And over time, this led to an increasingly larger, more complex and socially restrictive human containment system wherein simple tasks such as attaining a banana are now more difficult than when we had lived only in grass huts or caves — as we earlier determined by comparing our money-centric lifestyles to that of a chimpanzee in the wild.

As a result, despite their inherent complexity, every mental empire becomes a comfort trap for both its leaders and followers. This ensures a near certain death struggle in trying to inspire change in any system of governing as this will be interpreted by our fearful human minds as an invitation to suffering from discomfort, inconvenience and a loss of control. We may therefore reject even positive changes that promise to elevate our collective quality of life in fearing that they will disrupt our predictable daily survival routines and thereby threaten our existence.

Today, we all live in various cages of comfort that may also cause us to resist positive social progress in any form if, like institutionalized prisoners, we also fear to leave our familiar cages.

What this also means is that human slavery will stay with us in its many forms until our minds have broken free from a dependence upon our automated governing machinery and its scripted, identity-based control systems that justify all such selfish crimes against humanity for the sake of our collective convenience — and discount store prices.

Fortunately, the primary role of the IPSFA Sequence is to give us a simple psychological tool to visually deconstruct our many restrictive forms of social, cultural and political identity. Better still, it does this in a life affirming way that avoids inciting existential panic as we free our minds from their historic restraints. This then allows us to begin the longer process of freeing our bodies and future joy potential from our collective mental captivity. In short, there is hope for our future.

As a simple experiment, we can create an IPSFA scripted simulation of a newly-revised future human identity based on the most appealing aspects of personal freedom within a free global society. Naturally, such an identity script would be much longer and more comprehensive:

I	**Human Being** (A free-roaming member of a global society governed by a direct democracy).
P	To live or work anywhere in our world limited only by our physical or intellectual ability; to be accepted as a member of any global community based only on our human identity and equal and fair treatment of others in our host community; to be a global citizen belonging to our world.
S	Never knowingly cheat or abuse other human beings; Never exploit or destroy natural ecosystems and wildlife for profit; Always eat as you like any food harvested with respect for wildlife and a balanced ecology; Never litter or pollute the air and water of others, including that of animals in the wild; Always get regular blood tests to identify toxic threats in the local community or environment; Never discriminate against the opposite gender; Never discriminate against the consensual sexual expressions of others; Always protect children from violence, sexual and mental abuse at any cost to adults; Always pay regional taxes to support free basic healthcare for all, local infrastructure and services for the elderly and those in genuine need of community assistance; Always seek a balanced joy economy in all relationships to ensure equal and fair treatment; Never intentionally kill or injure anyone — never carry a weapon for killing other humans; Never engage in war or the hunting or hurting of animals for profit or recreational pleasure; Always believe as you like but never force your beliefs on others using fear or threats; Always seek a joyful life for yourself — respect other people's right to do the same; Always do your best to help others seek a joyful life by not oppressing their body, mind or spirit; Always treat others in the most respectful way that you could imagine treating yourself; Always love yourself and others without selfish expectation or victory in mind; Always educate yourself to understand the world, how it works and how we think; Always vote to ensure that your voice is heard in decisions that affect your future; Always ensure your government is a direct democracy that seeks your input on all decisions; Never allow those with greater money or power to silence the voices of their victims; Always allow all opinions to be heard in a fair-minded and time-efficient manner; Punish remorseless white collar criminals to a lifetime of lawfully helping to enrich others.
F	To live a scripted life of being told where to go, what to do and who to be without justification or fair compensation; to have no voice in political decisions or progress; losing our newly-gained freedoms for committing a serious crime against nature or other human beings.
A	Having to accept that our participation in any social, political, religious or economic group has no affect on the power of our individual vote in a direct democracy; being treated with equal respect by everyone, regardless of who we claim to be or what we have achieved; having to accept the inherent value of other human beings, their right to exist, and their right to seek joy.

We can then continue our experiment by using the IPSFA Sequence to deconstruct our current human identity scripts, perhaps beginning with our identity of national citizenship and what it offers in return for the demands it makes on our lives. We can then analyze our various social identity scripts based on religion, vocation, gender, etc., in order to compare their lists of promises and behavioral restrictions to that of the far more relaxed, inclusive and mutually respectful human identity script cited in our previous ideal example. We might then ask:

- ☑ Are there notable differences between this new script and our own?
- ☑ Are they rewarding enough to warrant changing our old scripts?
- ☑ What would need to happen to broadly implement such changes?

Understandably, it may take a few generations to implement such an ambitious rezoning of the human mind and its joy potential. It would also require the warlords and political dictators of our world to die of old age as they are unlikely to surrender their lucrative rackets for the sake of anyone's greater good. It will also require all industries to stop destroying our planet for profit and enter into a new era of respect for our natural world and life itself. Unchecked greed would also not be allowed to flourish — no one needs to own an entire planet.

Our immediate challenge is to reach a global agreement on shared human and social values. Here we face the same problem as do many species in regards to violent male selfishness and glory-seeking. We see this among boastful world leaders as they claim ideological dominance over one another's mental empires. As such, their pride, greed and fear of losing power inhibit our collective future progress. Moreover, even the lowest performing political systems of militaristic dictators and theocratic tyrants loudly boast of being humanity's best option for the future — an attitude also shared by every cult leader. Instead, we find that the more successful a government is in offering citizens a higher standard of living, the less noise it makes on the local or global stage. Conversely, those with a poor record of social progress, be it respect for human life, low infant mortality rates, or a fair living wage, tend to be more boastful in having to convince their captive citizen-slaves to believe with mere words what their eyes have yet to see. In short, our governments and their political leaders must stop trading in illusions. Facing reality is essential, whereupon we can begin to elect the highest qualified of humanitarian freethinkers into governing seats of power as we implement *globally* a more direct form of democracy.

Prisoners Of Denial

In concluding our overview of the captive society, it will be helpful to review some of its critical points. To begin, slavery arises from a selfish desire for ever-greater comfort, convenience and control. This has the selfish forcing others into an unbalanced trading relationship wherein they must invest their time and energy to serve that person's needs in return for unequal repayment, or none at all. This can culminate in the creation of a mental empire, whose pyramid-like governing structure forces those below to serve the needs of the person or group at the top. Noteworthy is that we share this distinction with *slave-making* ants, who also exploit other species for selfish gain — even if it is ultimately to their own detriment by sacrificing their ability to be self-sufficient.

We also learned that human slavery is facilitated using isolation and fear, including isolation from reality or other cultures, and fear of being persecution or expelled from our groups. There are also many reasons why we may be willing to remain within the exploitive confines of a slave-based mental empire. Familiarity is an important one, because at least we have learned the empire's way of thinking and are accustomed to its means of captivity. Apathy is another, wherein we may have little enthusiasm for joining local groups to discuss the problems of society if we cannot even solve our own — even though many are related.

Furthermore, who has the time and energy to fight *the system* after working all day, only to get tear-gassed and beaten bloody by licensed government killers? Clearly, our fatigue and self-preservation instincts favor the efforts of any tyrant seeking our wholesale surrender.

And so, our constant want for comfort, convenience and control may see us passively accepting our fate and hoping instead to be rescued by some heroic savior of the downtrodden — a fresh-faced politician, a promised religious messiah, or a spaceship full of benevolent aliens. In the meantime, we can even hope for an early, painless death.

And so we wait. And then we wait some more. And eventually a new election cycle comes around with yet another happy-talking champion of the people promising to make life better for all of us by fixing the rigged system of which they also claim to be a victim. This often leads to a comical irony wherein a greedy businessman who has spent his life exploiting the same voters he now seeks to charm, must pretend to side with his victims against "the enemy" — greedy people like himself.

But as the years pass and despite constant reassurances to the voting public, our businessman-turned-political-leader has likely done little or nothing to improve *the system* for anyone except his wealthy donors by giving them tax breaks. In fact, the only change we may ever see is that this counterfeit *man of the people* has amassed even more money and real estate holdings while we have amassed only more wrinkles.

And while credit lenders, psychiatrists and liquor stores continue to thrive in servicing a society in spiritual decline, many of us will begin to exhibit some of the same traits seen in caged zoo animals.

Unable or unwilling to escape our confinement, we will also wander aimlessly back and forth, gnawing at ourselves with hurtful thoughts or self-destructive behaviors, lashing out in frustration or anger, falling into depression, or hiding in some dark corner of wasting addiction or obsessive delusion. But it all goes largely unnoticed as long as we still have our "bread and circuses" to keep us thoughtlessly distracted.

And yet, we need only one key to free ourselves and that is to change the restrictive life routines and beliefs that form these illusory walls of our mental prisons. Moreover, it will be humankind's greatest tragedy if we fail to realize that everything holding us captive, from mounting national debts to any contrived sense of human superiority that seeks to oppress us is just an illusory state of mind that we could change by the time we reach the end of this sentence.

...

While we wait for the others, let me introduce a pet project of mine entitled *"Citizen Based Social Planning": The next step in the evolution of democracy.* This is a system of governing based on a direct democracy framework wherein we as citizens no longer vote for politicians but on ideas and social objectives to improve our quality of life. Instead of one night of pageantry and a popularity contest, we engage in an extended survey process that gives every citizen an equal voice in guiding the future of their society. (For more info, visit: www.cbsp.rolandk.ca).

CHAPTER 19
The Greater Good

Whether to free an enslaved nation or feed a hungry stray cat, someone has to take action, otherwise nothing will change for the better. That is why our world needs heroes, those extraordinary individuals who exemplify the best of our humanity and human potential.

In setting a higher standard and leading by example, they inspire us to excel with them by offering hope that our life can also be more than just a random journey of suffering toward imminent death. In return for helping to promote those values that our society holds in highest regard, we favor these heroic top performers above all others, and this has created a symbiotic relationship in every culture between its people and their beloved celebrities.

For example, in many nations, media advertising presents beautiful fashion models as heroic icons for us to worship. As part of the "greater good" of our society, they embody the values of beauty that young girls must emulate to win their own share of male sexual attention. Yet in acting as commercial bait for the beauty industry, they not only lure young women into adopting a shallow stereotype of their human value as mere sex objects, but they also promote the idea that starvation is a viable option for remaining competitively thin. And so, as a parent watching our daughter commit nutritional suicide by refusing to eat, we can at least take comfort in knowing that she is competing with the very best of them for the greater good of our society.

Further presented for our daily public worship are the heroic images of police officers, soldiers in combat and wealthy businessmen whose values young people must likewise emulate to win their future share of social admiration and respect. Yet when those police officers brutalize unarmed citizens, those soldiers massacre innocent civilians or those leaders of industry lay waste to vast areas of wildlife habitat by their reckless looting of natural resources, then surely these predatory values will also be absorbed by anyone seeking guidance for their own future crimes against humanity or our global ecosystems. After all, even the worst among us need someone to look up to for inspiration.

Obviously there is no hope for any society that celebrates selfishness and self-destruction as measures of human greatness. Subsequently, let us examine this concept of "the greater good" to ensure that what we value as a society and species is not just good for the greater among us, but also for everyone else.

To Serve And Protect

In any nation, we are trained from early childhood to treat the police as the embodiment of society's "greater good." Acting as the enforcers of our mental empire's consensual reality, their presence is meant to be a constant lethal threat in the lives of ordinary citizens to ensure that we obey the laws of our leaders and their subjective notions of "justice."

Yet these celebrated defenders of the law and social order are being recruited from the same anonymous sea of humanity from which every manner of criminal arises. Subsequently, there are many documented cases of cold-blooded killers passing undetected through the academy to prey upon the public from behind an official badge. We may then see such rogue law enforcers committing crimes against civilians that may be ignored for the greater good of the institution's own protection. And instead of helping us, our political leaders may likewise look the other way, thereby acknowledging an unspoken truth that the primary role of a nation's police force is to protect the powerful by keeping the powerless in their place — as any bloody-faced protestor can attest.

As a victim of police brutality, we may then ask: "But who is policing the police?" — for which no satisfactory answer has yet been found.

This threat of being *victimized by our protectors* confronts us in many aspects of our lives given our utter dependency on others for anything from food and shelter to our transportation and communication needs. In short, we are completely helpless without those goods and services being sold to us by complete strangers — mostly to profit themselves.

This is why we must be equally concerned whenever the food, fuel, mining, and other industries exert pressure on our governments to give them *the political freedom* to police themselves instead of having their operations overseen by credible regulators to ensure the public's safety. Such industries play a vital guardianship role within society, yet their obligation is not to public safety but only to shareholders. As such, we risk our future survival upon this planet by allowing any industry that is profit-driven to police itself given the catastrophic damage that their wrongdoing can incur — as evidenced by the devastating oil spills in our oceans. After all, how long before there are no more whales left to wash up on our oil-stained beaches; their stomachs full of plastic trash; their blood streams full of industrial chemicals?

And lest we forget, we live in a blameless society where confessions of guilt can infringe upon our freedom to make those profits. As such, any concern for our safety will typically be dismissed lest we endanger the livelihood of the guilty parties and their government facilitators. In the meantime, armed police and crisis management PR firms will keep us too far away from the scene of the crime to count the dead bodies. In short, we cannot trust anyone driven by selfish ambition.

In that regard, human group dynamics and our selfish urges all but guarantee that nothing will be done until it is too late. For instance, the fear of losing our income can keep us from reporting even the most serious violations of our employer — from their sexual assaults to their poisoning of our city's water supply. Ironically, the unsuspecting public may then interpret our silence as a good sign rather than a symptom of our fear to speak out and endanger that company's existence and our weekly income — even as it knowingly engages in destroying us.

This reflex by predatory companies and their employees to keep such crimes *within the family* is to be expected given the extremes to which dependent groups of people will go to keep a "family" secret.

Let us consider, for example, how unlikely it would be for a young girl to report her father's sexual abuse to the police. Even less likely is that her father will go to the police to report himself. But most tragic of all is when her mother also knows, yet chooses to remain silent to serve and protect her own selfish interests. And if a parent can refuse to protect their child at the cost of its greater good, then how can we trust selfish industrialists or any reckless looter of natural resources to willingly confess to us their crimes of greed-fueled excess? It will never happen as long as *selfishness* remains in charge of public policy.

And so, whether in context of family life, profit-driven commerce, or the gainful governing of a nation, there is proof in every society that group intimidation and a fear for our own self-preservation can allow any number of heinous crimes to be perpetrated against the innocent and most vulnerable of our world.

In that regard, our society and any remaining areas of wilderness on our overcrowded planet are also like innocent children that require a similar protection from the predatory practices of rogue industries and economic opportunists. As such, even if most business owners were to behave as exemplary guardians of society, we would still need powerful systems in place to ensure that those tempted to abuse the public trust could quickly be neutralized from doing further damage, whether it be to the health of our families, the land and water, or the many animals who must also trust that we will not poison them out of existence.

Ultimately, we must all be accountable to one another to ensure that we do not live in a perpetual state of victimhood at the hands of those remorseless economic predators roaming our nations. Furthermore, we are unlikely to hear a public outcry against stronger environmental regulations for businesses by our government. Instead, such counter arguments typically arise from habitual offenders having an extensive record of committing industrial crimes against nature and humanity on a global scale with the aid of compliant government officials.

Rebranding The Slaughter

In regard to our victimhood on a national scale, we have already seen examples of how governments, religions and marketers can exploit us as groups by triggering our fear-based instincts and herd mentality. We must therefore arm our minds with greater knowledge of ourselves and our world as a purely defensive measure. In doing so, we will also save the lives of countless young men from an early grave by understanding the *Bio-Psychological* origin of men's primal urge to conquer and kill other men — which our leaders have long exploited to increase their own personal power over rival mental empires.

In this regard, we can summon the learned wisdom of Jane Goodall, an iconic defender of the greater good of all wildlife and perhaps the world's foremost expert on primate behavior. In her decades of study, she discovered a disturbing parallel between the behavior of humans and chimpanzees, our nearest genetic equivalent in the wild. What she and others came to realize about these endearing creatures is that they are natural born killers who also engage in organized exterminations of their own kind. In fact, the dominant males of chimpanzee troupes form marauding armies to target and kill the alpha males of other rival troupes by beating them to death and repeating those raids until all competitors are eliminated — thus leaving them with more females.

Lacking a moral or economic motive, we can deduce that their own violent acts of warfare are not carried out for altruistic reasons, such as a desire to promote "freedom" for chimpanzees worldwide, or to carry out the divine plan of their monkey God as part of a growing religious movement among primates. Instead, they prove yet again that the only purpose of such savage murder sprees is to create mating opportunities for the victorious by eliminating their rivals. As such, chimpanzees also have no need to rebrand their slaughter as being a noble act serving the greater good of ape society. Knowing this, we can see what a farce it is when the purveyors of human warfare pretend otherwise by stirring up our fear and hatred of foreign nations and their leaders to engage us in these biologically-ingrained calls to violence. And with them comes a flood of money from weapons sales and resource looting that always only serves the greater good of our own alpha male leaders in politics, finance and the war-making industries.

Further confirming this underlying sexual motive is any male lion who enters the territory of a rival dominant male to take possession of his female pride using violent aggression — even killing the offspring to bring those females back into estrous. As is typical, sex is that lion's primary motive as part of nature's strategy to ensure that the genetic seed of the dominant is planted for the greater good of the species and its long term survival. And for any young man who needs more than violent sport to satisfy his biological bloodlust for dominance, he can also experience the thrill of being a natural born killer by going off to war with full immunity from the criminal laws of a peaceful society.

Throughout history, territorial invasion, murder and sexual conquest were the intended goal of these marauding troupes of armed human males. As such, rape is a historic aspect of male warfare, though not as celebrated in media as are their heroic deeds of mass murder.

Ironically, this reckless urge to eliminate one's rivals can also get out of hand in the wild. In one documented case, a roaming coalition of brother lions killed fifty-six resident males to gain sexual access to their females. In acting as an army, they had the strength in numbers to defeat their rivals without needing to prove their own individual qualifications as a candidate to unseat the alpha male. Like humans, they also found a loophole in their biological contract with nature by working as a group to claim genetic victory over "the better man."

In human societies, this male urge to dominate other men is further complicated by an equally hostile climate of competition for economic supremacy among the wealthiest in our monetary ecosystems. As such, any successful arms manufacturer must constantly promote a need for war by provoking our fear of being invaded. This creates a demand for the guns, fighter jets, bombs and other killing implements they supply for the government sanctioned mass murder industry. As in sport, this requires a team effort by marketers, government officials and industry leaders to provoke the public's fear and urge for conquest, especially in young men, who are already fighting among themselves. But instead of directing that winning urge toward the sporting field, it will now be directed toward the battlefield to serve both the political and financial interests of those who always remain safely out of range of enemy fire. Clever media marketing will then *rebrand* this shameless grasping for profit and power as an act of patriotic heroism and source of national pride — in short, a child's death that any parent can be proud of.

But after countless blood-soaked centuries of these organized mass murder sprees, many are coming to realize that the only victors in war are the bullet makers and bankers sitting comfortably upwind from the smell of rotting flesh as they profit with every shot fired and body bag filled. And perhaps this reveals the most clever war strategy of all in that by sending those strong, young, healthy males off to die, the ruling class of dominant males also rids itself of their rivals at home — thus leaving more fertile females for them to inseminate.

And so, wherever a nation spends more on weapons than education while its wealthy politicians speak in tones of praise for the poor boys they have just sent off to war instead of to a better school, we might do well as citizens to ask ourselves — *is this also for the greater good?*

Larger Than Life

In reflecting upon our war-scarred history of tribal violence, we find that leaders often cloaked their selfish ambitions for conquest beneath a veil of patriotism or claiming to act on behalf of a loving God with a suspiciously human appetite for war. In clearing a path to a peaceful conquering of organized male violence in our societies, we must also address the acts of war being perpetrated on the battlefields of business and finance where similar conquests of foreign lands and people are taking place in the name of yet another almighty god — "Greed."

This reckless human predatory impulse to constantly seize ever more power beyond our needs has broken the spiritual backbone of many cultures by promoting human slavery and dire ecological destruction. Toward that end, we must first find a verifiable explanation as to why our human species alone hoards energy beyond any practical future need only to recklessly squander it on excesses of material acquisition — and often just on gambling, prostitution and recreational drugs.

Mimicking the behavior of a demented squirrel hedging against an endless winter of want, our obsessive human grasping for ever more land and material gain is also an outward symptom of the biological need to intimidate our rivals in dominating a territory.

For instance, in the wild, the bodily design of many animals includes some feature that allows them to appear larger and more intimidating to discourage attack by a potential predator or rival. The hairs of a cat, for instance, can bristle outward to strike an intimidating pose, while a bear can rise high on its back legs to tower over an opponent of lesser stature. Others, like the common toad, can inflate their bodies with air to appear too large to be eaten by a small snake or other creature.

By humble contrast, our human capacity to appear larger is limited to increasing our muscle mass and walking with our arms spread apart in that familiar pose of bodybuilders and insecure men. More comical and less effective is the cocky pose associated with "snobbery" wherein we proudly stride with our noses high in the air and our chins strutting out to appear tall and confident. Ironically, our brains interpret seeing the underside of someone's nose as their being taller in stature. And by not lowering our head, we also appear less as timid prey.

Beyond these discount forms of visual intimidation, we also require some external means to appear larger than life to our social rivals for status and glory. As history reveals, it was our vain leaders who were first to promote *material-based* greed to create a facade of incontestable dominance in defending their holdings of fertile land and females.

Deploying nature's own defensive bloating strategy, they also began wearing oversized hats and robes to appear taller and wider than those serving them. They further enhanced this visual illusion by sitting atop elevated thrones in rooms decorated with proof of their excess wealth and physical might, including jewel encrusted crowns and flattering portraits of them dressed for military battles that others had fought.

Language also underwent a fine tuning to ensure that every time we addressed our leader, we would be reminded of how much bigger and better they were than the rest of us. And so, such blatantly lofty terms as "Your Highness" and "Your Excellency" began to enter the cultural vernacular to ensure that we would subjugate ourselves in both word and deed before our supreme ruling masters.

This boastful strategy of malignant self-inflation also extended to a leader's home lest we mistake it for the abode of some lesser mortal. And so it came to pass that our glorious leaders demanded to live in massive dwellings, as exemplified by the castles of bygone kings sitting high atop a hill. Beyond acting as a display of their elevated status and excessive wealth, these hilltop towers also served a practical purpose as a lookout for angry mobs of the overtaxed coming to collect on their king's broken promises. And as their self-serving reigns of power came to an end, our glorious leaders also demanded to be buried in some extravagant, oversized tomb to ensure that, even in death, they would continue to live a better life than all the living combined.

Bigger, Better And More

Once our flamboyant rulers had set the visual standard for how social dominance was to be measured, we intuitively began mimicking their boastful displays of material excess in our own street-level battles for social glory and sexual favor. Today, this association between size and status continues to inspire comical extremes of materialistic gluttony in our instinct-driven, subconscious contests of self-promotion.

For example, an oversized house is a minimum requirement to prove ourselves financially superior, while a lofty title of authority must be prominently displayed lest we be mistaken as a member of some lowly caste of illiterates. And after a long day of parading our oversized gold watches and diamond rings in the courtyards of society, we must also sleep only on the largest of beds — also aptly named *King-size*. And as we prepare our bodies for their final repose, our reserving of a burial tomb of royal dimensions in some exclusive upper class boneyard will ensure that our prestigious remains do not accidentally mingle with those of the lesser dead.

Elsewhere, our quest for a prestigious "trophy kill" in sport hunting requires us to defeat *the largest male* of other species, while marketers train women to hunt for the biggest diamond ring by using oversized breasts as sexual decoys to flush out the wealthiest of male suitors to pay for the largest, most costly wedding anyone has ever attended.

And knowing that these measuring sports originate from men's urge to rank higher as a mate, we can also understand why they might pay a king's ransom for magic pills and potions that promise to elevate their penile stature to that of leadership proportions. Going to great lengths to qualify for a top position, their concern is less for a woman's pleasure than being shamefully disqualified from yet another form of male status-seeking competition to claim the highest score.

And if ill-suited for such battles, we can still strive for dominance in a virtual world of computer gaming as we conquer distant lands from the comfort of a cushioned chair without risk of injury or criticism.

Out in the real world, however, the stakes are much higher, as are the qualifications for winning. As earlier revealed, by moving our contests for genetic dominance into a monetary ecosystem, we have inspired a bloodless form of materialistic gamesmanship that infects our society at every level. Herein, we use consumerism-based visual bluffing as the primary means by which to measure male and female dominance.

I	**Fashion** (A competitive means of display for the purpose of attaining social dominance).
P	Promise: To win the rewards associated with being noticed and admired by others.
S	Buy the newest clothing styles; discard clothing previously displayed, or worn by a rival female.
F	Being ignored for appearing ugly, old, poor or "common."
A	Defining joy as other people's positive reaction to our outward appearance.

And as we each fight to prove ourselves "better" than our rivals, it is not only our societies that are forced to pay a high price, but also our strained ecological systems in having to feed our ever-growing want for land and natural resources from their finite supply. In short, we are running out of room for our greed to grow.

Furthermore, to facilitate this kind of materialistic posturing on a global scale, we have begun to standardize not only the means of our production, but also our values, beliefs and attitudes. We see this in the revised portraying of "the greater good" as a constant state of *economic growth* and *growing profits* for businesses while minimizing the value of basic social protections for ordinary citizens, such as healthcare and healthy food. Today, profit and growth are all that seem to matter.

Yet in repurposing society as a game board to facilitate this symbolic global race for what is essentially "the best sperm donor" among rival business empires and well-born elites, we can predict that the ultimate victory of this war will require the complete submission of the human race to its victor, lest a truce be called for the greater good of our world and its many species. In the meantime, everything from the motive to the means are already well in place and fully engaged at this moment.

Consuming The world

There is little doubt that the military establishment would be the clear winner in any contest for social dominance or ownership of the land and resources of our nations. Historically, their penchant for forcibly taking the reigns of government in a "military coup" represents a threat to any democracy. It also proves that, as in the wild, one man's physical might over another is the only proving ground for dominance and any other form of victory is little more than a theatrical performance of our might as illusory as the money sitting in our bank accounts. Yet nature demands that a winner be chosen and awarded the female prize, which is why our symbolic human battles for glory began and continue on.

In aspiring to a top position in any bloodless war for economic glory, the corporate gladiator must also inflate himself to visually intimidate his rivals and prove his dominance. This begins by wearing the most expensive brand of suit available while sitting at the head of the largest boardroom table high atop the tallest, most costly office building in the largest, most expensive city in the world — everything must always be *bigger, better* and *more than* even the day before.

And just like the mission statement of cancer, his company's agenda must be to maintain a constant state of growth to outsize every rival company in its quest to seize the largest market share in serving the greater good of its wealthiest shareholders. Unfortunately, the reality of every morbidly obese business is that with increased size also comes an increased appetite and need to consume ever-larger portions of our natural resources at an unnaturally high rate. In short, it must break every law of nature to keep on *winning*. Herein, moderation, balance and any notion of sustainability are the purview of losers.

Under these economic combat conditions, greed becomes a virtuous necessity to ensure the daily feasting of countless strategically-bloated companies in all sectors of industry. And to ensure their continuing growth in both profits and stature, they must somehow persuade us to over-consume their products in excess of our needs. The result is that we are inundated by media advertising from companies desperate for ever more money to feed their growing hunger and future ambitions.

We experience the symptoms of this economic hoarding strategy in many ways, such as when companies offer us less yet charge more. And so, food portions become smaller while quality ingredients are replaced with cheaper substitutes. Products are also made less durable to ensure their frequent need for replacement. Yet nowhere to be found among these underhanded "smash and grab" business strategies is a blueprint for a more joyful world not mired by greed and selfishness.

As citizens, we are the foot soldiers in this economic war for glory among the wealthiest of society. Our only obligation is to sustain their perpetual state of symbolic warfare, no matter its consequences to our own quality of life. In this way, we also validate their acts of economic aggression against us, whether in stealing our land resources and future health, or our mental freedom to focus on more than just *winning*. For this reason, many of us have stopped caring about joy or healthy living, or even the damage we do to others as we renounce our own humanity. Meanwhile, the fear of losing our position to others keeps many of us from slowing down to reconsider our role in this tragic story wherein no one lives happily-ever-after and all the heroes die young.

Nor is there hope in our waiting for corrupted politicians to impose stronger legislative reforms on businesses engaged in economic slavery or ecological suicide. After all, they create the two perennial favorites of every government — taxpayers and taxable goods. And when even our seats of government are filled with status-hungry materialists and greedy businessmen working to rig the system in their favor, then the combined weight of their self-serving interests will ensure that we remain on this trajectory toward the extinction of most life forms on our planet — at least those needing clean water and air to survive.

Beyond the damage being done to wildlife and our ecology, the situation is also dismal for humankind spiritually, with some likening it to watching our planet enter hospice care — knowing that this is the end and that there is little we can do but offer comfort in its passing.

For those needing a way to frame our current predicament, we can encapsulate the cause of our planet's decline under the stewardship of rampant greed by amending a familiar old proverb:

Give a man a fish and he will eat for a day;
Teach a man to fish and he will eat for a lifetime;
But pay a man to fish, and by tomorrow, all the fish will be gone.

Surviving Our Attitude

In witnessing the hostile power struggles between divorcing couples or siblings fighting over an estate, there seems little hope in our trying to organize millions of equally selfish, status-hungry individuals into a cohesive, sharing society. Yet there is even less hope in our continuing to engage in militarized warfare for the glory of a few greedy men. Nor is there more hope in designing our societies as economic battlefields to serve the selfish aims of those same greedy few. Ultimately, they will always win if they can keep us doing as they want, which is to submit and obey out of our fear of doing otherwise.

As such, we now stand at a critical crossroads in the evolution of our human societies wherein we are forced to choose between our selfishly competitive biology — guided by greedy human predators — and our future survival as a species. Whether we survive matters not in the least to our planet or its wildlife — they have no need for us, whereas we cannot live without them. So how do we attain a more peaceful state of coexistence as a compulsively embattled species? And how can we slow down our reckless destruction of a planet wherein men plan ever more glorious ways to rape its resources for the sole selfish purpose of making themselves appear larger than life to their economic rivals?

The obvious solution is a worldwide change of mind; a re-evaluation of our social priorities beyond the vague, aimless notions of "economic growth" and "more jobs" being used to justify all manner of abuses against humans, animals and ecosystems in our free fall of decline. We have run out of time to keep pretending that this is a *normal* way of life for lack of logical answers or a guiding vision for our collective future — both of which are now desperately needed.

This process of planetary reclamation must begin by first teaching all citizens not to cower before authority. Instead, we must demand equal seats of power at a genuine democratic table to negotiate for a greater balance for all, including our ailing natural world. As it stands, we live as disposable game pieces in a political game of chance wherein its top players know not even why they seek to win the game, let alone care what greater good it serves the rest of us for them to win it. Their only goal is to stay on top, even as it all begins to fall down around them.

That is why ordinary citizens must now take the reigns before all is lost, for we can no longer afford to gamble our precious time away by counting on angels or hoping that our selfish dominators will one day be magically transformed by feelings of empathy and remorse. It could happen for some of them, but without a worldwide reawakening to the importance of our connection to nature and an inspired revisioning of our human purpose to a more inclusive way of life, there is little hope that any of us will survive our present attitude into the future.

CHAPTER 20
Life in the Balance

Sitting around an oval table under the bright studio lights, a panel of celebrity "experts" is about to begin their weekly televised debate on some pressing social issue; a kind of ritualized mental boxing match whose ultimate goal is to hold the attention of its viewing audience between bouts of paid advertising. Ironically, what we learn most from watching these staged clashes of opinion is not so much the solution to any lingering social problem but rather why such problems remain unresolved in the first place.

Our first clue is that none of these well-informed panel members are showing any signs of changing their mind. Instead they appear intent only on continuing to promote their existing beliefs and opinions. And rightly so, because their role as celebrity debaters is to argue for our entertainment, not to have an ideological epiphany before the cameras. We might then ask *what is the value of such debates* if their only purpose is to seed conflict for the sake of ratings and ad revenue rather than to reach any kind of mutual consensus? And by further extension, what value has truth itself if we refuse to consider anything that conflicts with our own existing mental biases?

This is a dilemma that we all face in defending our mental fortresses of certitude against enemy attack. But as we know, certainty is also a highly uncertain thing, especially if our convictions are not based on provable facts or even personal experiences but only on faith, tradition or the hearsay of complete strangers with questionable motives.

In regard to the latter, let us recognize that we live in a human world wherein we are being exploited at every level of existence, whether by drug dealers, liquor vendors, pawn brokers and lottery cartels or at the upper levels by corrupt governments, religions or financial institutions that use our want for a better life to keep us serving their own interests. In accepting the truth of this, let us also recognize that we are acting as *street-level missionaries* for the contrived reality of every mental empire now exploiting us. This accounts for why many leaders want us to fear the otherwise good people living on "the other side" of their imaginary national or ideological borders. In this way we may reject all other ways of thinking to remain under their influence. In fact, most would not want us to read a book such as this, lest we free our minds from the exploitive circumstances that hold so many of us captive.

But most significantly, we cannot solve problems that we dare not speak about. And this is our greatest challenge to gaining a realistic view of our present human condition in that we are mostly addressing superficial symptoms — taxes; racism; misogyny, etc. — rather than underlying causes — biological selfishness; our urge to dominate, etc.

In arriving at this final chapter in Clearing a Path to Joy, we have not only proven our stamina for learning but also increased our awareness of such issues. Let us continue in that direction by seeing the collective struggles of our society as the outward manifestation of our individual struggles for balance in relation to life itself. This will allow us to better understand and accept why *we cannot change society for the better unless we first change ourselves.* And so, with life in the balance, let us confront those internal struggles so that we might also heal our polarized social attitudes and begin to elevate the joy of all those with whom we now share our planet.

The Great Divide

In stark contrast to the communal unity of our ancient tribal systems, success in a monetary ecosystem is marked by abandoning our homes and neighbors in graduating to the next economic class — like passing a grade in the school of materialism. This divisive, wealth-based kind of human stratification is a common feature of hierarchical societies wherein power is also distributed unequally to favor those perceived as being of a higher value than most, be they the leaders of government and industry, or those claiming to be of a privileged "royal" status.

This bias is confirmed by real world statistics wherein the top 1% of the wealthiest of a nation may disproportionately own most of its land and material assets. Yet societies are also living, breathing entities and if our hearts were pumping most of our blood to 1% of our body, we would all be dead. And yet, we expect our societies to function in such a precarious state of imbalance, despite their overt symptoms of failing health and inability to function without debt-generating assistive care.

To better understand why this imbalance is occurring, let us consider the differences in the underlying motives and psychological dynamics of various kinds of *social climbing*. For instance, a mentally balanced person will seek to improve their quality of life. We can see this in our choosing to drink from a cup rather than with our hands, or living in one location rather than being a nomadic hunter. Yet to the mentally unbalanced individual, the quality of their life may matter less than its quantity. A hoarder, for instance, is often driven by a selfish urge to cling to the perceived *future* value of their assets for fear of suffering. A glory seeker, by comparison, will hoard material assets of a *perceived* high value as a symbolic display of their social dominance over others. Obsessed with winning, their insatiable greed is also the cause of most human suffering in our world — from poverty to war and slavery.

As recently noted, greed is a manifestation of the desire to display our superiority; the more power we keep for ourselves, the less others will have to compete against us. This creates a demand for ever-greater displays of wealth by the top economic combatants of society whose vain sport of material acquisition is meant to undermine the prosperity of others to ensure their ongoing victory. In this way, they also ensure for the greater majority of "losers" a constant increase in our daily life struggles to survive and improve our economic circumstances. In short, they purposely create a state of social imbalance to disempower and defeat the rest of us — the bare minimum is good enough.

The result of all this selfish social climbing and its suppression of those below is that familiar imbalance between the rich and the poor wherein a few hold too many resources while the many hold too few. Meanwhile, the assets and self-interests of those hoarding far beyond their needs is protected by razor fences, self-serving tax laws and slack environmental regulations designed to favor their oversized economic exploits of our natural resources. And all of this is enforced by armed police, threats of prison for whistleblowers and protestors, and a media that shames us for questioning these institutionalized abuses of power as being anything but the just reward for good, honest, hard work by true patriotic lovers of our country and all for which it stands.

I	**The Gated Community** (A sanctuary from the discomforting symptoms of social inequity).	
P	To live a guarded life among higher income families away from the struggles of the poor.	
S	Buy a home in an exclusive community surrounded by a fence and an armed security detail.	
F	To be approached or attacked by desperate, needy people; to be forced to live among the poor.	
A	The irony of allowing those same poor, desperate people through our gates to work as servants.	

Notwithstanding ecological collapse from industrial pollution, the only genuine threat to this top-down monopoly on social power is the "middle" class, which represents a balancing point between desperate need and vainglorious excess. This strata of society has the educational and entrepreneurial savvy to demand a fair share of material wealth and political influence. As such, they threaten to undermine the selfish gains of those who depend on a slave colony power structure based on extreme polarities of economic greed and deprivation. This is why the greedy have always worked to destroy the middle class before they can climb further up the social-economic pyramid to become a nuisance to anyone's monopoly on power.

Unlike many conspiracy theories, we can find actual proof of this in the cyclical purging of the *almost-haves*. Here, we see a "survival of the financially-fittest" strategy being implemented to decimate the middle class with inflation, employment scarcity (perhaps by moving higher wage jobs to pro-slavery nations) and austerity measures to weaken basic social support services, including daycare for working mothers. The result is an overall increase in our cost of living a better life, which the wealthy can easily afford many times over. This allows for the ailing middle class to be reintegrated into the slave economy in return for a more meagre ration of hope, power and personal freedom; a cycle of economic castration that seems to occur too regularly to be passed off as the symptom of ordinary market forces.

Although governments may characterize such economic downturns as the fault of the poor demanding too much, they instead often arise whenever a greedy few have gamed the system to a point of collapse in taking ever more for themselves. As such, to make up for the losses of those high above, more is taken from those who exist below them.

Further proof of this conspiracy against the middle class is a history of "union busting" to prevent workers from creating a united front to negotiate a fair trade with wealthy employers. To further eliminate any threats to their market dominance, companies may also buy up smaller rival companies to dismantle them. As for predicting to what lengths a person might go to ensure their victory over us, our prison systems are a testament to the worst of such human inclinations.

As a system of governing, wealth-based social domination requires a constant state of inequity to protect its highest level patrons. This means that energy must constantly flow upward to enrich those at the top while draining those below so they cannot rise up to negotiate for greater social influence. This domination strategy is long familiar in its historic use against human slaves and women by disallowing them to vote or be educated. As such, wherever the values of greed reign, they reveal themselves in the low quality of life among the oppressed. And with human civilization now also utterly dependent on trans-national banking cartels and global trade, we can expect such manipulations to occur on a global scale to ensure that the balance remains in favor of the most wealthy and powerful in our world. And if a war is needed to ensure their victory, then the downtrodden will only be too happy to risk death in return for securing a fair living wage as a soldier.

Beyond excessive taxation and high interest rates, the importing of poor migrant workers further dilutes the power of ordinary citizens to negotiate for improvements to their collective quality of life — be it to demand higher pay, safer workplace conditions, or more free time with their families. In short, even today, many nations are not promoting a more prosperous state of independence for their citizens but rather a lifelong state of child-like impotence and economic slavery.

Having studied the nature of human selfishness, glory-seeking and greed in previous chapters, we may now see the absurdity in any debate to further increase the wealth of the privileged by way of tax cuts or government aid in a misguided belief that this will increase the quality of life for the poor. Instead, reality dictates that economic power is best maintained by hoarding one's wealth, not sharing it. Yet the idea of giving someone already bloated with excess even more is inversely akin to giving even less to those with nothing. But that is how many of our governing and economic systems work — or perhaps hobble along on their metaphoric equivalent of two broken legs and a twisted mind.

At this point, it would be fair to ask why no one seems to be working to solve these obvious problems of inequity. The simple answer is also the most ironic and embarrassing in that *we have been expecting our oppressors to improve our quality of life.* Here again, it is like waiting for the jailer to bring us the keys to our freedom. This also exposes the fakery of democracies that offer us the illusion of having a voice in all political discourse by voting for politicians who claim to represent our best interests. Such mental trickery already begins in childhood as we are taught to let authority figures make all important decisions for us. This deferring of responsibility then becomes habitual as we seek to be employed under other people's leadership. We then face a system of governing that makes it difficult for anyone but the well-financed and powerful to enter politics — and if we do make it through, we may be refused equal speaking time by commercial media for election debates. Subsequently, this forces us to always vote for the kinds of people who are engaged in keeping us down based on their campaign promises of wanting to help us. In reality, our goals as citizens conflict with their want for more power. This is why we must implement *direct democracy* on a global scale as there can be no future for a nation that allows only one person to decide its collective fate. History is our constant witness to this fact.

A further obstacle to greater social equality is our mental remoteness and apathy. Today, we are no longer a unified tribal community but an anonymous gathering of utter strangers whose private suffering is just a remote, abstract concern to those around us; we may not even know our immediate neighbors. Furthermore, we are so divided in terms of race, religion, politics or other differences that we may not believe that we are "in the same boat" with the others, even as we are all sinking in it together — much like the stratified victims on the Titanic.

And with far too many citizens to honor as unique individuals, it is also more convenient for our governments to treat us as just a faceless mass of sequentially-numbered tax-generating units. Ironically, their systems are far less effective at detecting our suffering than our refusal to pay those taxes that the wealthy seem so adept at avoiding. It is a needlessly sad state of human affairs that no marketer or politician can simply paint over with a smile or trivialize with a dismissive wave of the hand. But this is all we may get, aside from promises of a glorious future in societies run like a struggling business by profit-minded men who have no genuine interest in helping anyone but themselves.

But while this callous attitude has transformed the nature of human relationships, it has not changed our human nature or shared need for joy. This is why we may feel that there is something terribly wrong with how we are living. Yet in having been too long removed from a genuine tribal experience, we cannot know that our oppressive sense of social isolation and insignificance is largely the symptom of our *communal separation anxiety*. As a result, we may come to feel painfully alone in among millions of our fellow citizens as we silently mourn the loss of intimate human contact across a growing social divide.

Clearly, our collective path to future joy depends upon rejecting this social trend of growing farther apart. Instead, we must break down our isolating walls of identity to build a wider and more structurally sound bridge back to the founding values of our lost humanity so that we can begin to take our fellow human beings into greater consideration.

In doing so, let us also recognize that it was not the slave master who marched in the streets to demand freedom for his slaves, nor was it men who carried placards and shouted for women to have the equal right to vote or work for money outside the home. As such, we should also not expect any current generation of social oppressors to fight on behalf of improving our quality of life. Instead, we ourselves must take all such necessary action in that regard — as history clearly dictates.

A World Of Difference

On a more positive note, despite the efforts of a greedy few to divide, conquer and enslave our world, there are also many others working to unite us in greater harmony. One challenge in facilitating such a global unification are the differences in how each culture fulfills the needs of its citizens. After all, living in a desert requires a unique set of survival skills unlike those for living in a jungle. In short, we will always have some cultural differences, which also makes living in our world a more interesting experience for curious adventurers.

A far more critical challenge is overcoming the oppressive *emotional atmospheres* that political dictators may promote as a symptom of their own dysfunctional character and temperament. Here the threat is one of mimicry wherein an entire culture may copy the behavioral antics of a deranged psychopath in believing that his promised path to joy is the best one for all of us. Such behavior is also typical of religious cults wherein followers mimic the toxic mental effluent of some charismatic leader's insanity to become a unified mass of deluded escapists who are oblivious of their growing departure from reality.

As a point of reference, let us consider the following non-clinical, yet most practical definition of a psychopath and a sociopath: *A psychopath is someone who would enjoy watching us die, whereas a sociopath is someone who would offer a psychopath our phone number in exchange for free tickets to a hockey game. Our ability to tell the difference between them is largely based on whether or not we are still alive.*

Although intentionally humorous, this identifies a clear difference in the motivation for each type's behavior. We can then compare this to political leaders who are merely corrupt in selling our nation's future to private interests versus someone using mass executions and public shaming to keep us sacrificing our lives to serve his own insatiable lust for power and glory. As such, each type also promotes a different kind of *emotional atmosphere* within their respective societies.

Our first experience with emotional atmospheres is often as a child while visiting the home of a friend. Here we may notice a contrast in parenting style that can make a world of difference as to whether our friend enters adulthood as a well-adjusted person or a tortured soul. To understand how this could happen, let us consider three emotional atmospheres that we may encounter in visiting other people's homes:

Domination: In this home, the children may seem timid, sullen and defeated; perhaps exhibiting signs of physical or mental abuse at the misguided hand of a hostile guardian. Here, the dominant parent may be excessively selfish and territorial, using threats of violence or hurtful insults to intimidate weaker family members into submission. Aside from causing a hatred for their oppressor, this kind of mental terrorism also teaches children that "might makes right," and may cause them to adopt a similar attitude of tyrannical apathy in all future relationships. Sadly, in many cultures people are subjected to this *dysfunctional family* style of governing, wherein leaders treat their citizens more as enemies at the cost of everyone's mutual joy and emotional well-being.

Censorship: In this home, the children seem abnormally well-behaved as though afraid to disturb the well-managed facade of what is less a family home than a display case for their parents to prove how morally pure or civilized they are to visitors; an illusion that the children must not dare to disrupt. In this home environment, children are trained to act as lifeless ornaments of superficial display for overly-vain or fearful comfort seekers. In response, children may rebel against this fiction by developing addictions, eating disorders or sexual misbehaviors to win attention from their emotionally inept guardians. We see the same in nations that favor superficial social gestures and a pretense of civility to conceal deeper organizational flaws lurking underneath. Censorship in most cases arises from living in denial to avoid facing the truth. As a result, pressing social problems also cannot be solved if our leaders are pretending that such problems do not exist under their rule.

Reverence: Here, the children seem joyfully well-adjusted in a caring environment wherein they feel nurtured, secure and free to behave not only as children, but also as respected individuals. Such treatment feeds an appreciation for any parent who treats their child as an unformed adult rather than a helpless subordinate or extension of themselves to be exploited. Children treated with respect for their individuality will learn that their lives and happiness matter — that their existence has equal value. This avoids the need for secrecy, subversive behavior or angry protests to gain fair treatment. Some nations promote this kind of an emotional atmosphere, which is reflected in the self-esteem and tolerance of its people. Conversely, in more selfishly-oriented cultures, people may be more aggressive or cynical in feeling undervalued or unsupported in critical ways by their society or fellow citizens.

In viewing our nations and institutions from this perspective, we can see that most use the same hierarchical "family structure" to guide our development toward success. Here too, leaders act as parental figures to a public that lacks the same power of autonomy as children living at home. However, every leader has a choice whether to promote an atmosphere of joyful inclusion or one of terror. For this reason, our future success or failure is also directly linked to their social parenting style. Subsequently, we must take great care in selecting our leaders to prevent our regression as citizens to a helpless state of childhood.

Domination versus leadership

The *domination* and *censorship* parenting styles previously listed reveal a familiar obstacle to joy that exists in many nations and institutions wherein a leader does not actually lead but merely dominates followers to protect his own privileged access to power. This impedes both our collective evolution toward a genuine democracy and achieving higher states of consciousness beyond primal fear and selfishness.

Here again, the natural world offers clarity as to what can hinder our progress on these fronts. Among mammals in the wild, for instance, we find that mothers will mentor their young to a state of self-empowered independence; even surrendering their own dens or territory at times. By comparison, dominant males typically play no role in caring for the young and may even pose a threat to them by violently defending their status against new arrivals. This explains the common tension between many fathers and sons as their internal Bio-Psychology urges them to clash for dominance. However, due to men's individual character traits, we find a wide range of deviation from instinctive norms. As such, some men are highly skilled and caring fathers while others are not to be trusted in the vicinity of either woman or children.

As is also the natural order, we typically see mothers raising children while fathers play a more peripheral role as *group leader*, for better or worse. If his leadership style is to dominate, then we might see various negative outcomes, from a deprivation of basic material comforts to torture, humiliation, physical violence or even the murdering of one's own children to "win" custody in a divorce. At the mental end of the domination spectrum, some parents try to maintain lifelong control over their adult children for selfish reasons. On the global path, this motive is mirrored by repressive governments that keep citizens in a perpetual state of child-like impotence to discourage our independent thought or prevent our escape from captivity. Domination is also why we are violently suppressed for protesting any corrupt government and why members of cults are subjected to mental terror to induce a fear of leaving their false paradise. And while such sinister motives may be apparent to outsiders, they can seem a "normal" part of everyday life for those trapped in the role of playing the downtrodden victim.

Beyond brutal police forces and military mercenaries, the alpha male dominators of our societies also maintain control by having us believe in their supreme powers of leadership. This introduces us to a further trait of any unfit leader clinging to power. First, they conceal their sociopathic tendencies and motives beneath a scripted facade of civility. Then, if anything goes wrong, they defend their public image using "DARVO" — an acronym for a defensive behavior that is most often exhibited by male perpetrators of domestic violence.

Here the abuser **D**enies responsibility for his attack by **A**ccusing his victim for inciting it, thus **R**eversing the role of the **V**ictim and the **O**ppressor. In other words, nothing is ever the leader's fault, no matter the crime. Political dictators often play this DARVO blame game to justify violently oppressing citizens into lifelong submission. Here too, the victim is always at fault for being victimized — often for breaking trivial laws specifically designed to legitimize such government abuses. We may then even come to accept a woman's public beating for having worn *illegal clothing* that exposes her face or bare ankles.

Ironically, patriarchal domination of women in any form would not exist if women were larger and stronger than men. Unfortunately, men have long used their physical size to gain a winning advantage over women. But rather than admit to this and expose his self-serving motives, a man may instead blame the woman for why he beats her into submission. The same ploy is used by leaders in politics, religion or industry when they shamelessly defer blame for their transgressions to protect their media-friendly facade of incontestable authority or moral rectitude. In short, they abuse their power while blaming others for the inevitable negative fallout that ensues.

But finding a solution for these imbalances of social power is no easy task. Like confronting alcoholism or drug addiction, an admission of guilt or acknowledgement of the problem is critical to correcting the behavior of any abusive leader. Yet for those using terror-based systems of hierarchical domination to control us, such confessions are not to be expected. Instead, we may be met with more denial, ridicule, shouting, insults, threats of violence or outright murder. In short, they may do anything to win — or avoid losing their positions of power.

What does this mean for our efforts in clearing a path to global joy? Here we can look to *reality* for answers. For one, we have no historical record of hostile female armies invading foreign lands and destroying other cultures, nor of installing murderous regimes to maintain their power over others. On the other hand, we have an abundance of such evidence to prove that men will not only destroy their own nations but even their own families in their urge to win. For example, as he hid in a bunker after leaving Germany in ruins, Adolf Hitler poisoned his own dog to test his cyanide as propagandist, Josef Goebbels, killed his six children in his own final act as "man of the house." Would any sane mother have orchestrated such a horrific end for either her children or country? No, because she has been biologically programmed by nature to care more about sustaining life than fighting for status. Hence, it was not women who invented war planes or nuclear weapons because they were meant for destroying life rather than protecting it.

This causes us to face some uncomfortable yet necessary questions as to the future of humankind. For instance, did nature intent for men to be involved in raising children when there is little evidence among other species that females need help in this regard? Male chimpanzees play no such parental role, nor do most non-human males. Knowing this, we might then ask: *are men truly qualified to lead our societies based on their proven history of social and ecological destruction?* Even as you read this, women and children are being mercilessly slaughtered as "collateral damage" by men in their profit-driven military wars, or just for refusing to yield to the selfish demands of a tyrannical husband. Looking back upon centuries of catastrophic wars and environmental destruction, the only logical answer to that question is "NO!"

Moreover, animals in the wild agree. In matriarchal elephant society, for instance, males are cast out so as not to threaten the entire herd with their instinct for competitive violence. And while we can expect a noisy surge of DARVOesque denials if men are asked to account for their long history of inhumanity against humanity, necessity dictates that we must now engage in such debate given that the illusion of male supremacy in leadership roles is neither a credible nor proven solution for guiding our world toward a healthy state of social and ecological balance. In fact, we can easily predict our future under continued male domination by simply looking at our past. And realistically, it looks increasingly bleak because greed affords its purveyor no consideration for balance, be it within our societies, or our world ecology. And in the midst of crisis, it will do us no good to hear that typical callout of *every man for himself* which shows no regard for either women or children.

And so we must ask ourselves, should the future fate of our societies continue to rest on the rise or fall of stocks in some high stakes parlor game played by wealthy male gamblers? Or on which male-dominated political party is steering our society toward its own enrichment? As their political speeches often betray, male glory seekers are unaware that sustaining a healthy society or raising a child is not like running a for-profit business. Our focus must therefore be on our collective protection and nurture, not on serving the financial interests of a select few. This is how nature designed tribal societies to function and clearly we have entered into a life-threatening state of communal dysfunction.

The illusion of male exceptionalism has long-impeded the conscious evolution of our species in having *allowed male aggression to masquerade as leadership potential*. This is seen in nations conquered by dictators and the invading armies of foreign empires. And what is their interest in asserting such physical dominance — to promote social equality?

Now is the time for a gender-based regime change in the governing of our nations before it is too late. After all, what is the worst that can happen — children stop dying in wars? Or that we start focussing on social and environmental issues instead of short-term profits? As we prepare for this inevitable transition, let us be reminded that each day our world is being looted to meet the growing demands of men having no further need of money, yet addicted to the thrill of victory. As such, our access to a better life is often being blocked to feed this endless lust for more among those who already have too much of everything.

Winning The Human Race

As we near the end of twenty chapters of relentless fault-finding in our quest for greater joy, it is clear that our species has many obstacles to overcome, not the least of which is to ensure the responsible governing of our nations and local communities.

Yet changing a system of government is like trying to do mechanical repairs on a moving race car; inside that vehicle is an ambitious driver whose only goal is to cross the finish line before others claim the prize. In this male-dominated race, like most others, victory is symbolized by a sexy young female waiting at the podium, along with a backslapping chorus of sponsors, each riding the winner's coattails toward their own selfish ends. And whether in sport or politics, an idle majority sits on the sidelines watching the winners take it all. In short, business as usual in our competitive human world.

Also embedded in this racing analogy is the reason for the inequity between men and women in regard to political power. Contrary to popular belief, *gender prejudice is not the reason why governments are male-dominated.* Instead, we find that politics has long been used as the ultimate competitive sport to determine a nation's top symbolic *alpha inseminator* among ruling class males — much like a reigning tom cat with first penetration rights to a female. As such, lurking beneath the tailored suits and patriotic overtures of every ambitious male political climber is a nagging urge to prove his dominance that supersedes most other concerns, including those for money or the long term health of his society in becoming its ultimate leader.

Today, sports matches, political debates and military warfare are just another venue for men to claim alpha mating status over one another. Here, even money is only a means to that end; a way of keeping score and procuring more females. Subsequently, when stock markets crash or nations crumble, it is often just the symptom of men at the upper tiers of economic power playing too rough at winning.

Following this logic, we can then understand why men have wanted to keep women out of any competition for social dominance because such contests largely exist to grant the winner greater access to women.

In other words, for the typical glory-seeking male, politics is not about looking after the best interests of voters but proving their own genetic dominance through the seizing of power and territory. Even if we are unconscious or in denial of this goal, our selfish actions do not lie. In exposing this connection between a man's political ambitions and his procreative biology, we can begin planning for a new era in politics wherein the guardianship of our societies will predominantly be in the control of women. The rationale for this is reflected in women's inborn inclination toward nurture and community building as opposed to the use of competitive violence or systematic oppression of the majority to favor a privileged few. Females in the wild offer similar proof.

Naturally, the prospect of losing control of the political game board has long scared men since they first realized how expendable they truly are once insemination is complete and mother and child are surviving by their own self-sufficient ingenuity. After all, what future awaits an unemployed king? Yet once men's battles for control of our political systems end, so will many of our lingering social problems as well.

But rather than drum up fears of a mass extermination of obsolete male politicians, we can take a more enlightened view of our global evolution toward a less selfish form of governing. For one, with more women in change, we may see a world where citizens are more equally empowered; a world wherein our needs can be met in ways that no longer disqualify us from the right to exist now that politics and social progress are no longer being hijacked as a showcase for men's vain posturing and inclinations toward class warfare. Instead, what we may see is a movement toward our becoming more of what we were meant to be, both as individuals and as a modern tribal community focussed on protecting its young rather than acting as a battleground ruled by the selfish violence of power hungry men.

In preparing for this inevitable social transformation, our challenge as joy-seeking global citizens is to keep lust-fueled male competitions for sexual advantage from distorting the role of governance. In short, we must not allow this unconscious male drive to continue steering our world toward communal disintegration and ecological disaster.

Adam's Nipples

Unsurprisingly, the notion of male exceptionalism has permeated most aspects of our cultures — even God is claimed to be a member of that esteemed gender. This would explain the origin of the creation myth of Adam and Eve, which is shared by several religions. In one popular version, God creates Eve from Adam's rib; a claim accepted as a true account of our human origins by many of the faithful. The historical introduction of this story allows us to address a number of issues that will make our future transition to a more equal-minded and peaceful world less of a challenge for both faithful and doubtful alike.

The first issue is that this creation myth declares that women were born of men via a masculine God — thus also crediting men with her creation. Yet such thinking is problematic and explains why religion has a strained relationship with science, which can bring some of its long-standing "truths" and faith-based claims into question.

For one: *if Eve was created from Adam, then why does Adam have Eve's nipples?* The honest answer is *because of reality*. In more modern times, scientists discovered that all human life begins from a generic *female* template. That is why men are born with nipples as it allows them to become either gender at birth until the Y chromosome transforms them into a sexual counterpart for females. Hence, the creation of an Adam with worthless nipples and so, in some sense, a broken woman.

The importance of addressing this topic is manifold and begins with that familiar presence in our mental lives — stereotyping. As we noted earlier, stereotyping is the lazy mind's attempt to economize thinking for the sake of convenience. The negative fallout of processing reality this way includes a polarized debate over "nature versus nurture" that has researchers finally agreeing that both are critical, while failing to address individual character traits whose influence may be even more critical in determining if we become a nurturer or destroyer of life. In short — there are no fast, free and easy black or white answers.

Unfortunately, due of its mental ease of use, stereotyping remains a primary method for maintaining the gender imbalances of power that exist between men and women in every patriarchal society. And this has also led to our being governed as a reflection of *stereotypical male behavioral traits* — defined by our competing against others in a selfish quest for personal glory as opposed to promoting a peaceful state of mutual support and balance in society, which is more a female trait.

Referring back to scientific study, female chimpanzees do not fight for dominance — a pro-social attitude — whereas males chimpanzees kill one another to win alpha status — an anti-social stance. Again, this is also why male elephants are ejected from the herd's matriarchal society due to their ruthless aggression. In this way, some things will never change because human males suffer the same urge to fight for dominance, thus negatively affecting everyone else around them. This also explains why our world is being destroyed by armies of invading men having weapons, industrial equipment and banking systems at their disposal. And all this destruction is governed by a male-centric ideology that prioritizes one man's wants over everyone else's needs in a world whose *emotional atmosphere* is defined by rampant *selfishness*.

Ironically, while stereotyping is neither fair nor thoughtful, it would be fair to suggest that women are predisposed by nature to be superior to men in their nurturing impulse toward others. As sole guardians of their offspring in the wild, we see this inborn caregiving inclination among the females of many species, including bears, elephants and even snakes and alligators. In human females, this often extends to caring for needy husbands, the elderly, family pets, hospital patients, animals requiring rehabilitation and young children entering school. Women are also more likely to organize family and social gatherings for peaceful purposes rather than to engage in competitive sports or to stir up hostility in preparation for political, military or class warfare.

This is what makes women's current circumstance so ironic. Given her invaluable natural assets in tending to home and communal affairs, we would expect women worldwide to be holding influential seats of power in every society due to their knowledge of protecting life. But instead, she continues to be minimized, marginalized and victimized in a world dominated by male combat for ownership of her lifelong sexual favor and domestic servitude.

This brings us full circle to the issues concerning the story of Adam and Eve in that men have also long-dominated religion, thus turning spirituality into yet another competitive male sport that keeps women out of its winner's circle. As such, few religions define spirituality as is done in chapter 13, *The Silent Partner*. Instead, we see it used as another means to dominate our societies with violence and mental terrorism. And so, after centuries of bloody warfare, it remains a venue for male status-seeking that hides within its message of loving forgiveness the threat of violence for those who refuse to submit to its male leaders.

Ironically, the mere suggestion of a women having mystical powers has seen her being burned as a witch by groups of *hysterical* men. As such, despite centuries of denial and reassurances, we can see that men have long engaged in a planet-wide effort to undermine and devalue the life-giving and nurturing powers of womankind. And the results speak for themselves — we stand on the verge of our mass extinction.

Would religion have retained its purity had women been in charge from the onset? Would there have been killing crusades or a murdering of its most noted prophets and peacemakers? What we do know is that human history, under male rule, is a story of unfolding tragedies.

Keeping this in mind, one cannot fail to notice the irony of women in freer societies clamoring aboard the male testosterone bandwagon by covering their bodies with muscles and tattoos. Meanwhile, feeling their territory being encroached upon, men have resorted to doing the one last thing at which few women excel — growing a beard. In short, we are seeing women trying on male stereotypes of dominance, which is not the direction we need to go to rescue our world from the violent and ecologically destructive clutches of an insatiable lust for power.

Female rule over human society is supported by nature's own logic. Here, to protect their offspring, the females of most species do not engage in violent altercations. After all, a dead mother cannot feed her hungry baby. Yet nature did not design men for nurturing duty, which is why few of our top economic male predators have any regard for the well-being of our communities or natural environments. Instead, most feel no remorse in leaving us to exist in the toxic aftermath of their greed-fueled paths of destruction. What they and the rest of us must accept is that women are made to rule human societies based purely on their instinct to protect what is most important in life — life itself.

This is why the worlds of politics and business are in urgent need of "the feminine touch" so that we can all begin to regain our balance as families, nations and stewards of a planet wherein the mothers of all species want their offspring to survive.

In response to the increasing global destruction from men's reckless contests for dominance, women must now be more politically active in every society. This begins with tearing down the Gender Wall and its blatant attempts to stereotype women as helpless "stick people" born to serve the sexual appetites of men as shaved party dolls wobbling on pencil thin heels. Women can do themselves a further service by not watching media programming that portrays them as incompetent or foolish. This is just cultural propaganda disguised as entertainment. Instead, it is far more helpful to learn about independent-minded and intelligent women, such as those whose sharp minds helped men reach the moon — thereby also disproving two long-held stereotypes about our innate human potential based on race and gender.

What women cannot afford to do is become a laughable caricature of the same unrealistic male ambitions that have destroyed the lives of countless men in betraying their own true identity. Instead, we must embrace each other's right to authenticity as we work toward a reunion of the embattled sides of this long-outdated gender war. In this way, we will attain a more joyful state of balance in all future societies.

God Loves Science

And finally, in clearing a global path to joy, our greatest challenge in guiding our societies toward greater balance and unity are the values, beliefs and attitudes we promote as members of any institutionalized mental empire. The states of mind they promote are the greatest source of division among our species and the most critical issue we need to address to overcome their divisive manifestations. After all, we now act as though *thought* alone creates reality, which, as revealed in chapter 2, can have us dismissing whatever threatens to disrupt the tranquility of our preferred interpretation of life, including reality itself.

Our need to heal such divisions is embodied by the philosophical war between science and religion. Here, devout believers on either side may stop seeking the truth to protect those beliefs upon which their entire existence is built. This is further infected by male glory-seeking among men using these institutions as yet another form of team sport.

As such, each side may dismiss the other with close-minded derision rather than the open-minded curiosity required to ensure their mutual conscious evolution. And so, as one side laughs away credible reports of UFOs and growing evidence for a spiritual after-world, the other closes its mind to the pursuit of wisdom via the scientific exploration of its extraordinary claims. And this is all being done in a misguided effort to defend against that most terrifying of all intruders; our feeling of uncertainty and its threat of changing all that we think we know and rely on to navigate our way through life. And for some it means a loss of power and authority in having convinced countless others that we have all the answers they seek — that our leadership is true.

Collectively, our challenge on either side of this mental divide is to begin deprogramming our institutionalized minds and scripted senses of social identity; to uncover our own truths by revealing *ourselves to ourselves* and rediscovering the authentic person waiting underneath.

As a gentle reminder, time continues to consume our days and lives at a relentless, unforgiving pace. We must therefore not waste another precious minute denying ourselves that bounty of bliss inherent to our human joy potential. And as we venture forth, let us embrace the gift of humility in case we should ever believe that we have arrived at some final conclusion when our quest for wisdom has only just begun.

As emboldened visionaries clearing a path to future joy, let us also not become a stubborn obstacle obstructing our way but instead allow ourselves to be guided by the unfailing compass of our inner joy — for in that wise and welcoming direction also awaits our destiny.

Epilogue

It is October, 2021, as I prepare this book for its public release. *I have done my best to do my best* in terms of its development, from writing and editing to typesetting and the cover design. In this way, I rest assured that my vision for this book has not been compromised by commercial concerns or agendas. As a project now 28 years in the making, beyond its technical aspects, what I also learned through this process is that I can trust myself to get the job done.

What I cannot predict, however, is how others will receive this book. Have I done a good job to explain my ideas? Will others even care about what I've written? In that regard, I'll cross my fingers and hope for the best…

This public aspect of the book's journey matters most to me because, as I sit here putting on the final touches, another oil spill has occurred off the coastal waters of California, USA. Seeing images of floating "booms" being used to contain the spill reminds me again that there is no profit in inventing clean up technology. Hence, there is none. And so we see the same clumsy response each time this habitat destroying industry fails us: warnings to stay off the beach until all the dead marine animals has been cleared away.

It's hard to stay hopeful in a world such as ours where suffering seems inevitable, whether by our own design or at the selfish hands of others. We also seem to have picked the worst time for hope, given the current mental state of our world wherein the craziest among us are awarded the power to decide our collective fate. Such craziness has always been in abundance here, but it has recently reached epidemic proportions fuelled in part by an actual epidemic. There is little sense to be found here in a world where many of us are engaged in a heroic mental war against reality itself.

As such, and given our mental climate, I cannot predict what this book will do for you or me. What I do know is that I was meant to write it and that I met my obligation with a degree of dedication that I have given to nothing else in my life. However, I do plan to spend some quality time in the future recording my songs and enjoying the sights and sounds of nature.

In the meantime, based on my own experiences, I want you to know that there is far more to our human story than we know and that no matter what happens — *it's going to be okay*. But this doesn't mean that you should stop trying to make life better. After all, that is where our joy lies. I know this first hand from the joy I felt in writing this book. It also rewarded me with a life of meaning and creative fulfillment wherein I never gave up trying to make it better for you and the others to read.

I wish you the same joyful determination in your endeavours. Now please, hurry and fix our broken world before things get out of hand. Someone has to do it, and maybe you are the one that we have all been waiting for.

Good luck. And always keep a copy of this book nearby — just in case.

Glossary

As a tool of reference, here is a list of significant concepts or terms that were introduced in this book. Also included for clarification are a few familiar terms with CPJ book-specific definitions. Also, denoted in parentheses is the chapter number in which a term is first introduced or more fully explained.

Acquired Social Identity (ASI)
(ch 4) Any form of externally-imposed group identity not inherent to our inborn human "fixed" biological identities of species, gender and race. ASIs are the basis of our professional, religious, political and other group identities based on the shared scripted thoughts and behaviors of an IPSFA Sequence. ASIs are adopted by way of mental recruitment.

Bio-Psychology
(ch 1) The default aspects of human behavior internally directed by biological urges instead of mindful conscious choices; primarily related to the survival and procreational urges. Ex. Engaging in public displays of our physical or financial dominance to solicit sexual attention, or allowing fear to limit how we choose to live or speak in public.

Note: This is a CPJ book-specific definition *unrelated to other disciplines.*

CBSP (Citizen-Based Social Planning)
(Ch. 18) A new form of governing based on direct democracy wherein voters choose ideas for improving society rather than political representatives.

Comfort Seeker
(ch 7) A person driven to seek comfort in various forms as an expression of their biological fear of death or suffering. Such a person may become entirely focussed on seeking material comfort through economic security or group conformity to the detriment of their spiritual life. This is an aspect of human Bio-Psychology also evident in most wild animals, but uniquely expressed in humans through the influence of culture, personal beliefs, etc.

CPJ
Acronym for *Clearing a Path to Joy* book or its related topics.

Cropping
(ch 2) A term derived from photography used herein to describe the mental process of our selectively ignoring evidence or events that contradict our beliefs or what we want to believe is true. Ex. Avoiding debates based on scientific evaluation to protect our faith-based religious beliefs, or conversely,

avoiding topics such as spirituality or UFOs to protect our objectivity-based interpretation of reality — or tenuous hold on a shared definition of sanity.

Note: This is a CPJ book-specific definition *unrelated to other disciplines.*

Dandelion (its symbolic meaning in this book)
(ch 1) The dandelion reminds us that nature always wins. It symbolizes our actions to suppress or control nature, including our own. It also represents the often harmful actions we engage in to deny reality, as demonstrated by poisoning the water, land and animal life with toxic chemicals to maintain the facade of a perfectly green lawn — which is an *unnatural* phenomenon.

The Deconstruction of Acquired Identity
(ch 4) The process of reverse-engineering Acquired Social Identities in order to return to the core essence of our authentic being and its founding values. This process uses the *IPSFA Sequence* to identify the elements of the scripted thoughts and behaviors in which we engage to maintain such identities. The result is a realistic tool for promoting global peace by removing restrictions in our thinking created by the adoption of any socially-acquired identity.

Funnelling
(ch 2) The mental process by which a child's mind is subjected to a gradual narrowing of its joy potential. This occurs by way of mental recruitment to various inhibitive beliefs and the adopting of Acquired Social Identities that restrict one's thoughts and behavior as based on gender, class, religious caste, or any other kind of social distinction.

The Gender Wall
(ch 2) An artificial social barrier of acquired values, beliefs and attitudes used to divide humans for the purpose of assigning each gender its specific social role and duties. In most cases, the gender wall favors men's domination over society by disempowering women via restrictions on their behavior, such as denying them the right to vote or earn their economic independence.

Glory Seeker
(ch 6) A person driven to seek social glory as an unconscious expression of their biological urge to be a dominant inseminator of females. This can take the form of public displays of wealth or killing our rivals through acts of war. Glory-seeking is an aspect of our fundamental animal Bio-Psychology.

The Inverse Reality Principle
(ch 13) The process of creating our reality and identity from the inside-out to safeguard against others imposing their own reality upon us. The purpose

here is not to be a non-compliant outcast, but to protect ourselves against the mental threat posed by manipulative social groups and institutions.

The Invisible Economy

(ch 2) Relating to the mind's *subjective* symbolic conversion of various forms of energy into others. Example: turning a gift of flowers into feelings of love or acceptance, thus material objects into emotions. It also guides us toward specific goals based on the kinds of energy transactions we prefer.

The IPSFA Sequence

(ch 4) Discovered and offered here as a diagnostic tool by Roland Kriewaldt, it defines a sequence of scripted thoughts and actions inherent to forming all Acquired Social Identities (ASIs). IPSFA is an acronym for its five elements, which are the psychological basis for creating all human social identities for the sake of organization and mind-control. The IPSFA Sequence is the basis for creating "Mental Empires," of which nations are a familiar example.

Joy Bureaucracy

(ch 4) Mental obstructions to joy created by Acquired Social Identities that guide us with opposing motives or behaviors. For example, our identity as a person of religion may oppose *killing* while our identity as a soldier demands that we engage in such behavior — hence, which is the "right" action?

Joy Compass

(ch 1) The inborn guidance system for recognizing our unique path to joy; an individualistic sense of what makes us feel happy or content. Where it leads us may oppose the destinations chosen for us by others. As such, other people's meddling in our self-development can cause emotional distress and suffering, from anger and depression to thoughts of suicide.

The Joy Coordinates

(ch 4) The symbolic energy conversions — thoughts and actions leading to positive emotional states — that we must engage in to achieve feelings of joy or inner contentment. These are subcategorized as *The Joys of Inspiration* and *The Joys of Contentment* and are the basis for living a happy life.

Joy Potential

(ch 1) The inborn conscious ability of any healthy child to experience joy and engage in activities that result in joyful feelings throughout its lifetime; based on engaging the Spiritual States of Being: curiosity, creativity and the seeking of communion with other sentient beings.

Mental Empire
(ch 17) A hierarchal system for controlling people as groups using an IPSFA Sequence of scripted thoughts and actions that is mentally transferred by way of recruitment. Governments and religions offer familiar examples of this group-based "mind control" process wherein we can create imaginary empires by adopting scripted social identities that help to support their existence.

Monetary Ecosystem
(ch 5) Any artificial environment, such as a large city, wherein food and other natural energy resources cannot be hunted or gathered directly but must be obtained from outside agencies by trading in the symbolic energy of money. This also creates an unnatural dependency on those who control the flow of incoming and outgoing energy resources — including the money that we require to pay for them.

Object Value Training
(Ch 5) The mental programming of children for their future immersion in a money based, material-centric economy. This is achieved by training us from infancy onward to have positive emotional reactions to material objects such as toys, clothing or even diamonds, guns and cigarettes, by associating them with various positive emotions, especially happiness and self-confidence.

The Physics of Psychology
(ch 2) An understanding of human behavior based on our physical, mental and emotional relationships to energy in any kinetic, potential or symbolic form. These relationships shape our values, beliefs and attitudes throughout our lifetime and represent a core teaching of this book.

Psychopath vs Sociopath
(ch 4) A psychopath is someone who would enjoy watching us die, whereas a sociopath is someone who would offer a psychopath our phone number in exchange for free tickets to a hockey game. Our ability to tell the difference between them is largely based on whether or not we are still alive.

Note: This is a CPJ book-specific definition *unrelated to other disciplines.*

The Sexual Mascot
(ch 8) Refers to a sexually attractive young woman of fertile age used in media advertising to draw men's attention to any product or service. Ex: Bikini girls presented in ads for beer, cars, sports, etc. The sexual mascot's presence also provokes rivalry among women in competing for male attention. This creates opportunities to market beauty products and fashions that allow women to

mimic these *sexually* dominant women presented in media. Ultimately, she is a tool of manipulation used by marketers to stimulate our spending.

The Six States of Being (C–SIX)

(ch 5) The six primary motivators of human activity, based on three physical and three spiritual states of being whose agendas are directly opposed. While our body directs us to engage in the physical quests for comfort, convenience and control, our mind directs us to satisfy our spiritual urges toward curiosity, creativity and communion. This results in both internal and external conflicts of interest and becomes a part of our mind's *Joy Bureaucracy*.

Superstition

(ch 1) Our belief or engagement in any comfort-seeking ritual wherein we hope to influence the outcome of an event over which we otherwise have no control. Ex. Trying to increase our chances of winning by wearing a "good luck" charm. Whether through the use of prayer, incantations or physical props and accessories, what we are doing is trying to counteract our feelings of uncertainty — and vulnerability — in the face of the greater unknown.

Wedging

(ch 2) As the opposite of mental "cropping," this is the process by which our mind selectively attributes evidence or events in ways that favor our existing beliefs or mental biases. Ex. When we give God credit for healing our illness or blame our lack of joy in life on somebody else.

Index

acquisition 5, 94, 270
alcohol 8, 75, 108, 118, 164, 208
anger 2–3, 12, 85, 147, 262, 301
animals 2, 21, 26, 42, 65, 69, 72, 87, 195–196, 203, 207, 230, 243, 246, 256, 270, 276, 289. See also: relationships, mother, animal mothers
   cat 74, 128, 157, 206, 263
   chimpanzee 117–118, 153, 253, 267
         Chimpanzee warfare 267
   dog 1, 84, 158, 203–204
   dogs and cats 147, 149
   lion 29, 193, 251
   pets 7, 11, 149–150, 186, 212, 294
   rabbit 7, 9, 60
   zoo 2, 8, 262
attraction 40, 42, 48, 72, 75–76, 93, 101, 105, 139, 144, 154–155, 157, 219, 235, 244, 302
authenticity 88, 130, 133, 146, 296
   integrity 72, 89, 116, 121, 132–133, 137, 141, 174, 187
Bio-Psychology 1, 5, 15, 25, 168, 213, 219, 238, 287, 299
brain 146, 196, 223. See also: freedom, mental freedom
   conscious evolution 10, 64–65, 99, 179–180, 187, 189, 208, 218, 220–221, 227, 229
   consciousness iv, 2, 4, 9, 44, 83, 90, 114, 131, 133, 146, 180, 184, 186, 188, 200, 206, 211, 223, 299, 301
   cropping 18, 60, 65, 248, 299, 303
   intelligence 65, 185
   wedging 18–19, 90, 303
C–SIX or the Six States of Being v, 63, 127, 132, 136, 225, 229, 241, 303
certainty 9–10, 13–14, 19, 34–36, 49–50, 64, 87, 91, 184, 186, 193, 196, 231, 297, 303
childhood 7, 17, 41, 46, 48, 59, 61, 98, 107, 123, 141, 162, 192, 236, 238–239, 264
Citizen Based Social Planning 262
comfort 5, 58, 64, 73, 77, 81, 112, 124, 204, 219, 257, 261
   hoarding 26, 73–74, 124, 269, 274
   mental comfort 64, 85, 87, 132, 194. See also: certainty
   physical comfort 83–84, 191
Comfort Seeker 77, 82–85, 88, 299
community 1, 53, 60, 97, 117, 164, 226, 259, 280
competition 5, 31, 36, 44, 70, 72, 75, 77, 141, 149, 161–162, 168
conditioning 172, 189, 194, 208, 239. See also: social, conditioning
   brainwashing 223, 249. See also: freedom, mental freedom
   mental conditioning 18, 48, 105, 185. See also: Mental Empires

mind control 49, 210, 236–238, 240, 243, 246, 249, 252
control 16, 18, 25, 35, 60, 64. See also: certainty
convenience 23, 26–27, 30, 43, 64
   haste 23–24, 31, 43, 64
   laziness 24, 30–31, 33, 64, 188
   procrastination 198. See also: selfishness
creativity 2, 18, 24, 65, 222–225, 227–229
   art 54, 222
   happy accidents 220
   playing with God 220
culture 130, 164, 220, 222, 226, 249, 255, 299
   competitive culture 67, 69, 78, 102, 220, 229, 263, 276, 294. See also: Glory Seeker
   consumer culture 61, 223
   cultural myths 35, 100. See also: religion
   cultural reality. See: Mental Empires
   cultural recipe 6, 222
   cultural stereotype 105, 120, 242. See also: Gender Wall
   cultural traditions 90, 120, 154, 163, 193, 231, 255
   foreign cultures 33, 242, 267, 269, 289
   homogenous cultures 89, 222
   mental culture 63, 189
death 26, 32, 44, 53, 74, 83–84, 124, 134, 174, 180, 186, 191, 197–199, 202, 253, 257
   near-death experience iv, 199, 209
debt 29–30, 53, 61–62, 71, 79, 94, 173, 216, 257, 262, 279
democracy 62, 74, 79, 238, 282, 287
   direct democracy 30, 239, 259, 262, 283
denial 38, 50, 124, 131, 181–182, 261
depression 1–2, 164, 262, 301
distractions 8, 15, 24, 31–32, 74, 95, 151, 169, 189, 200, 205, 251
DNA 47, 50
dominance 30, 35, 69, 78, 138–139, 161, 168, 247, 253, 268, 270, 276, 287, 299–300
   adolescent males 70
   alpha male 76, 167, 214, 238, 267–268, 288
   class dominance, 165, 223
   DARVO 288
   dominant male 76, 104–105, 267–268
   dominant predator 29, 41, 87
   economic dominators 70, 74, 257, 299
   genetic dominance 75, 78, 272, 292
   military dominance. 74, 81, 103, 151, 172, 197, 207, 273, 289, 294
   patriarchy. See: Mental Empires, Gender Wall
   social domination 49, 236, 281

territorial dominance 68–69, 153, 178, 229, 246, 249, 268, 285
emotions 14, 22, 25, 43, 57, 59, 63, 68, 85, 106, 112, 126, 134, 145, 161, 168, 184, 195, 200, 212, 223, 301
   emotional atmospheres 284–285
   Emotional Illiteracy 122–124
   Emotional Legacy 174
   emotional suffering 1, 126, 186. See also: depression, suffering
   emotional trauma 147, 186–187, 209
expectations 48, 58, 115, 119, 123, 127, 132, 141, 144–145, 149–150, 173, 259, 294
extinction 63, 215, 255, 275, 295
faith 6, 19–20, 35, 37, 53, 152, 185, 205, 239, 293, 299
fear 3, 9, 16, 27, 34, 63, 73, 77, 81, 84, 92, 106, 135, 147, 177, 191, 194, 198, 208, 246, 255, 267, 299
   fear drug 201, 204
   fear economy 41–42, 83, 107
   fear fencing 35, 244, 246
   fear of death 5, 82–83, 86, 90, 150, 177, 197–199, 201, 299
   fear of losing 25, 32, 41–42, 64, 68–69, 72–73, 75, 194, 265
   fear of rejection 40, 68, 108, 160
   fear porn 201–202
   fear-programming 204
   fight or flight 69, 73, 80, 194, 244. See also: fear, fleeing
   fleeing 33, 68, 81, 150, 169, 195, 201
   horror 32, 194–196, 199, 201
   self-consciousness 3
   shame 108, 126–127, 131, 154, 161, 165, 272, 280
   terror 70, 83–84, 86, 152, 191, 195, 197, 203, 216, 254
freedom 8, 22, 49, 64, 141, 148, 189, 236, 238, 251, 253, 256, 259, 267
   mental freedom 5, 47, 120, 179, 183, 208
   of choice 7, 18, 25, 32, 46, 64, 68, 132, 223, 232, 257, 299
   of movement 6–7, 17
Gender Wall 36, 105, 163, 241, 296, 300
genetic 47–48, 75, 78, 115, 153, 157, 267
Glory Seeker 77–78, 137–138, 167, 178, 227, 250, 279, 290, 300
government 12, 13, 18, 25, 30–31, 36, 46, 49, 63, 78, 91, 104, 125, 130, 162, 189, 197, 239–240, 242–244, 246, 248, 251–252, 259–260, 266–267, 275
greed 28, 79, 82, 104, 266, 269–270, 274. See also: control
grief 85, 138, 186–187
happiness 1, 5, 42–43, 53, 58, 61, 83, 93, 96, 111, 126, 130–131, 134, 144–145, 160, 261, 301
haste. See: convenience
hunger 5, 21–22, 44, 59, 61, 64, 68, 81, 84, 159, 193
hunting 29–30, 60, 256

angler fish 93. See also: marketing
economic sport 29. See also: Glory Seeker
hunting humans 167. See also: psychopath
sport hunting 195, 259, 272
the Bear Hunt 87

hypocrisy 20, 76, 85, 133, 150, 208, 247

inspiration v, 1, 3–4, 10, 15–16, 21, 43–44, 64, 83, 114–115, 148, 179, 186, 205, 217, 222–223, 263, 301. See also: joy, Joy Coordinates

intuition 4, 46, 117, 147–148, 181, 184, 217, 230, 253, 271

IPSFA Sequence (the) v, 47–50, 85, 101, 125, 167, 181, 194, 207, 241, 246, 258–259, 299–301

Acquired Identity Conflicts 133, 137, 248
Acquired Social Identities 35, 46–47, 49, 63, 300–301

isolation 61, 73, 105, 117, 120, 158, 164, 184, 196, 255–257, 261, 283–284. See also: freedom, mental freedom, creativity

joy

balanced joy economy 111–112, 121–122, 259. See also: relationships
counterfeit happiness 63, 93–94, 96. See also: marketing
definition of joy 3. See also: spirituality, love
Joy Bureaucracy 46, 119, 133, 248, 301, 303. See also: C–SIX or the Six States of Being
Joy Coordinates v, 43–45, 63, 112, 126–128, 136, 301
joy decoys & symbolic substitutes 53, 59, 136, 222. See also: marketing
joy potential 2, 14, 38, 47, 54, 63, 83, 92, 113, 127, 131, 136, 139, 146, 148, 178, 200, 224, 258, 300–301
mental barriers to 4, 10, 36, 87, 179. See also: fear
need for 1–2, 11–12, 15, 25, 81, 136, 283
role of spirituality 6, 177
The Four Paths to Joy 5
The Joy Compass 3. See also: intuition, inspiration

kindness 27, 171–172, 174, 217–218, 251

generosity 172, 174, 206

laughter 9–10, 96, 128, 148

love 22, 44, 59, 114, 143–144, 146–147, 152, 160, 171, 179, 209, 212, 259

marketing 31, 93–96, 99–100, 104, 236, 269, 272

advertising 23, 31, 55, 59, 62, 77, 95, 97, 103, 108, 145, 151, 157, 203, 205, 263, 274, 302
commercials 96, 98, 102, 106, 108, 202, 235, 263
television 41, 77, 96–97, 106, 122, 202, 235

marriage 45, 113, 115, 127, 137, 151, 154

meaning & purpose 1, 14–15, 53, 68, 76, 129, 134–136, 159, 182, 187, 205

Mental Empires 241, 245–247, 251–252, 296, 301

money 6, 22, 26, 29, 47, 58, 62, 67, 76, 94, 117, 144, 160, 221, 237, 239, 255, 257, 302

credit 29, 37, 55, 68, 143, 262

taxes 12, 60, 103, 118, 236, 262, 280, 282–283
nature & natural 2, 11, 67, 69–70, 72, 81, 84, 154, 195, 249
  artificial 8, 12, 47, 60, 67, 72, 98, 164, 170, 172, 300, 302
  dandelion 11–12, 300
  ecology 61, 91, 164, 232, 249, 259, 266, 272, 275, 280, 289–290, 295
  human body 5, 8, 16, 21, 50, 63, 68, 81, 85–86, 97, 151, 156, 160, 195, 270, 303
  instincts 1, 68, 77, 79, 261, 267, 294
  natural law v, 11, 25, 29, 34, 69, 133, 157, 232, 238, 274
  natural resources 60–61, 79, 94, 257, 273
  natural world 11, 24, 54, 58, 61, 85, 164, 260, 276
normal 57, 103, 115–116, 125, 151, 163, 181, 222
orgasm 3, 66, 75, 96
passion 13, 123, 144. See also: meaning & purpose, joy, Joy Coordinates
peace 1, 20, 32, 57, 61, 63, 68, 92, 103–104, 146, 191–192, 199, 207, 212, 230, 236, 248, 250, 269, 293–295, 300
playing 1, 8, 112, 118, 149, 163, 192, 219, 223, 228–230
political 13, 19, 28, 62, 66, 71, 79, 98–99, 105, 120, 197, 210, 236–237, 246, 249, 254, 258, 260, 276, 299
  campaigns & elections 99, 104, 232, 245, 250, 261–262, 283
  matriarchy 292, 294–296
  politicians 6, 61, 74, 98, 129, 189, 239, 275, 296
prejudice 32, 34, 36, 58, 158, 179, 188. See also: fear, fear fencing, social, status
  hatred 180, 217, 267, 285. See also: selfishness, fear, fear of losing
  homophobia 36, 180, 245. See also: culture, cultural stereotype, Gender Wall
  misogyny 74, 121, 127, 150–155, 163, 165, 263, 281, 284, 288, 291, 293, 295–296, 300. See also: Gender Wall
  racism 32, 163. See also: fear, fear fencing, social, status
pride 22, 57, 67, 119, 140–141, 149, 160, 186, 269
promises 37–38, 42, 55, 59, 70, 77, 95, 97, 99, 102, 125, 143, 157, 163, 178–179, 198, 238, 240, 246, 255, 272
psychopath 38, 88, 122, 167, 196, 248, 285, 302
Reality Checks 124, 126, 152, 198
  A Spiritual Reality Check 221
Relationship Ledger (the) 127
relationships 5, 26, 47, 61, 84, 111, 113, 118, 120, 123, 125, 131–132, 143, 148, 159, 164, 168, 173, 192, 217, 254, 302
  father
        father and son rivalry 287
        father figures in leadership 250, 252, 266, 287
        fatherly voice in commercials 106
        male stereotypes 105. See also: Gender Wall
  friendship 115, 132, 147
  mother 97, 158, 171, 252–253
        animal mothers 17, 39, 287, 289, 294

        caregiving inclination 294
        cultural prejudice against. See: prejudice, misogyny
        motherhood theme in milk commercials 107
        substitute mother figures 5, 154
        vain mothers 108
    parental nurturing and protection
        adolescent male risk taking. See: dominance, Glory Seeker
        losing a child 70, 187
        sexual abuse 266
        sharing vs selfishness 227
religion 6, 18, 28, 36, 55, 57, 107, 151, 154, 183, 185, 189, 196, 209, 215, 232, 247, 255, 267, 297
    charlatans 6, 91, 166, 239
    God 6, 8, 19, 34, 50, 139, 150, 152, 180, 184–185, 192, 205–206, 211, 219, 236, 246, 267, 269, 296, 303
    superstition 6, 34–35, 184, 303
self-esteem 28, 87, 94, 128, 160–162, 164, 167–168, 170–171, 192, 216, 230, 244
selfishness 1, 16, 72–74, 80, 83, 90, 144, 149, 168, 173, 179, 206, 240, 248, 254, 259–260, 264, 275
sex 10, 37, 40, 78, 151, 153–154, 208, 242, 252, 263, 268
social
    attention 38, 40, 42, 58, 67, 70, 77, 85, 93, 96, 98–100, 166, 171, 219, 221, 227, 235, 263, 299, 302
    conditioning 9, 55, 212, 236. See also: conditioning, mental conditioning
    dominators 71, 74, 79, 191, 271, 273
    engineering 155, 249, 300. See also: Mental Empires
    evolution 262
    hunting and gathering 22, 29, 272, 302
    identity 33, 49, 99, 116, 119, 125, 127, 132, 181, 208, 284. See also: IPSFA Sequence (the)
    predators & manipulators 30, 72, 94, 118, 162, 171, 174, 219, 236, 239, 244
    programming 7, 57, 131, 161, 164, 202, 223, 296–297, 302
    status 9, 40, 67, 70, 75, 78, 87, 102, 138, 165, 229, 250, 254, 270, 275, 287, 289, 291, 294
    values, beliefs and attitudes 16, 18, 35, 38, 42, 46–47, 87, 89, 98, 130, 169, 236, 243, 246–247, 273, 296, 300. See also: culture
socialization 4, 46, 85, 88, 132, 207, 221, 249. See also: conditioning, mental conditioning
    childhood training 39, 41, 171
        happy mommy face 96
        mimicry 42, 63, 100–101, 119, 271
        Object Value Training 59
sociopath 57, 94, 167, 172, 250, 288, 302

spirituality
   Kundalini Awakening iv, 138, 186, 206, 208, 210, 212, 217
   reverence 132, 205–206, 209, 212, 216, 218
   Spiritual States Of Being 64, 83, 126, 147, 225, 303
   The Inverse Reality Principle 180
   thoughtfulness 178, 216, 226, 294
   transcendence 3, 65, 146, 206, 211–212
   transformation v, 65, 138, 186–187, 208
   wisdom 6, 19, 64, 97, 178, 185–186, 192, 206, 210, 212, 217, 225, 297
suffering 5, 15, 26, 34, 64, 72, 82, 92, 122, 144, 186, 192, 252, 299, 301
sustainability 61–62, 213–214, 274, 289–290
trauma. See: emotions, emotional trauma, grief
trust 3, 16, 28, 37, 44, 65, 94, 114, 118, 123, 130, 141, 148, 154, 161–162, 167, 200, 238
truth 5, 11–12, 13–14, 18–19, 65, 72, 97–99, 116, 129–132, 141–142, 143, 154, 178, 185, 210, 232, 297
   honesty vi, 131, 141, 236
UFO 189, 297, 300
vanity 9, 41–42, 62, 64, 69, 79, 82, 102, 139–140
war 2–3, 27, 30, 36, 67, 70–71, 103, 150, 251, 259, 269, 273, 300. See also: dominance, animals, chimpanzee
   weapons 57, 62, 70–71, 80, 81–82, 84, 103–104, 191, 195–196, 259
work 12, 24, 42, 45, 112, 118, 126, 167, 220, 240, 254, 259, 261
   career 2, 27, 40, 45, 98, 113, 115, 122, 223
   factories & machinery 5, 24–25, 60, 164, 224, 257–258
   professional 105, 116, 127, 141, 166, 299

About the author:

Roland Kriewaldt is a German-born Canadian author and musician residing near Toronto, Canada. Aside from writing, he has spent years touring the US and Canada with live bands and also worked in graphic and web design. He also tries to make life easier for wild animals.

CPJ Book website:
www.ClearingAPathToJoy.com

Upcoming books by Roland Kriewaldt:
www.AuroraSkyPublishing.com

Roland's personal website:
www.RolandK.ca

BOOKS:
Reality Checks for Everyday Life — A series of books featuring "loaded questions" to enlighten and entertain the thinking class.

MUSIC:
Too Big To Fail — Music & Info-Motion Video Project
(Written and performed by Roland Kriewaldt).
(More info: www.music.Rolandk.ca)

OTHER PROJECTS:
Citizen-Based Social Planning.
(More info: www.cbsp.Rolandk.ca)

www.ingramcontent.com/pod-product-compliance
Lightning Source LLC
Chambersburg PA
CBHW031407290426
44110CB00011B/292